AMERICAN LEGAL REALISM

Skepticism, Reform, and the Judicial Process

AMERICAN
LEGAL REALISM

Skepticism, Reform, and the Judicial Process

By WILFRID E. RUMBLE, JR.

Cornell University Press

ITHACA, NEW YORK

For My Father and Mother

Acknowledgments

The publication of this book would not have been possible without the help of a number of people. I am delighted to have this opportunity to acknowledge their assistance. Rose Tucker of the Vassar College Library aided in several ways. Nancy Stirling, senior law librarian at the splendid New York State Law Library at Albany, cheerfully assisted on more than one occasion. Melody Allen, my student assistant for the academic year 1966–1967, performed various tasks quickly and effectively. Ian R. Macneil of the Cornell University Law School was kind enough to write me several long and instructive letters. They were in response to one of my articles, but were very useful in the preparation of part of Chapter V. The editorial staff of Cornell University Press gave me much helpful encouragement and advice. Mildred Tubby was of extraordinary service as the typist of several versions of the book. Cathy Rumble, my daughter, aided me in verifying some of the quotations. Last but far from least, Kirk Fobes Rumble gave me the kind of invaluable assistance which only an unselfish wife can render. Without her sacrifices I would not have had that most precious of assets, uninterrupted time for work. None of the individuals listed above is, of course, to be held in any way responsible for possible errors and infelicities in the subsequent pages.

A few paragraphs in Chapter II first appeared in the *Journal of Public Law* and are reprinted with its permission. Quotations from Karl N. Llewellyn's *The Common Law Tradition: Deciding Appeals* are used with the permission of Little, Brown and Company. Selections from *Law and the Modern Mind* by Jerome Frank (copyright 1930, 1933, 1949 by Coward McCann, Inc.; copyright 1930 by Brentano's, Inc.) are from the Anchor Books edition (1963); copyright renewed in 1958 by Florence K. Frank; reprinted by arrangement with the estate of Barbara Frank Kristein.

WILFRID E. RUMBLE, JR.

Vassar College
August 1967

Contents

CONTENTS

CONTENTS

Abbreviations Used in Notes

Academy of Political Science Proceedings	*Acad. Pol. Sci. Proc.*
American Bar Association Journal	*A. B. A. J.*
American Law Review	*Am. L. Rev.*
American Law School Review	*Am. L. Sch. Rev.*
Annals of the American Academy of Political and Social Science	*Annals*
California Law Review	*Calif. L. Rev.*
Columbia Law Review	*Colum. L. Rev.*
Connecticut Bar Journal	*Conn. B. J.*
Cornell Law Quarterly	*Cornell L. Q.*
Fordham Law Review	*Fordham L. Rev.*
George Washington Law Review	*Geo. Wash. L. Rev.*
Georgetown Law Journal	*Geo. L. J.*
Harvard Law Review	*Harv. L. Rev.*
Howard Law Journal	*How. L. J.*
Houston Law Review	*Houston L. Rev.*
Illinois Law Review	*Ill. L. Rev.*
Iowa Law Review	*Iowa L. Rev.*
Journal of American Judicature Society	*J. Am. Jud. Soc'y*
Journal of Legal Education	*J. Legal Ed.*

Journal of Public Law	*J. Pub. L.*
Law and Contemporary Problems	*Law & Contemp. Prob.*
Maryland State Bar Association Bulletin	*Maryland S. B. A. Bull.*
Michigan Law Review	*Mich. L. Rev.*
New York Law Forum	*N.Y. L. F.*
New York Law Journal	*N.Y. L. J.*
New York University Law Review	*N.Y.U. L. Rev.*
North Carolina Law Review	*N.C. L. Rev.*
Northwestern University Law Review	*Nw. U. L. Rev.*
Political Science Quarterly	*Pol. Sci. Q.*
Rutgers Law Review	*Rutgers L. Rev.*
St. Louis University Law Journal	*St. Louis U. L. J.*
Temple Law Quarterly	*Temp. L. Q.*
Texas Law Review	*Texas L. Rev.*
Tulane Law Review	*Tul. L. Rev.*
United States Law Review	*U.S. L. Rev.*
University of Chicago Law Review	*U. Chi. L. Rev.*
University of Florida Law Review	*U. Fla. L. Rev.*
University of Toronto Law Journal	*U. Toronto L. J.*
Vanderbilt Law Review	*Vand. L. Rev.*
Villanova Law Review	*Vill. L. Rev.*
Virginia Law Review	*Va. L. Rev.*
West Virginia Law Review	*W. Va. L. Rev.*
Wisconsin Law Review	*Wis. L. Rev.*
Yale Law Journal	*Yale L. J.*

AMERICAN LEGAL REALISM

Skepticism, Reform, and the Judicial Process

I

The Realist Movement in American Jurisprudence

In a now celebrated address delivered in 1932, Mr. Justice Cardozo observed that "one of the most significant signs of the times is the ferment of present-day interest in problems that are bound up with the nature and origin of law, problems of judicial method, problems of judicial teleology, problems of legal philosophy." The writers whose heterodox ideas form the basis of this study constituted the chief manufacturers of this ferment of interest. The significance of the brew which they concocted has seldom been denied. As Cardozo went on to point out, "The most distinctive product of the last decade in the field of jurisprudence is not in anthropology. It is not in any social science that is merely historical or descriptive. The most distinctive product of the last decade in the field of jurisprudence is the rise of a group of scholars styling themselves realists." [1] The perceptiveness of this insight

[1] "Jurisprudence," *Selected Writings of Benjamin Nathan Cardozo*, ed. Margaret E. Hall (New York: Fallon Publications, 1947),

1

AMERICAN LEGAL REALISM

has been amply confirmed by the passage of time. In the 1930's the legal realists made an even larger mark upon American jurisprudence. To be sure, in the postwar period their movement tended to lose its dynamic force: the call for a "realistic jurisprudence" has been considerably

---

pp. 7–8, 10. This address was delivered in 1932 to the New York State Bar Association and constitutes Cardozo's most systematic appraisal of legal realism. There is no infallible method to determine who is a legal realist. In general, this study is based on the writings of men listed as such by Karl N. Llewellyn in a celebrated article on the movement. See Llewellyn, *Jurisprudence: Realism in Theory and Practice* (Chicago: University of Chicago Press, 1962), pp. 74–76. Edwin W. Patterson, who was the friend and colleague of many of the legal realists, has pointed out that "to Llewellyn's list might be added, with justification, Thurman Arnold and Felix Cohen." Patterson, *Jurisprudence: Men and Ideas of the Law* (Brooklyn: Foundation Press, 1953), p. 538, n. 7. For the purposes of this book Arnold and Cohen are regarded as legal realists, as is Fred Rodell. There is no standard account of the nature and development of legal realism. For interpretations of some of the men upon whom this study is based, see Llewellyn, *Jurisprudence*, pp. 3–76; Llewellyn, *The Common Law Tradition: Deciding Appeals* (Boston: Little, Brown, 1960), pp. 11–18, 508–520; Jerome N. Frank, *Law and the Modern Mind* (Garden City, New York: Doubleday, 1963), pp. viii–xxx, 46–52, 283–306; Lucy Kramer Cohen (ed.), *The Legal Conscience: Selected Papers of Felix S. Cohen* (New Haven: Yale University Press, 1960), pp. 33–94; Jerome N. Frank, *If Men Were Angels: Some Aspects of Government in a Democracy* (New York: Harper, 1942), pp. 276–315; and Max Radin, "Legal Realism," *Colum. L. Rev.*, XXXI (1931), 824. For other accounts of legal realism, see Myres S. McDougal, "Fuller v. the American Legal Realists: An Intervention," *Yale L. J.*, L (1941), 827; Eugene V. Rostow, *The Sovereign Prerogative: The Supreme Court and the Quest for Law* (New Haven: Yale University Press, 1962), pp. 3–45; Patterson, *Jurisprudence*, pp. 537–555; Edwin N. Garlan, *Legal Realism and Justice* (New York: Columbia University Press, 1941); Fred V. Cahill, Jr., *Judicial Legislation: A Study in American Legal Theory* (New York: The Ronald Press, 1952), pp. 97–148; Julius Paul, *The Legal Realism of Jerome N. Frank: A Study of Fact-Skepticism and the Judicial Process* (The Hague: Nijhoff, 1959);

muted in the last twenty years.[2] A new climate of opinion, the death of major realists, and various other factors have taken their toll. Nonetheless, realism is generally regarded today as the most significant development in American legal theory in the years between the two world wars. Moreover, its impact is still visible. Finally, some of the most basic doctrines espoused by the realists retain contemporary relevance.

A movement about which all of this can be said is of obvious importance. Unfortunately, it has not received the kind of systematic study that it deserves. The purpose of this book is to contribute to such a study through an analysis of the answers given by the realists to the following questions: How are judicial decisions reached? What is the role of established rules? How objectively do courts find the facts of concrete cases? How can the prediction of

---

Moses Aronson, "Tendencies in American Jurisprudence," *U. Toronto L. J.*, IV (1941), 90; Roscoe Pound, "The Call for a Realist Jurisprudence," *Harv. L. Rev.*, XLIV (1931), 697; Lon L. Fuller, "American Legal Realism," *U. Pa. L. Rev.*, LXXXII (1934), 429; Herman Kantorowicz, "Some Rationalism about Realism," *Yale L. J.*, XLIII (1934), 1240; Harry W. Jones, "Law and Morality in the Perspective of Legal Realism," *Colum. L. Rev.*, LXI (1961), 799; Grant Gilmore, "Legal Realism: Its Cause and Cure," *Yale L. J.*, LXX (1961), 1037; Hessel E. Yntema, "American Legal Realism in Retrospect," *Vand. L. Rev.*, XIV (1960), 317; Bernie R. Burrus, "American Legal Realism," *How. L. J.*, VIII (1962), 36; Ralph J. Savarese, "American Legal Realism," *Houston L. Rev.*, III (1965), 80; David H. Moskowitz, "The American Legal Realists and an Empirical Science of Law," *Vill. L. Rev.*, XI (1966), 480; David H. Moskowitz, "The Prediction Theory of Law," *Temp. L. Q.*, XXXIX (1966), 413; and David E. Ingersoll, "Karl Llewellyn, American Legal Realism, and Contemporary Legal Behavioralism," *Ethics*, LXXV (1966), 253.

[2] See Jerome Hall, *Studies in Jurisprudence and Criminal Theory* (New York: Oceana, 1958), pp. 136–142.

judicial decisions be made more accurate? What methods should courts use in reaching and justifying decisions? These are not, of course, the only questions which the realists asked. Nonetheless, an analysis of the answers given to them is of vital significance. The judicial process is the area of law which was of greatest interest to the legal realists [3]; their analysis of it has had a profound impact; and no book-length study of this analysis has yet been published. Before such an inquiry can be undertaken, however, the precursors and general nature of the realist movement must be explained.

Impact of Pragmatism

In 1958, Jerome Hall wrote that in "the recent past . . . the obvious fact is the influence of Pound, Holmes, and the Legal Realists." He went on to point out that Holmes "occupied the place of unique distinction as the catalyst, while Pound, in 25 years of scholarly publication, established sociological jurisprudence as the characteristic mode of thought among legal scholars in this country." [4] The names of William James and John Dewey should also be added to Hall's list. Their impact upon American legal thought in this century has been profound. Pound, Holmes, James, and Dewey are, then, the men who more

[3] To be sure, the importance of other areas of the legal process was fully admitted. See Llewellyn, *Jurisprudence*, pp. 65–68. As Harry W. Jones has pointed out, however, "what happened after 1930 is that realist scholarship came to be concentrated on the judicial process and to deal only incidentally with the work of nonjudicial officials and hardly at all with the area of contact between official action and societal behavior." "A View from the Bridge," *Law and Society: A Supplement to the Summer Issue of Social Problems* (1965), p. 40.

[4] Jerome Hall, "The Present Position of Jurisprudence in the United States," *Va. L. Rev.*, XLIV (1958), 322.

than anyone else shaped the climate of progressive juristic opinion which formed the background to the realist movement. In light of this, the indispensable first step for any study of the legal realists is clear. It is to trace the impact upon them of the pragmatism of James and Dewey, the sociological jurisprudence of Roscoe Pound, and the views of Mr. Justice Holmes.

The philosophy of James and Dewey had, of course, a marked effect upon Pound and, to a lesser degree, upon Holmes. The latter, while a great admirer of Dewey's thought, was rather critical of some of James's ideas.[5] In any event, the influence of pragmatism upon the realist movement is unmistakable. It was the dominant current of philosophical thought in the 1920's and 1930's. The realists were not, in general, philosophers who applied ready-made systems to the law. They were lawyers first and

[5] Holmes once wrote of James that "I never could make anything out of his or his friends' advocacy of his nostrum [pragmatism] except either that in motives depending upon human conduct effort affects the result—which we have heard—or that by yearning we can modify the multiplication table, which I doubt. . . . But I think as little of his philosophy as I do much of his psychology." Mark Dewolfe Howe (ed.), *Holmes-Laski Letters: The Correspondence of Mr. Justice Holmes and Harold J. Laski* (Cambridge: Harvard University Press, 1953), I, p. 70. Holmes described Dewey's *Experience and Nature,* however, as "truly a great book." For Holmes, Dewey "seems . . . to hold more of existence in his hand and more honestly to see behind all the current philosophers than any book I can think of on such themes." Howe, *Holmes-Laski Letters,* II, pp. 904–905. Dewey had, in turn, great respect for Holmes and once described him as "one of our greatest American philosophers." *Experience and Nature* (Chicago: Open Court, 1925), p. 417. For good accounts of the relationships between Holmes and pragmatism, see Philip P. Wiener, *Evolution and the Founders of Pragmatism* (Cambridge: Harvard University Press, 1949), pp. 172–189, and Morton White, *Social Thought in America: The Revolt against Formalism* (Boston: Beacon, 1957).

foremost. But they were lawyers who read what some philosophers had to say and used the ideas which were found for their own purposes. No one was referred to more than James and Dewey.

To begin with, the legal realists inherited from the founders of pragmatism a distaste for formalism, deduction, and abstractions. When James wrote that the pragmatist "turns away from abstraction and insufficiency, from verbal solutions, from bad *a priori* reasons, from fixed principles, closed systems, and pretended absolutes and origins," he described very well the spirit of legal realists as well. If pragmatism means "the open air and possibilities of nature, as against dogma, artificiality, and the pretence of finality in truth," then realism is pragmatism in law.[6] Moreover, the emphasis of both James and Dewey upon evolution and change is also reflected in the literature of realistic jurisprudence. Dewey once wrote that the "problems with which a philosophy relevant to the present must deal are those growing out of changes going on with ever-increasing rapidity, over an ever-increasing human-geographical range, and with ever-deepening intensity of penetration."[7] If "legal thought" is substituted for "philosophy" in this quotation, then it represents a very accurate statement of the views of the realists. Still further, their result-orientation in the study and evaluation of law also reflects themes which the leaders of pragmatism reiterated. For James, the "pragmatic method" means an "attitude of orientation." Its essence is *"looking away from first things, principles, 'categories,' supposed necessities;*

---

[6] William James, *Pragmatism and Four Essays from the Meaning of Truth* (New York: Meridian Books, 1955), p. 45.

[7] *Reconstruction in Philosophy* (New York: New American Library, 1948), p. 9.

and of looking towards last things, fruits, consequences, facts." [8] The consequence of this attitude for decision-making was well expressed by Dewey. For him, the "problem is not to draw a conclusion from given premises; that can best be done by a piece of inanimate machinery by fingering a keyboard. The problem is to *find* statements of general principle and of particular fact which are worthy to serve as premises." For this reason, the "logic of rigid demonstration" must be replaced by a "logic of search and discovery," an "experimental logic," a "logic relative to consequences rather than to antecedents," a "logic of inquiry into probable consequences." Human decisions should not be reached by deduction from pre-established norms, but through "inquiry, comparison of alternatives, weighing of facts." [9] Similar recommendations for judicial decisions abound in the literature of the legal realists.

The final element in pragmatism which had a profound impact upon the realists is the particular creation of John Dewey. Eric Goldman has pointed out that "James, a patrician who was scarcely a patrician reformer, had come to his revolt against absolutes with no reform urge except a vague irritation against 'the bitch-goddess, success' and a compassion in thinking of human problems." The same cannot be said of Dewey.

Clergymen or economists, anthropologists or lawyers, reform thinkers wanted to replace an evolution that stopped at the present with an evolution that raced on; an environment that predetermined men and women with an environment that human beings manipulated to meet their needs; the dreary inevitabilities of Conservative Darwinism with the radiant

[8] James, *Pragmatism and Four Essays,* p. 47.
[9] Dewey, *Philosophy and Civilization* (New York: Milton-Balch, 1931), pp. 134, 126.

7

hopefulness of Reform Darwinism. And now John Dewey had swept all their specific pragmatisms into a system from which each reformer, working away in his own field, could draw comfort and strength. "We were all Deweyites before we read Dewey," J. Allen Smith phrased the fact, "and we were all the more effective reformers after we had read him." Dewey was the Herbert Spencer of Reform Darwinism, and if there were no banquets at Delmonicos, a thousand other signs pointed to the fact that he was rapidly becoming the most important philosopher in the United States.[10]

By the 1920's and 1930's, Dewey had become the most important philosopher in the United States. Like reformers in other fields, the legal realists drew particular comfort and strength from his conviction of the imperative need for the application of scientific methods to the study of social problems, and his faith in "organized intelligence" as a vehicle of social reform. When Dewey claimed that "the reconstructive work to be done by philosophy" is "to undertake to do for the development of inquiry into human affairs . . . what the philosophers of the last few centuries did for promotion of scientific inquiry in physical and physiological conditions and aspects of human life," he defined very well how the realists viewed the reconstructive work to be done by legal study. The same can be said of his contention that "approximation to use of scientific method in investigation and of the engineering mind in the invention and projection of far-reaching social plans is demanded." [11]

[10] Erich F. Goldman, *Rendezvous with Destiny: A History of Modern American Reform* (New York: Knopf, 1952), pp. 156, 158–159.
[11] Dewey, *Reconstruction in Philosophy*, p. 18; *Liberalism and Social Action* (New York: Putnam, 1935), p. 73.

Roscoe Pound's Sociological Jurisprudence

By the end of the first decade of this century Pound had outlined the essentials of his new approach to law. It reflects, too, much of the pragmatic temper. The planks in the platform of sociological jurisprudence, as Pound defined it, can be classified into two different kinds of proposals. The object of one is the study of law, the other of its application. The sociological jurists stressed a variety of changes in methods of study. One of the most important is to switch the focus of juristic analysis from mere doctrine to the social effects of legal rules and practices. The objective must be a "scientific apprehension of the relations of law to society and of the needs and interests and opinions of society of today." [12] The need for greater factual information about the operation and impact of law is crucial. In 1907, Pound lamented that

no one can obtain statistics at all complete nor at all authoritative upon the most everyday points in judicial administration. . . . There are no endowments for juridical research. There are no laboratories dedicated to legal science whose bulletins shall make it possible for the scholar to obtain authoritative data and for lay public to reach sound conclusions.[13]

Also, the ex-Dean of the Harvard Law School emphasized again and again the desirability of utilization of the methods and concepts of the social sciences. This theme has been echoed throughout this century in American jurisprudence, and Pound was one of its first and most influential advocates. As he wrote in 1910, "Let us look the facts

[12] Pound, "The Need of a Sociological Jurisprudence," *Green Bag*, XIX (1907), 610–611.
[13] *Ibid.*, p. 608.

of human conduct in the face. Let us look to economics and sociology and philosophy, and cease to assume that jurisprudence is self-sufficient. . . . Let us not become legal monks." [14]

The second kind of proposal was directed at norms for judicial decisions. Its essence is "equitable application of law" rather than mechanical deduction from preordained premises. Advocates of the new movement, Pound wrote in 1912, "conceive of the legal rule as a general guide to the judge, leading him toward the just result, but insist that within wide limits he should be free to deal with the individual case, so as to meet the demands of justice between the parties and accord with the general reason of ordinary men." [15] Three years earlier he had outlined the background to this demand. In a celebrated passage he claimed:

Jurisprudence is the last in the march of the sciences away from the method of deduction from predetermined conceptions. The sociological movement in jurisprudence, the movement for pragmatism as a philosophy of law, the movement for the adjustment of principles and doctrines to the human conditions they are to govern rather than to assumed first principles, the movement for putting the human factor in the central place and relegating logic to its true position as an instrument, has scarcely shown itself as yet in America.[16]

These two proposals constitute the essence of sociological jurisprudence as viewed by Pound. What was its ultimate objective? How was that objective to be achieved?

[14] Pound, "Law in Books and Law in Action," *Am. L. Rev.*, XLIV (1910), 35–36.

[15] Pound, "The Scope and Purpose of Sociological Jurisprudence," *Harv. L. Rev.*, XXV (1912), 515.

[16] Pound, "Liberty of Contract," *Yale L. J.*, XVIII (1909), 464.

What was the impact of it all upon the legal realists? These questions must be answered if the realist movement is to be placed in its appropriate context.

No one can read the many articles and books of Roscoe Pound without concluding that the major aim of his program is the reform of the positive law itself. This is obvious insofar as equitable application is concerned. It is less apparent but equally true of his methodological proposals. Their immediate goal was to inform the judge and the legislator of the effects of law, and the degree to which legal rules and institutions had in fact achieved their presumed purposes. This objective was, in turn, pursued so vigorously because the sociological jurists felt that ignorance of the effects of law is perhaps the chief reason for unwarranted legal conservatism. Both Pound and Brandeis were prone to cite the statement of Arthur Henderson that "a lawyer who has not studied economics and sociology is very apt to become a public enemy." The explanation for their belief is not obscure. It is the conviction that "bad" law is primarily the result of ignorance. As Pound himself asserted in two of his early articles:

More than anything else, ignorance of the actual situations of fact for which legislation was provided and supposed lack of legal warrant for knowing them, have been responsible for the judicial overthrowing of so much social legislation.[17]

The entire separation of jurisprudence from the other social sciences . . . was not merely unfortunate for the science of law on general considerations . . . but was *in large part* to be charged with the backwardness of law in meeting social ends, the tardiness of lawyers in admitting or even perceiving such

[17] *Ibid.*, p. 470.

11

ends, and the gulf between legal thought and popular thought on matters of social reform.[18]

Given these views, the great emphasis which Pound placed on knowledge of the effects of law and integration of jurisprudence and the other social sciences is not surprising. They were the indispensable methods for bridging the great gulf between legal and popular thought on matters of social reform. In perfect harmony with the spirit of the Progressive Era, of which he is such a typical example, Pound pinned many of his hopes for reform on education. It was to be the great catalyst for the changes which he regarded as so necessary. As he put it, "The remedy is in our law schools. It is in training the rising generation of lawyers in a social, political, and legal philosophy abreast

[18] Pound, "The Scope and Purpose of Sociological Jurisprudence," *Harv. L. Rev.*, XXV (1912), 510 (italics mine). For the views of Mr. Justice Brandeis, see Osmond K. Fraenkel (ed.), *The Curse of Bigness: Miscellaneous Papers of Louis D. Brandeis* (New York: Viking, 1935), and Samuel J. Konefsky, *The Legacy of Holmes and Brandeis: A Study in the History of Ideas* (New York: Macmillan, 1956). The Brandis brief is, of course, the classic attempt to devise a method by means of which the courts' "ignorance of the actual situations of fact" could be overcome. Oddly enough, however, the work of Brandeis in this regard was seldom mentioned by Pound. As Konefsky has pointed out: "The curious fact is that Pound did not recognize Brandeis for the leader of the new jurisprudence that he was. As one of Brandeis' law secretaries has suggested, Brandeis was 'living proof' of the kind of jurist Pound was seeking. In the constitutional sphere, Brandeis was the prophet of the new approach. . . . But even if Louis D. Brandeis had not been afforded the opportunity to apply his methods and his ideas within the judicial laboratory, the social importance of the techniques he initiated would have assured him a lasting reputation as a master of sociological jurisprudence." *Ibid.*, p. 92. The most celebrated application by Brandeis of his ideas and methods occurred, of course, in his brief in *Muller* v. *Oregon*, 208 U.S. 412 (1908).

of our time. . . . Must not a philosophy of law founded on
a sound knowledge of the elements of the social and political science of today form part—and a necessary part—of
the equipment of the trained lawyer?" [19] Only in this way
will the great gap between the needs of the day and the
substance of law be lessened. For this reason,

the modern teacher of law should be a student of sociology,
economics, and politics as well. He should know not only what
the courts decide and the principles by which they decide, but
quite as much the circumstances and conditions, social and
economic, to which these principles are to be applied . . .
[and] the state of popular thought and feeling which makes
the environment in which the principles must operate in practice. Legal monks who pass their lives in an atmosphere of
pure law, from which every worldly and human element is
excluded, cannot shape practical principles to be applied to a
restless world of flesh and blood. The most logical and skillfully reasoned rules may defeat the end of law in their practical administration because not adapted to the environment in
which they are to be enforced.[20]

Sociological Jurisprudence and Legal Realism

Once it is realized that this outline of a sociological
jurisprudence had been formulated in the first dozen years
of this century, the debt of the legal realists to Pound
becomes clear. To a degree the realist movement was
quite obviously a vigorous reassertion of doctrines the
lineage of which leads back to him. As he once wrote, so
far as the realists

[19] Pound, "Do We Need a Philosophy of Law?" *Colum. L. Rev.,* V
(1905), 352–353.
[20] Pound, "The Need of a Sociological Jurisprudence," *Green Bag,*
XIX (1907), 611–612.

think of law (in all its senses) functionally . . . urge study of the actual social effects of legal institutions, legal precepts, and legal doctrines . . . advocate sociological study in preparation for lawmaking . . . call for psychological study of the judicial and juristic processes . . . demand study of the social background and social effects of legal institutions, legal precepts, and legal doctrines and argue for recognition of the importance of individualized applications and of just solutions of individual cases—in all these respects they were anticipated by the sociological jurists of a generation ago.[21]

All of these proposals and propositions were advocated by the legal realists. All of them had also been advanced earlier by Pound. This is why the late Karl Nickerson Llewellyn wrote in 1960 that the pioneering work of Pound "is the basis of our forward-looking thought of the 20's and 30's and has provided half of the commonplace equipment on and with which our work since has builded." [22] There are, of course, genuine differences in some of the ideas advanced by the legal realists and Pound. Indeed, knowledge of these points of disagreement is the key to comprehension of the distinctiveness of the realist movement. Nonetheless, it is important to recognize *that* and *how* it constituted the attempt to develop and apply theories which Pound had done so much to propagate.

One of the most significant signs of the impact of Pound upon the realists took the form, ironically, of a criticism. Its essence is that he had failed to implement the approach which he so persuasively advocated, and which urgently needed to be applied. Typical is the lament of Llewellyn.

---

[21] Pound, "Fifty Years of Jurisprudence," *Harv. L. Rev.,* LI (1938) , 791.

[22] Llewellyn, *Jurisprudence,* p. 496.

In his mind, Pound's "buddings" were "brilliant"; but in the main they have "not come to fruition." [23] Thus, Llewellyn once implored, "What would one not give for the actual appearance of the long-awaited *Sociological Jurisprudence,* if its author would integrate it in terms of those pioneering thoughts of his which thus far have been waiting to be called together in a Constituent Assembly?" [24] Not surprisingly, it was the claim and to a degree the inspiration of some of the realists to have succeeded where Pound, they felt, had failed. As Herman Oliphant wrote in 1933, their objective was to convert " 'sociological jurisprudence' [into] a fact rather than a mere aspiration." [25]

The concrete ways and means devised to achieve this goal are far too varied to survey here. Still, a brief examination of the Institute of Law of the Johns Hopkins University may be appropriate. It is an excellent illustration of the kind of endeavors to which this facet of the realist movement led. Moreover, it has been described as "probably the most important of all attempts by legally trained personnel to develop significant social research on the operation and functioning of law." [26] Established in 1928, the Institute collapsed in 1933, one more victim of depression-induced economies. Its staff consisted largely of prominent legal scholars. Most of them, such as Walter Wheeler Cook, Herman Oliphant, and Hessel Yntema, played important roles in the realist movement.

The stated purposes and methods of the Institute faith-

[23] *Ibid.,* p. 7, n. 3.   [24] *Ibid.,* p. 8.

[25] "Parallels in the Development of Legal and Medical Education," *Annals,* CLXVII (1933), 162.

[26] Frederick K. Beutel, *Some Potentialities of Experimental Jurisprudence as a New Branch of Social Science* (Lincoln: University of Nebraska Press, 1957), p. 105.

fully reflect the kind of sociological approach urged by Pound. In an article written in 1927, Walter Wheeler Cook pointed out that

its primary purpose would be the non-professional study of law, in order that the function of law may be more clearly understood, its limitations appreciated, its results evaluated, and its future development kept more nearly in touch with the complexities of modern life. . . . The aim of the school would be . . . the development of the scientific study of law. All else would be incidental.[27]

As has been indicated, Pound in 1907 had criticized the absence of judicial statistics about the administration of law. He had deplored the lack of "endowments for juridical research" and "laboratories dedicated to legal science." The same cry pervades the literature stating the goals of the Institute. Thus one of the major justifications for its establishment was the fact that present collections of judicial statistics "are as a few scattered cases of information in a Sahara of ignorance with respect to the grist being ground by the judicial machine." And again, "If one looks for far-reaching interpretations of data, and especially if one looks for illuminating correlations of judicial data with other types of data, he finds a void that is absolute and of Stygian darkness." [28] The primary need is more knowledge about how the legal and especially the judicial system actually operates. It is a need which the traditional style of legal research cannot fulfill. Only the accumulation of facts through field research can close the gap. For

---

[27] "Scientific Method and the Law," *A. B. A. J.*, XIII (1927), 309.
[28] *The Johns Hopkins University Circular: The Institute of Law, 1930–31* (Baltimore: Johns Hopkins, 1930), p. 11.

the only way to find out what anything does is to observe it in action and not to read supposedly authoritative books about it, or to attempt by reason to deduce it from fundamental principles assumed to be fixed and given. The consequences of this assumption is that only a small part of the work of the staff of the Institute will be with books in libraries: by far the larger part will be concerned with the difficult, time-consuming, and expensive task of gathering and interpreting the facts concerning the operation of our legal system.[29]

Moreover, the founders of the Institute justified this kind of research in terms identical to those advanced by Pound. Time and again it was defended as indispensable for intelligent reduction of the law's "cultural lag," to use the famous phrase coined by William Ogburn in 1922.[30] As Hessel Yntema wrote, "The elemental factor in the need for research which the Institute . . . has been planned to meet is that legal science has lagged behind the times. . . . The world has been changing at a rate which

---

[29] Cook, "Scientific Study and the Administration of Justice," *Maryland S. B. A. Bull.,* XXXIV (1929), 148.

[30] See Ogburn, *Social Change with Respect to Culture and Original Nature* (New ed.; New York: Viking, 1950), p. 200. According to Ogburn, "the thesis is that the various parts of modern culture are not changing at the same rate, some parts are changing much more rapidly than others. . . . Where one part of culture changes first . . . and occasions changes in some part of culture dependent upon it, there frequently is a delay in the changes occasioned in the dependent part of culture. The extent of this lag will vary . . . but may exist for a considerable number of years, during which time there may be said to be a maladjustment. It is desirable to reduce the period of maladjustment, to make the cultural adjustments as quickly as possible." *Ibid.,* pp. 200–201. Significantly, Ogburn cited the facts of laws on workmen's compensation as prime evidence for his hypothesis. For an interesting critique of his thesis, see Lawrence M. Friedman and Jack Ladinsky, "Social Change and the Law of Industrial Accidents," *Colum. L. Rev.,* LXVII (1967), 72–77.

has left the lawyer, the judge, and the law-teacher breathless." [31] For this reason the function of the Institute of Law was sometimes compared to that of the world-famous Medical School of the Johns Hopkins University.

The purpose of the Medical School was the training of men equipped for observation and accurate deduction, the gathering of correct data, followed by close and accurate study. Its objective was the prevention of disease. If we substitute "social maladjustment" for "disease" . . . could the Institute . . . ask for any better formula? While it may be true that the law cannot create happiness, it can certainly promote, retard, and even destroy it.[32]

Given these objectives, it is not surprising that the methods of study advocated by the founders of the Institute also bear a strong similarity to those recommended by Pound. "An Institute committed to the study of the impact of law upon life must, by the very nature of the case, build upon intimate and substantial contacts with the other social sciences." The great need is for the "application of methods similar to those which scientists in other fields have so fruitfully used [and which] will yield a rich harvest in the legal field." The studies of the Institute thus "require the cooperation not only of judges, practicing lawyers and scientific students of the law, but also of students of heredity, of psychology, of psychiatry, of sociology, of criminology, and perhaps others." [33]

Unfortunately, the achievements of the Institute, as

[31] *The New York Times,* July 29, 1928, #8, p. 11.
[32] *The Johns Hopkins University Circular: The Institute for the Study of Law, 1929–30* (Baltimore: Johns Hopkins, 1929), p. 14.
[33] Cook, *op. cit.,* pp. 148, 153.

18

measured by its published results, at best but partially realized these very ambitious goals. While several of the studies received the acclaim of legal scholars, the vast majority passed rather soon into oblivion. In general, they were rather unexciting factual inquiries about certain limited phases of judicial systems.[34] Little interdisciplinary cooperation was in fact elicited. A sympathetic student of the Institute has contended that its "scientific work . . . reached approximately the same stage as Botany would, had its efforts been devoted wholly to counting leaves on trees." [35] Most of the work of the Institute did not advance, in short, beyond a rather crude form of empiricism.

In part, this was due to its short existence. Five years is hardly long enough to convert sociological jurisprudence from an aspiration into a fact. In part, the rather unspectacular achievements of the Institute stem from more basic factors. One has been pointed out by Felix Cohen. In 1933 he wrote that " 'sociological jurisprudence' remains in large part a pious program rather than a record of achievement." In his mind, "at the root of this failure" is "the lack of any definite criterion of importance which will dictate which of the infinite consequences of any legal rule or decision deserve to be investigated." [36] Another reason has been adduced by Mr. Justice Douglas. In 1936 he asserted that "no real fusion of law and . . . other social sciences . . . has been accomplished . . . in no sin-

---

[34] For a bibliography of the studies produced by the Institute of Law, see Wilfrid E. Rumble, Jr., "The Foundations of American Legal Realism" (unpublished Ph.D. dissertation, Dept. of Political Science, The Johns Hopkins University) , p. 73, n. 105.

[35] Beutel, *Experimental Jurisprudence*, p. 112.

[36] Felix S. Cohen, Review of *Bentham's Theory of Fictions*, by C. K. Ogden, *Yale L. J.*, XLII (1933) , 1150–1151.

19

gle field of law has there been any substantial integration." For him the basic cause is the "volatile character of the phenomena being studied." [37] More important than either of these reasons is the extraordinarily ambitious character of the goals of a sociological jurisprudence as defined by Pound and as urged by the legal realists. It is difficult to disagree with David Riesman's statement that "the early advocates of sociological jurisprudence were unduly sanguine. Many of them hoped to storm the fortress of the law without extensive empirical work but with what now appear as semantic and epistemological slogans. The effect of these slogans was at first stimulating . . . [but] now . . . the tasks loom in their true magnitude." [38] It is one thing to demonstrate the desirability of a sociological approach to the study of law. Interdisciplinary analysis of the effects of "law" upon society is a noble goal. But it is also a very difficult goal to achieve. The history of American jurisprudence in this century is ample testimony to the complexity of the obstacles to be overcome.[39]

[37] James Allen (ed.), *Democracy and Finance: The Addresses and Public Statements of William O. Douglas* (New Haven: Yale University Press, 1940), pp. 285, 281.

[38] David Riesman, "Law and Sociology: Recruitment, Training, and Colleagueship," *Law and Sociology: Exploratory Essays,* ed. William M. Evan (New York: Free Press of Glencoe, 1962), p. 15.

[39] As Philip Selznick has written, "In this country, the premises of sociological jurisprudence achieved a rather quick and general victory. . . . This victory, such as it is, has had but little to do with the actual researches of sociologists; nor does it reflect the particular concepts and funded knowledge of the field. It is a point of view, an approach, a sensitivity that has been accepted." "The Sociology of Law," *Sociology Today: Problems and Prospects,* ed. Robert K. Merton, Leonard Broom, Leonard S. Cottrell, Jr. (New York: Basic Books, 1959), p. 115. This judgment is not as true now as it was in 1959, but it still has an important core of truth.

Contribution of the Realists

Even so, the contribution of the realist movement, *viewed from the limited perspective* of the attempt to implement the kind of sociological studies urged by Pound, is not insignificant. In the first place, some valuable empirical work was produced. Aside from the studies of the Institute of Law, the investigations of Charles E. Clark, Harry Schulman, and Underhill Moore are perhaps the most outstanding examples.[40] In the second place, the realists provided a stimulus to further research. They were effective propagandists for a most worthwhile objective. The studies at the University of Chicago on the operation of the jury system are one illustration among many which could be cited. The authors of the most recent of these studies have described their work, for example, as "a contribution to what has often been called realist jurisprudence; it is an effort to find out how the law in operation, as contrasted to the law on the books, is working." [41] According to Hans Zeisel, a participant in this effort, the magnitude of the tasks is now generally recognized.

In the law schools, empirical social research . . . has now reached a second phase . . . it is characterized by the inclusion of topics that are not necessarily in the passing limelight of litigation or in the political debates of the day; by an aspiration to use the very latest developments in social science technique; and by a sober realization of the limitations of such

[40] See Clark and Shulman, *A Study of Law Administration in Connecticut* (New Haven: Yale University Press, 1937); Underhill Moore and Charles C. Callahan, "Law and Learning Theory: A Study in Legal Control," *Yale L. J.*, LIII (1943), 1; and the studies by Moore cited *infra*, p. 162, n. 45.

[41] Harry Kalven, Jr., and Hans Zeisel, *The American Jury* (Boston: Little, Brown, 1966), p. 11.

inquiry into the law. . . . The yield from these efforts is still modest.[42]

Finally, the plea of the realists for sociological study has had an important impact upon legal education. Brainerd Currie has written that "the most significant development in American legal education since 1870 is the movement toward reorganization of courses along functional lines and toward the broadening of law school studies to include nonlegal materials, chiefly from the social sciences, which are relevant to legal problems."[43] It is a development for which the legal realists can take a good deal of credit. In the 1920's and 1930's, certainly, they were the most avid exponents of a functional and interdisciplinary approach.[44] Indeed, according to Edwin W. Patterson,

[42] Zeisel, "Social Research on the Law: The Ideal and the Practical," *Law and Sociology: Exploratory Essays*, ed. William M. Evan (New York: The Free Press of Glencoe, 1962), pp. 142–143. The yield becomes greater, however, each year. For a good bibliography, see Anne Rankin, "A Selected Bibliography in the Sociology of Law," *Law and Society: A Supplement to the Summer Issue of Social Problems* (1965), pp. 54–57. For interpretive essays, see Jerome H. Skolnick, "The Sociology of Law in America: Overview and Trends," *Law and Society*, p. 4; Harry W. Jones, "A View from the Bridge," *Law and Society*, p. 39; Carl A. Auerbach, "Legal Tasks for the Sociologist," *Law & Society Review*, I (1966), 91; and Skolnick, "Social Research on Legality: A Reply to Auerbach," *Law & Society Review*, I (1966), 105.

[43] "The Materials of Law Study," *J. Legal Ed.*, VIII (1955), 1.

[44] See Fred Rodell, *Woe Unto You, Lawyers!* (2d ed.; New York: Pageant, 1957), pp. 138–150; Jerome N. Frank, "What Constitutes a Good Legal Education?" *Am. L. Sch. Rev.*, VII (1933), 894; Frank, "A Plea for Lawyer Schools," *Yale L. J.*, LVI (1947), 1303; Frank, "A Disturbing Look at the Law Schools," *J. Legal Ed.*, II (1949), 189; Karl N. Llewellyn, "On What Is Wrong with So-Called Legal Education," *Colum. L. Rev.*, XXXV (1935), 651; Llewellyn, "McDougal and Lasswell Plan for Legal Education," *ibid.*, XLIII (1943), 476; Llewellyn, "The Current Crisis in Legal Education," *J.*

the most important immediate consequences of legal realism were in the field of legal education. While outside of academic halls the realists seemed to many to be merely cynics or icono-clasts, within those halls legal realism was a vital constructive influence. . . . To claim for legal realism all of the innovations in legal education after 1930 would be an exaggeration; to restrict the influence of legal realism to those who became its avowed followers would be no less misleading. A good many law teachers who rejected the extreme positions of legal real-ism were moved to incorporate more moderate versions of its ideas in their own work.[45]

Legal Ed., I (1948), 211; Herman Oliphant, "Legal Research in Law Schools," *Am. L. S. Rev.*, V (1924), 293; Oliphant, "The Future of Legal Education," *ibid.*, VI (1928), 329; Oliphant, "Parallels in the Development of Legal and Medical Education," *Annals*, CLXVII (1933), 156; Charles E. Clark, "Law Professor, What Now?" *A. B. A. J.*, XX (1934), 431; and Clark, "Legal Education in Modern Society," *Tul. L. Rev.*, X (1935), 1. Llewellyn once denounced American legal education as "blind, inept, factory-ridden, wasteful, defective, and empty. . . . It blinds, it stumbles, it conveyor belts, it wastes, it mutilates, and it empties." "On What Is Wrong with So-Called Legal Education," p. 653. The shrill character of the language of this criticism is not representative either of Llewellyn or the other realists. All of them were, however, very dissatisfied with the state of American legal education. The spirit of the kinds of reforms which they urged is nicely caught in this statement: "First, law should not be studied and taught as an isolated body of doctrine, but problems of law and government should have cast upon them whatever light can be obtained from any and all bodies of human knowledge. Those likely to throw most light . . . are the ones which . . . deal with human relations and human behavior, i.e., the other social sciences. . . . Second, . . . we should not limit ourselves to those tools of study which have hitherto been available to the lawyer but should seek and devise more exact and objective methods and techniques. . . . Third, we must 'return to the patient'; legal prob-lems would not be studied in the cloistered seclusion of academic halls, where they are not, but in the field where they are." Oliphant, "Parallels," p. 162.

[45] Patterson, *Jurisprudence*, p. 554.

Signs of this impact are varied. Patterson's testimony, as the friend, associate, and perceptive observer of many of the realists, merits special attention. He has singled out three developments as of particular importance. First of all, a new type of casebook emerged. One of its major features is the inclusion of a considerable amount of factual or "extralegal" material. " 'Cases and Materials' became the standard heading for the classbook, revised to include, besides the traditional collection of reported judicial decisions, 'materials' showing economic or social theory or fact, relevant business practices, excerpts from works on psychiatry, forms of contract, and frequently just straight legal text from law reviews or treatises." Another important development was "the 'functional' grouping of cases and materials, rather than a doctrinal, chronological or historical grouping."[46] In addition to this, important revisions in the curriculum were devised under the leadership of prominent legal realists. The changes initiated at Columbia, in which Herman Oliphant played a key role, and those at Yale, a hotbed of legal realism, are perhaps the most famous examples.[47] Finally, the practice developed of

[46] *Ibid.*, pp. 554–555.

[47] See *Summaries of Studies in Legal Education by the Faculty of Law in Columbia University* (1928) ; Clark, "Educational and Scientific Objectives of the Yale Law School," *Annals*, CLXVII (1933), 165; Currie, "The Materials of Law Study," *J. Legal Ed.*, III (1951), 331; and Currie, "The Materials of Law Study," *ibid.*, VIII (1955), 1. According to Currie, the movement "for reorganization of the law curriculum along 'functional' lines and for the broadening of law school studies to include non-legal materials, drawn principally from the social sciences . . . may be said to have its beginning in the studies of legal education undertaken in the years 1926–28 by the Faculty of Law of Columbia University." "The Materials of Law Study," *J. Legal Ed.*, III (1951), 332. "This was the institutional beginning of the movement for integration of nonlegal materials with the course of law study." *Ibid.*, p. 334, n. 3. Currie has also

appointing distinguished social scientists to the faculties of the law schools. The appointments of Walton Hale Hamilton and Harold Lasswell at Yale, of Robert L. Hale at Columbia, and of Sheldon Glueck at Harvard are but a few illustrations.

All of these changes cannot be credited to the legal realists or those under the influence of their ideas. The magnitude of the reforms should not be exaggerated either. Thus in his excellent study of American legal education Currie concluded in 1955 that "two things are clear: first, the events of the late Twenties were the stimulus to a remarkable productivity, imaginativeness, and vitality in legal education; and second, the goals of the more ambitious planners were far from realized." Among the factors which he felt were responsible for this failure are: the fear that law schools would be converted into mere research institutes "for the 'scientific' study of law as an aspect of social organization"; the sheer magnitude of the problems involved in a functional reorganization of the curriculum; the difficulties which confront interdisciplinary cooperation in the study of law; and "the lack of any sharp conception of the purpose to be served by such materials and, more particularly, the frustrations and defections which resulted when the more ambitious conceptions of the goal were disappointed." [48] In 1964 the editors of the *Columbia Law Review* reached a somewhat similar conclusion. In a study of American legal education, they contended that "prospects for further progress in the integration of law and social sciences remain uncertain. Problems

---

pointed out that "clearly, the driving force" for the movement at Columbia "was supplied by Oliphant." "The Materials of Law Study," *J. Legal Ed.*, VIII (1955), 9.

[48] *Ibid.*, 64, 74.

of collaboration exist; a coherent methodology has yet to evolve; and articulations of fundamental aims and purposes continue to be vague." Nonetheless, it was also felt that "the interdisciplinary approach will surely continue to evolve, and remain a dominant factor in modern legal education." [49] To the degree that such a prediction is valid, the legal realists deserve a good deal of credit. They were the major pioneers of such an approach in the interwar period. The trail which they blazed is not yet completed, unforeseen obstacles have been encountered, and progress remains slow; but much has been accomplished.

The Interpretation of Karl N. Llewellyn

The purpose of the foregoing pages has been to explain how the legal realists tried to implement the sociological jurisprudence first outlined by Roscoe Pound. The general conclusion which was reached is that these efforts were not wholly successful. Regardless of this, the realist movement represents much more than the attempt to develop ideas first enunciated by Pound. The theories formulated by the advocates of "realistic jurisprudence" have a richness and uniqueness of their own. What accounts for this distinctiveness?

The logical place to begin the search for an answer to this question is in the interpretations of the movement advanced by the leading legal realists. One of the most important is Karl Llewellyn's notable article, "Some Realism about Realism—Responding to Dean Pound." [50] Its purpose was to rebut certain criticisms leveled against the legal realists by Pound, in the first of his many critiques of

[49] "Modern Trends in Legal Education," *Colum. L. Rev.*, LXIV (1964), 726, 726–727.

[50] *Harv. L. Rev.*, XLIV (1931), 1222.

their work.[51] The achievement of this objective required a description of the nature of the movement. Its goal was to demonstrate that the realists did not in fact hold many of the views for which Pound criticized them. It is this part of the article which for present purposes is of greatest relevance.

At the outset, Llewellyn described the general character of legal realism. He insisted that it is erroneous to construe it as a school of jurisprudence. "One thing is clear. There is no school of realists. There is no likelihood that there will be such a school. There is no group with an official or accepted, or even with an emerging creed." The doctrinal diversity among the legal realists is immense. Still, he pointed out, "there is . . . a *movement* in thought and work about law." It consists of "individual men, working and thinking over law and its place in society." Moreover, the work of these men begins from certain "common points of departure." Also, it exhibits "a cross-relevance, a complementing, an interlocking of their varied results 'as if they were guided by an invisible hand.'" Finally, there is the "fighting faith" of the realists "in their methods of attack on legal problems."

Llewellyn then described nine "common points of departure" of the legal realists. He viewed four as "common to the workers of the newer movement" but not "peculiar to them." He regarded five as "the characteristic marks of the movement. Men or work fitting those specifications are to me 'realistic' whatever label they may wear. Such, and none other, are the perfect fauna of this new land." The four points of departure which are common but not peculiar to the realists are: an insistence upon the reality of

[51] See Pound, "The Call for a Realist Jurisprudence," *Harv. L. Rev.*, XLIV (1931), 697.

legal change, and of judicial creation of law; the conception of law as a means for the achievement of social ends, to be evaluated in terms of its purposes and effects; an emphasis upon the rapidity of social change, and the likelihood that for this reason law stands in need of constant updating; and "distrust of traditional legal rules and concepts insofar as they purport to *describe* what either courts or people are actually doing." The items in the agenda of the realists which are both common and distinctive are: the temporary divorce of *Is* and *Ought* for purposes of study; distrust of the theory that traditional prescriptive rule-formulations are *the* heavily operative factor in producing court decisions, and tentative adoption of the theory of rationalization for the study of opinions; emphasis upon the need to group cases and legal situations into narrower categories than has been the practice in the past; insistence on the necessity to discover the effects of law, and to evaluate it in terms of these effects; and *"sustained and programmatic attack* on the problems of law along any of these lines." [52]

The value of this interpretation of the realist movement is considerable. It still is one of the best accounts ever written. For example, Llewellyn has correctly pinpointed a fact which any student of the legal realists ignores at his peril. This is their diversity in point of view. The legal realists were a heterodox lot. Most generalizations about their work are subject to numerous exceptions. At the same time, Llewellyn was also correct to point out that some convergence of results did exist. He was right, too, to speak of the "fighting faith" of the realists in their approach. Indeed, the militant character of this faith adds a rather different *temper* to the realist movement than that

[52] Llewellyn, *Jurisprudence,* pp. 53, 54, 57, 56, 57.

which characterized, say, Pound's sociological jurisprudence. This stridency was not without its disadvantages. Often it reached such heights that students of the new movement—particularly in its great days of the 1930's—missed its positive elements.[53] Nonetheless, the

[53] For the critical reaction of the 1930's and early 1940's, see the literature cited *supra,* note 1. Also, see Pound, *Contemporary Juristic Theory* (Claremount, Calif.: Ward Ritchie, 1940) ; John Dickinson, "Legal Rules: Their Function in the Process of Decision," *U. Pa. L. Rev.,* LXXIX (1931), 833; Dickinson, "Legal Rules: Their Application and Elaboration," *ibid.,* LXXIX (1931), 1052; Walter B. Kennedy, "Functional Nonsense and the Transcendental Approach," *Fordham L. Rev.,* V (1936), 272; Kennedy, "More Functional Nonsense—A Reply to Felix S. Cohen," *ibid.,* VI (1937), 75; Kennedy, "Realism, What Next?" *ibid.,* VII (1938), 203; Kennedy, "A Review of Legal Realism," *ibid.,* IX (1940), 362; Kennedy, "Psychologism in the Law," *Geo. L. J.,* XXIX (1940), 139; Kennedy, "The New Deal in the Law," *U. S. L. Rev.,* LXVIII (1934), 533; Kennedy, "The Scientific Approach in the Law," *ibid.,* LXX (1936), 75; Frances J. Lucy, "Natural Law and American Legal Realism: Their Respective Contributions to a Theory of Law in a Democratic Society," *Geo. L. J.,* XXX (1942), 493; Philip Mechem, "The Jurisprudence of Despair," *Iowa L. Rev.,* XXI (1936), 669; Pound, "The Ideal and the Actual in Law—Forty Years After," *Geo. Wash. L. Rev.,* I (1933), 431; Pound, "Fifty Years of Jurisprudence," *Harv. L. Rev.,* LI (1938), 777, 784 (n. 26), 791–792, 800; Pound, "Philosophy of Law and Comparative Law," *U. Pa. L. Rev.,* C (1951), 1, 3; Pound, "How Far Are We Attaining a New Measure of Values in Twentieth-Century Juristic Thought?" *W. Va. L. Q.,* XLII (1936), 81, 89–90; Pound, "What is Law?" *ibid.,* XLVII (1940), 1, 4, 10; Pound, "Law and the Science of Law in Recent Theories," *Yale L. J.,* XLIII (1934), 525; Pound, "The Future of Law," *ibid.,* XLVII (1937), 1, 7, 13; and Pound, "Sociology of Law," *Twentieth Century Sociology,* ed. Georges Gurvitch and Wilbert E. Moore (New York: Philosophical Library, 1945), p. 337. The attitude of Pound toward the legal realists was not wholly negative. Thus he once praised the efforts of the late Karl Llewellyn as "much the best outline of the task of a sociology of law and the way of going about its performance which has yet appeared." *Ibid.* Nonetheless, he was critical of the realists' interpretation of the judicial process and, in particular, what

vigor with which the advocates of realism denounced prior views and propagated their own adds a zest to their writing which American jurisprudence has seldom seen.

Llewellyn's account of the common but not distinctive points of departure of the legal realists is also important. He was right to point out that they did emphasize heavily the existence and rapidity of social change, and the consequent need for legal flexibility in meeting that change. Moreover, his analysis of their distrust of traditional legal rules as descriptions of what courts or people have in fact done captures a recurring theme in their literature. His emphasis on their result-orientation in the evaluation of law merits the same classification. His analysis of the common *and* distinctive points of departure of the realists is also significant. In particular, it highlights two crucial themes in their work. This is "rule-skepticism" and what I shall call "opinion-skepticism." These ideas constitute much of what was distinctive and, it will be argued, of greatest value in the realists' analysis of the judicial process. Also, his emphasis upon the need to formulate more precise and narrower categories for legal rules and doctrine accurately reflects a persistent and distinctive theme of the exponents of "realistic jurisprudence."

Still, Llewellyn's article has some limitations. Most of these stem from the fact that it was written in 1931, before the great outburst of realist literature in the 1930's. Indeed, given this date, the fact that he saw as clearly and as perceptively as he did is a remarkable testimony to his brilliance. The limitations are important, however, and need to be pointed out. To begin with, Llewellyn placed

---

he felt to be the extremism of their rule-skepticism. For his final evaluation, see Pound, *Jurisprudence* (St. Paul, Minn.: West Publishing Co., 1959), I, pp. 247–287.

little emphasis on the "fact-skepticism" of Jerome Frank. Since this only became a *major* theme in Frank's work after 1931, its omission is hardly a reason for criticism—particularly in light of the fact that Frank, according to Llewellyn, participated significantly in the preparation of the article.[54]

Moreover, Llewellyn placed insufficient emphasis upon the extent to which the realists were under the influence of new and distinctive models of legal science. The impact of Pound's conception of sociological jurisprudence upon the realist movement has been stressed. The fact that the legal realists were also influenced by a somewhat different kind of image of a science of law also needs emphasis. Many of them felt that the most imperative need was the development of an approach rather different from that envisaged by Pound. One way to express the difference is to say that some of the legal realists advocated a sociology of law, modeled along the lines of a natural science. The subject matter of such a science would be the behavior of officials rather than antecedent norms; its objective would be the description, explanation, and prediction of such behavior; and its students would not be concerned with the evaluation of law. For this precise reason, indeed, Pound reacted strongly against the model of legal science propounded by some realists. For him,

The conception of every branch of organized knowledge as a science, where it has been thought of as a philosophy . . . did nothing less than eliminate from the social sciences their real fundamental problem. For if the physical sciences have for their function to discover what is, the social sciences have for theirs to discover what ought to be and how to bring it about.

[54] Llewellyn, *Jurisprudence,* p. 42*.

. . . What-ought-to-be has no place in physical science. It has first place in the social sciences.[55]

In any case, the model of a natural science of law can be found in the literature of legal realists such as Llewellyn, Oliphant, Moore, Cook, and Bingham.[56] More important for present purposes, it induced an interest in the prediction of decisions which is not characteristic of Pound's work. Today this interest finds expression in the work of the judicial behavioralists.[57] They are the step-children of the legal realists in the development of a sociology of law.

[55] Pound, *Contemporary Juristic Theory*, pp. 35–36.

[56] Llewellyn, *Jurisprudence*, pp. 3–41, 77–100, 352–371; Llewellyn, "The Conditions for and the Aims and Methods of Legal Research," *Am. L. S. Rev.*, VI (1930), 670; Llewellyn, "The Normative, the Legal, and the Law Jobs: The Problem of Juristic Method," *Yale L. J.*, XLIX (1940), 1355; Llewellyn, "The Theory of Legal 'Science,'" *N.C. L. Rev.*, XX (1941), 1; Oliphant, "Facts, Opinions, and Value-Judgments," *Texas L. Rev.*, X (1932), 127; Oliphant, "A Return to Stare-Decisis," *A. B. A. J.*, XIV (1928), 71, 159; Joseph W. Bingham, "What Is the Law?" *Mich. L. Rev.*, XI (1912), 1, 109; Bingham, "The Nature of Legal Rights and Duties," *ibid.*, XII (1913), 1; Bingham, "Legal Philosophy and the Law," *Ill. L. Rev.*, IX (1914), 98; Bingham, "Science and the Law," *Green Bag*, XXV (1913), 162; Bingham, "Law Schools and the Future," *J. Legal Ed.*, VI (1954), 486; Walter Wheeler Cook, "The Possibilities of Social Study as a Science," *Essays on Research in the Social Sciences* (Washington, D.C.: Brookings Institution, 1931); Cook, "A Scientific Approach to the Study of Law," *Essays in Political Science in Honor of Westil Woodbury Willoughby*, ed. John Mabry Mathews (Baltimore: The Johns Hopkins University Press, 1937); Cook, "Scientific Method and the Law," *A. B. A. J.*, XIII (1927), 303; and the articles by Underhill Moore cited *infra*, p. 162, n. 45.

[57] For two good anthologies of the writings of the judicial behavioralists, see Glendon Schubert (ed.), *Judicial Behavior: A Reader in Theory and Research* (Chicago: Rand McNally, 1964), and Glendon Schubert (ed.), *Judicial Decision-Making* (Glencoe, Ill.: Free Press, 1963). For analysis of the relationship between judicial behavioralism and legal realism, see *infra*, pp. 169–179.

Finally, the role which the realists felt the judge ought to play does not have the prominence in Llewellyn's article which it merits. This topic is treated, though not in the section of the article analyzed in this chapter. Apparently, Llewellyn classified this theme as one of the "interlocking varied results" rather than a common point of departure. But if this classification is valid for the role which the realists ascribed to the judge, then it would seem also to apply to doctrines which he classified as common points of departure. Their "distrust of the theory that traditional prescriptive rule formulations are *the* heavily operative factor in producing court decisions" [58]—the essence of "rule-skepticism"—is an example. Certainly this distrust is as much a result of research as a common point of departure. In any case, the methods by which the realists felt judges should reach and justify decisions does not receive the emphasis which it merits. The recommendation of new techniques in this regard constitutes one of the distinctive and most important of their contributions.

Another major attempt by Llewellyn to identify the nature of legal realism occurs in the appendix of his magnum opus, *The Common Law Tradition*, which appeared only two years before his untimely death and thus represents his final attempt to delineate the movement to which he contributed so much. According to Llewellyn, the particular reason why he included such an appendix is that the realist movement, "which was vibrant and vocal when the study began, was violently misunderstood and misrepresented, and today, even where partly understood and recognized, is tending in modern American jurisprudential writing to be treated as an episode to be relegated to history." For Llewellyn, however, the interpretation of

[58] Llewellyn, *Jurisprudence*, p. 56.

legal realism constitutes no problem. "The situation is astoundingly simple, and the amount of print wasted on it [the nature of legal realism] is equally astounding." The reason for this is that "realism was never a philosophy, nor did any group of realists as such ever attempt to present any rounded view, or *whole* approach." Rather, "what realism was, and is, is a method, nothing more, and the only tenet involved is that the method is a good one. 'See it fresh,' 'See it as it works'—that was to be the foundation of any solid work, to *any* end."

Of all of these things, only "see it fresh," "see it clean," and "come back to make sure" are of the essence. They go to method. *That method is eternal.* That is point 1. The method may have come into first discussion among lawyers in relation to rules and judicial decision, but it is no more limited to that area than it is to matters legal. It applies to anything. That is point 2. But *the method* includes nothing at all about whither to go. That is point 3. *Realism* is *not* a philosophy, but a *technology.* That is why it is eternal. The fresh look is always the fresh hope. The fresh inquiry into results is always the needed check-up.[59]

Throughout this book my admiration for the genius of Llewellyn will be obvious. A strong case can be made for the proposition that he was the most brilliant and the most signficant of a brilliant and significant group of writers. As such, he deserves high standing in the annals of the jurisprudence of this century. The interpretation of realism advanced in *The Common Law Tradition* constitutes, however, a curious deviation from this general pattern of excellence. To be sure, the legal realists were not philosophers; they did not as a group develop a "whole"

[59] Llewellyn, *The Common Law Tradition,* pp. 508, 509, 510.

or "rounded" approach; they favored the pragmatic method described by Llewellyn; and the utility of this method is not limited to "matters legal." Nonetheless, any *definition* of realism as the method of "seeing it fresh," "seeing it clean," and "come back to make sure" is unsatisfactory. In the first place, such a definition is inconsistent with the much more fully documented interpretations of the realist movement forwarded by Llewellyn in his articles of the 1930's. In the second place, to define realism as a method is historically inaccurate. The advocates of "realistic jurisprudence" did believe that the use of the method so vividly described by Llewellyn is desirable; but they shared a number of other assumptions and theories as well. In the third place, to define realism in terms of the particular method alluded to in *The Common Law Tradition* is to reduce a rich and vital movement to something of almost trivial importance.

In light of these facts, one can only speculate why someone as perceptive as Llewellyn tried to picture legal realism simply as a method. In the last analysis only he knew, but guesses of varying plausibility can be advanced. Perhaps the most plausible explanation is a desire to disarm the critics of the realists. What better way to do this than by contending that realism is only a method, and is incapable of identification with any set of doctrine? The desire itself is understandable. A perennial criticism of the legal realists has been their failure to formulate a "philosophy" of law. More important, those who have advanced this criticism have sometimes in the process ignored the very real contributions of the movement as a whole. It is this fact which probably and justifiably bothered Llewellyn. Nonetheless, one need not make the false assumption that realism was only a method in order to appreciate its value.

The Account of Jerome N. Frank

The final interpretation of the realist movement to be examined here is that of Frank. It appeared in the Preface to the sixth printing (1949) of his classic *Law and the Modern Mind*. Frank began by reiterating what Llewellyn had emphasized eighteen years earlier: the legal realists hold too heterogeneous views to be classified as a school. Frank then went on to argue that "these so-called realists have but one common bond, a negative characteristic . . . a skepticism stimulated by a zeal to reform, in the interest of justice, some court-house ways." In light of this "zeal," he proposed that the realists should be called "constructive skeptics." These skeptics fall into two groups. They are either "rule skeptics" or "fact skeptics."

For Frank, Llewellyn is the most outstanding representative of the first group of realists. Their objective is to increase legal certainty, in the sense of the capacity to predict decisions in cases not yet commenced. For the rule-skeptics the inability to predict decisions stems primarily from the fact that "the formal legal rules enunciated in courts' opinions—sometimes called 'paper rules'—too often prove unreliable as guides in the prediction of decisions." What must be done, therefore, is to peer behind the paper rules and discover the "real rules" of judicial behavior. These rules are descriptive of uniformities or regularities in judicial behavior. They "will serve as more reliable prediction-instruments, yielding a large measure of workable predictability of the outcome of future suits." The major focus of the "rule skeptics," according to Frank, is "upper-court opinions."

The "fact skeptics," Frank contended, do not differ entirely from the "rule skeptics." "They, too, engaging in 'rule skepticism,' peer behind the 'paper rules.' Together with the rule skeptics, they have stimulated interest in factors, influencing upper-court decisions, of which, often, the opinions of those courts give no hint." Nonetheless, significant differences exist between the two groups. In the first place, the primary interest of the fact-skeptics is in trial rather than appellate courts. In the second place, the fact-skeptics insist that "it is impossible, and will always be impossible, because of the elusiveness of the facts on which decisions turn, to predict future decisions in most (not all) lawsuits, not yet begun or not yet tried." In the third place, the fact-skeptics, "thinking that therefore the pursuit of greatly increased legal certainty is, for the most part, futile—and that its pursuit, indeed, may well work injustice—aim rather at increased judicial justice." [60]

The major value of Frank's account is its clear grasp of the dual character of the realist movement. When he wrote that the bond which united the realists is skepticism toward traditional legal theories, stimulated by a zeal for reform, he caught as trenchantly as any single sentence could the *spirit* of the movement. The sentence is, of course, deficient as an account of the views of the realists. It does not indicate what traditional theories they were skeptical of, the reasons for their skepticism, or the nature of the alternative theories which they wished to substitute for traditional doctrine. No single sentence could do all of this. If Frank's had, there would be no reason for this book. Nonetheless, he articulated in one sentence the underlying *motif* of the realist movement—skepticism toward tradition in the interest of reform.

A less favorable verdict must be rendered upon his distinction between "fact skeptics" and "rule skeptics." It is

[60] Jerome N. Frank, *Law and the Modern Mind*, pp. x, xi.

true that some of the realists were more interested in trial than in appellate courts. It is also true that they were not united on the degree to which legal certainty could be increased, or how it could be increased. Nevertheless, they cannot be divided into the two categories which Frank has spelled out. "Fact-skepticism" is his particular creation. It constitutes a notable achievement and will be analyzed in detail in the third chapter of this book. But it is not a doctrine espoused by other legal realists. This is true, even, of those who were mainly interested in trial courts. Their primary concern is "rule-skepticism," and for this reason I have placed heavy emphasis on that particular doctrine. It constitutes a large part of the cement which tied the legal realists together, whatever their disagreements. Moreover, it is also rule-skepticism which primarily interested Frank, in his early work in the 1930's. This is the period which produced *Law and the Modern Mind.* It was not until later in his life, a period symbolized by his book *Courts on Trial,* that fact-skepticism became his predominant concern.[61]

The Impact of Mr. Justice Holmes

One inference to be drawn from these three accounts is that skepticism toward conventional views of the judicial process is a distinctive mark of the realist movement. Distrust of the classical view of judicial decision-making was felt, of course, before the legal realists emerged. Roscoe Pound and Benjamin N. Cardozo are convenient examples. Both of these distinguished jurists had begun the war against "mechanical jurisprudence" before the realist

[61] See Frank, *Courts on Trial: Myth and Reality in American Justice* (Princeton: Princeton University Press, 1949).

movement evolved as a force to be reckoned with in American jurisprudence. Nonetheless, it will be demonstrated that the legal realists prosecuted this war more vigorously, more radically, and on a wider front.[62] Thus the crucial need to understand their analysis of the judicial process in order to grasp the distinctiveness of their movement.

To assert that this analysis accounts for much of the distinctiveness of the realist movement is not to suggest that it is completely novel. Indeed, it is precisely with respect to the realists' view of the judicial process that the shadow of Mr. Justice Holmes looms large. No man was more consistently or generously extolled. The adulation became so great, indeed, that in 1941 one scholar compared the impact of Holmes upon legal thought to that of Kant upon philosophical reflection. As Moses Aronson put it, "The cumulative movement of revolt in American jurisprudence came to a head in the personality of Oliver Wendell Holmes. His influence upon contemporary legal thought is reminiscent of the effect which Kant had upon the development of philosophy in the nineteenth century."[63] In the eyes of the legal realists it was Holmes, more than any other figure, who had adumbrated their views.

The elements in the thought of Holmes which had the greatest impact on the realist movement were:

(1) His skepticism toward general rules as means to compel particular decisions—a skepticism expressed in the classic epigram, "General propositions do not determine concrete cases," and in the statement that "I always say in conference that no case can be settled by general proposi-

---

[62] See *infra*, pp. 83–88.

[63] "Tendencies in American Jurisprudence," *U. Toronto L. J.*, IV (1941), 92.

tions, that I will admit any general proposition you like and decide the case either way." [64]

(2) His emphasis upon the vast role of extralegal factors. In his almost immortal words,

the life of the law has not been logic: it has been experience. The felt necessities of the time, the prevalent moral and political theories, intuitions of public policy, avowed or unconscious, even the prejudices which judges share with their fellow-men, have had a good deal more to do than the syllogism in determining the rules by which men should be governed.

In substance the growth of the law is legislative. And this in a deeper sense than that what the courts declare to have always been the law is in fact new. It is legislative in its grounds. The very considerations which judges most rarely mention, and always with an apology, are the secret root from which the law draws all the juices of life. I mean, of course, considerations of what is expedient for the community concerned. [65]

(3) His insistence upon the role of unconscious factors. For Holmes, the process through which decisions have been reached "has been largely unconscious"; "the unconscious result of instinctive preferences and inarticulate convictions." Again, the "decision will depend on a judgment or intuition more subtle than any articulate major premise." [66]

(4) His relativistic view of legal certainty. While "the logical method and form flatter that longing for certainty and for repose which is in every mind," the fact remains

[64] *Lochner* v. *New York*, 198 U.S. 76 (1905); Howe (ed.), *Holmes-Laski Letters*, I, 243.

[65] Max Lerner (ed.), *The Mind and Faith of Justice Holmes: His Speeches, Essays, Letters, and Judicial Opinions* (New York: Random House, 1943), pp. 51–52, 54.

[66] *Ibid.*, and *Lochner* v. *New York*, 198 U.S. 76 (1905).

that "certainty generally is an illusion, and repose is not the destiny of man." The refusal to recognize this has simply been "to leave the very ground and foundation of judgments inarticulate, and often unconscious." [67]

(5) His awareness of the need to recognize the facts of judicial life and to proceed accordingly. In 1881 he wrote that

the philosophical habit of the day, the frequency of legislation, and the ease with which the law may be changed to meet the opinions and wishes of the public, all make it natural and unavoidable that judges as well as others should *openly discuss* the legislative principles upon which their decisions must always rest in the end, *and should base their judgments upon* broad considerations of policy to which the traditions of the bench would hardly have tolerated a reference fifty years ago.[68]

The correspondence between these ideas and those of the legal realists will become clear later in this study. The immediate purpose is simply to indicate those points in Holmes's overall picture of the judicial process which profoundly influenced the views of the legal realists. The parallel extends, moreover, beyond interpretations of the judicial process. A coincidence of ideas can also be found for the study of law. The legal realists, it has been pointed out, were to some degree trying to establish a sociology of law modeled along the lines of a natural science. They found support for this effort in three notions of Holmes.

The first is his predictive theory of law. For Holmes, "the prophecies of what the courts will do in fact, and nothing more pretentious, are what I mean by law." "The object of our study, then, is prediction, the prediction of

[67] Lerner (ed.), *Mind and Faith of Justice Holmes*, pp. 80, 81–82.
[68] *Ibid.*, p. 65 (italics mine).

the incidence of the public force through the instrumentality of the courts." "The primary rights and duties with which jurisprudence busies itself . . . are nothing but prophecies." [69] A legal right "is only the hypostasis of a prophecy—the imagination of a substance supporting the fact that the public force will be brought to bear upon those who do things said to contravene it." A legal duty "is nothing but a prediction that if a man does or omits certain things he will be made to suffer in this or that way by judgment of the court." [70]

The second idea is Holmes's insistence on the need to distinguish between law and morals. The word "distinguish" has been carefully chosen. The meaning of Holmes's thinking—as well as that of the legal realists—on this point has often been mistaken. The point of the celebrated first few pages of "The Path of the Law" is not that law and morals can be, or should be, completely separated. The purpose, rather, is to "dispel" the "confusion between morality and law." In Holmes's own words,

I take it for granted that no hearer of mine will misinterpret what I have to say as the language of cynicism. The law is the witness and external deposit of our moral life. Its history is the history of the moral development of the race. The practice of it, in spite of popular jests, tends to make good citizens and good men. When I emphasize the difference between law and morals I do so with reference to a single end, that of learning and understanding the law. For that purpose you must definitely master its specific marks, and it is for that I ask you for the moment to imagine yourselves indifferent to other and greater things.[71]

The third conception of Holmes of relevance here is his emphasis upon what courts do. In his typically pungent

[69] *Ibid.*, pp. 75, 72.　　[70] *Ibid.*, pp. 397, 72.　　[71] *Ibid.*, p. 73.

language, "When I talk of law I talk as a cynic. I don't care a damn if twenty professors tell me that a decision is not law if I know that the courts will enforce it." [72] Also of great importance is his famous admonition to "wash" legal concepts with "cynical acid," to "expel everything except the object of our study, the operations of the law." [73]

Any attempt to draw parallels between the views of Holmes and those of the legal realists is, of course, dangerous. It is likely for one thing to de-emphasize the tensions within Holmes's thinking. No one can deny his greatness. Yet, like most great thinkers, his ideas are not without their own inner stress. Precisely for this reason, indeed, both Pound and the realists could claim that the other had misinterpreted "what Holmes really meant." According to Pound, "too much has been claimed . . . for . . . Holmes as a skeptical realist." [74] But for the realists, it was Pound who had misinterpreted Holmes. Somewhat extreme but not uncommon is the claim of Jerome Frank that Pound "repressed" the "Holmes idea," "obstructed its full growth," "diluted it, mingled it with the watery substance of Holmes's predecessors. . . . He mangled his work because he compromised the heritage from Holmes, because he refused to recognize its essentially revolutionary character." [75] For this reason, Frank contended, "it was in the highest degree unfortunate that the first vastly influential teacher to take over Holmes's insight should thus have warped it." He concluded that "anyone who hopes to bring about fundamental change in . . . legal thinking

---

[72] Howe (ed.), *Holmes-Laski Letters*, I, 115.

[73] Lerner (ed.), *Mind and Faith of Justice Holmes*, p. 76.

[74] "Fifty Years of Jurisprudence," *Harv. L. Rev.*, LI (1938), 792.

[75] Frank, "Are Judges Human?" *U. Pa. L. Rev.*, LXXX (1931), 18.

. . . must . . . *rescue Pound's lasting contributions from Pound and his uncritical adulators."* An exposition of points of similarity is likely, also, to overemphasize the doctrinal unity within the realist movement. Finally, such an attempt may obscure the distinctiveness of the contribution of the realists. Many of their cues were taken from, or at least justified by reference to, Holmes. Yet these cues were developed and defended in ways which Holmes had not anticipated. How much he would agree with all of them is open to question. Nonetheless, the parallels are there, and they are too striking to be ignored in any account of the realist movement.

A Note on the Label "Legal Realism"

The term "legal realism" has been subject to endless controversy. Many of the legal realists were themselves dissatisfied with the phrase, and in some respects it conceals more than it reveals. Nonetheless, history and custom have dictated that it shall not easily be abandoned. The question to be answered here is what "legal realism" meant to the specific group of jurists examined in this study.

The best answer is that "realism" meant to them what it has meant in art and literature. It meant the attempt to represent things as they actually are. As Pound wrote in 1931, by "realism" the legal realists "mean fidelity to nature, accurate recording of things as they are, as contrasted with things as they are imagined to be, or wished to be, or as one feels they ought to be." [76] "Realism" means, according to Frank, representation of what is *"in opposition to 'romanticism,' 'fantasying,' 'prettifying,' and 'wishful*

[76] "The Call for a Realist Jurisprudence," *Harv. L. Rev.* XLIV (1931), 697.

thinking.' " [77] To explicate the meaning of "legal realism" is obviously, however, to say very little about the nature of legal realism as a specific movement in American jurisprudence. The mere desire or wish to record things as they are rather than as they appear or ought to be is not the monopoly of any particular group. As Cardozo pointed out in 1932,

I have said that the members of this group style themselves realists—realists because fidelity to the realities of the judicial process, unclouded by myth or preconception, is supposed to be, in a degree peculiarly their own, the end and aim of their endeavor. . . . I shall make bold to vary the description and speak of them hereafter as neo-realists instead. There were brave men before Agamemnon; and before the dawn of the last decade there were those in jurisprudence who strove to see the truth in the workings of the judicial process, to see it steadily and whole, and to report what they had seen with sincerity and candor.[78]

Cardozo's interpretation is unquestionably correct. Its chief implication for present purposes is that logomachy over "legal realism" is a cul-de-sac. The problem is not to explicate the meaning of a phrase but to determine what a specific group of jurists, loosely united under an ambiguous banner, thought had been imagined to be, wished to be, or ought to be. The task is to discover *why* they felt that what had been imagined, or assumed, or felt to have been the case does not correspond to what is the case. The job which needs to be done is to analyze the realists'

[77] Frank, "Are Judges Human?" p. 258, n. 70.
[78] Hall (ed.), *The Selected Writings of Benjamin Nathan Cardozo,* p. 10.

perceptions of reality. It is a job which, in this particular case, also involves examination of what these men hoped to do about what they found to be the case. *Then,* but only then, rather marked differences will emerge between the views of the legal realists and those of their predecessors. Prior jurists had striven to see and to report the actualities of the judicial process. Their perceptions and their reports as well as their prescriptions differed, however, from those of the legal realists.

Conclusion

The purpose of the foregoing pages has been to identify the major characteristics of the realist movement in American jurisprudence. If the interpretation advanced has been correct, then it is best understood as an outgrowth of pragmatism, sociological jurisprudence, and the ideas of Mr. Justice Holmes. In part the movement represents the attempt to apply to law the more general ideas initiated by the founders of pragmatism, ideas which Roscoe Pound had first developed for legal purposes. But in part the realist movement forged a distinctive chain of doctrine. Its central links are a thoroughgoing skepticism toward traditional views of the judicial process and, especially, the role of established rules; the development of new methods for the study of law and the prediction of decisions; and the formulation of a different role for the judge than found expression in even the writings of jurists such as Pound and Cardozo. The realists buttressed the ideas which they developed in each of these respects by an appeal to the majestic authority of Holmes. Yet his legacy for American jurisprudence is such that Pound and others could claim that the "neo-realists" distorted the teachings of the Yankee from Olympus. Regardless of who interpreted Holmes more correctly, the distinctive ideas of the legal realists form the subject matter upon which the student of the movement must focus his analysis. Only then can its unique contribution to the American jurisprudence of this century be fully grasped.

II

Rule-Skepticism

Skepticism toward traditional jurisprudence is, it has been suggested, a distinctive feature of the realist movement. The net of doubt cast forth covered a wide range. It encompassed judicial fact-finding, approaches to the study of law, methods by which decisions ought to be reached, and many other important areas of legal thought and practice. Disbelief in the impact traditionally ascribed to established legal rules is probably, however, the most significant form taken by the doubt of the realists. Rule-skepticism pervades their movement. Also, it is the root from which stem many of their most distinctive doctrines.

What precise role has traditionally been ascribed to antecedent rules? What exactly is rule-skepticism? What factors account for its prevalence among the legal realists? How does their analysis of the role of pre-established rules differ from that of their progressive predecessors? What criticisms have been leveled against rule-skepticism? What are its limitations and value? These are the questions which must be answered if the central thrust in the realists' analysis of the judicial process is to be understood.

48

Classical View of the Judicial Process

The traditional interpretation of the impact of established rules is an essential element in what can be called the classical theory of the judicial process. According to this theory the judicial decision is the rather mechanical result of the application of antecedent rules to the facts of particular cases. Judges have virtually no freedom in the selection or interpretation of these rules. The sources for their decisions are clearly fixed in a constitution, statute, or precedent. The meaning of the rules, once found, is unambiguous. To be sure, in some cases the application of a particular rule may not be beyond doubt. This uncertainty is not due, however, to any discretion or freedom which the judge has in the selection or interpretation of established rules. Rather, it stems from disagreement over what the facts in the case are. Otherwise, the process by means of which decisions are reached is mechanical, formal, and impersonal. The impact of established rules is decisive, and only because it is decisive are decisions uniform and predictable.[1]

The most celebrated exponent of this interpretation of the judicial process in Anglo-American jurisprudence is Sir William Blackstone. In his classic language,

What that law is, every subject knows, or may know, if he pleases; for it depends not upon the arbitrary will of any judge, but is permanent, fixed, and unchangeable, unless by authority of parliament.

The judgment, though pronounced or awarded by the judges, is not their determination or sentence, but the determination

---

[1] See Robert von Moschzisker, "Stare Decisis in Courts of Last Resort," *Harv. L. Rev.*, XXXVII (1924), 409, 410.

and sentence of the law. It is the conclusion that naturally and regularly follows from the premises of law and fact . . . which judgment or conclusion depends not therefore on the arbitrary caprice of the judge, but on the settled and invariable principles of justice.

For though in many other countries everything is left in the breast of the judge to determine, yet with us he is only to declare and pronounce, not to make or new model, the law.[2]

Moreover, one reason that the judge ought not to "make, or new model" the law is because of the mass of uncertainty which would thereby be created. Otherwise, there would be "an inlet to all manner of innovation in the body of the law itself." Men "would live in society without knowing exactly the conditions and obligations which it [the law] lays them under."[3]

This view of the judicial process has not been confined to the eighteenth century. A strong case can be made for the proposition that it was still the dominant view in the first two decades of this century. Thus in 1922 Charles Grove Haines wrote that the classical view of the judicial function "continues to hold sway in Anglo-American law as one of the strong determining forces guiding lawyers and judges." In his mind, American courts "have clung to the belief that justice must be administered in accordance with fixed rules, which can be applied by a rather mechanical process of logical reasoning to a given state of facts and can be made to produce an inevitable result."[4] In the

[2] William Blackstone, *Commentaries on the Laws of England* (London: Sweet and Milliken, 1821), I, p. 151; III, pp. 434, 359.

[3] *Ibid.*, I, p. 151; IV, p. 448.

[4] Haines, "General Observations on the Effects of Personal, Political, and Economic Influences in the Decisions of Judges," *Readings in Jurisprudence and Legal Philosophy*, ed. Morris R. Cohen and Felix S. Cohen (Boston: Little, Brown, 1951), pp. 461–462.

same year Roscoe Pound contended that the classical theory "has the largest following among practitioners and in dogmatic exposition of law. . . . Application is merely formulation in a judgment of the result obtained by analysis of the case and logical development of the premises contained in the reported decisions." [5] Finally, in 1933 Walter B. Kennedy asserted that "up to a decade ago it would be safe to say that logic, precedents, and the 'weight of authority' were decisive factors in determining . . . judicial judgments; it would be said that the judges made their decisions *after* reviewing the cases cited by the reason of the cumulative strength of an unbroken chain of precedents." [6]

Nature of the Realists' Revolt

The quotation from Kennedy implies that what could safely be said before the early 1920's could not later be confidently asserted. This is no doubt correct. By 1933 seeds of doubt had begun to flower, and they were cultivated with unusual diligence by the legal realists. The "theory that rules decide cases" may "for a century . . . have fooled not only library-ridden recluses, but judges. More, to have fooled even those skillful and hard-bitten first-hand observers of judicial work: the practitioners." [7] What may have been true of library-ridden recluses, judges, and practitioners is not true, obviously, of the exponents of "realistic jurisprudence." They delighted in contrasts between "what had been traditionally taught in

---

[5] *An Introduction to the Philosophy of Law* (rev. ed.; New Haven: Yale University Press, 1954), p. 61.

[6] "To Hunch or Not to Hunch," *N.Y. L. J.,* LXXXIX (1933), 742.

[7] Karl N. Llewellyn, "The Constitution as an Institution," *Colum. L. Rev.,* XXXIV (1934), 7.

law schools" or "said at bar association banquets" and what "in truth happens in court-houses"; [8] between "paper" rules and "real" rules; between what courts are supposed to do, or are assumed to do, and what they actually do. Many things have, of course, been taught, said, supposed, and assumed. None was more frequently assailed by the realists than the theory that established rules have determined specific decisions. In 1931 Llewellyn wrote that all of them distrusted "the theory that traditional prescriptive rule-formulations are *the* heavily operative factor in producing court decisions." [9] He went on to point out that this distrust, the essence of rule-skepticism, is also a distinctive mark of the realist movement. His judgment is difficult to disagree with. The war against "mechanical" jurisprudence has been, it is true, a conspicuous feature of the American jurisprudence of this century, and the legal realists were not the initial protagonists. That honor belongs to their predecessors such as Pound, Cardozo, and Holmes. Nonetheless, the advocates of realism waged a more militant, systematic, and radical campaign than any of their forerunners. Holmes is the one possible exception to this generalization. As has been indicated, however, the use which the realists made of his views is not beyond question.

In any event, the battle which they fought against the classical view of the judicial process has had a profound impact upon American jurisprudence. In the 1920's and 1930's the realists were the most insistent and influential critics of the traditional interpretation. In 1932 Cardozo

[8] Jerome N. Frank, *If Men Were Angels: Some Aspects of Government in a Democracy* (New York: Harper, 1942), pp. 56–57.

[9] *Jurisprudence: Realism in Theory and Practice* (Chicago: University of Chicago Press, 1962), p. 56.

perceptively wrote that they were concerned with "nothing less than revision to its very roots of the method of judicial decision which is part of the classical tradition." The revision has made an impressive mark. In 1960 Hessel Yntema wrote (with some exaggeration) that the realist "attitude toward legal problems . . . has dominated legal thinking in the United States during the past generation, even to the point of becoming commonplace." In 1961 Grant Gilmore maintained that the legal realists "did much to make of law a more useful and flexible instrument for the resolution of social conflicts." More recently David Riesman has contended that the "victory" of the legal realists is "now taken for granted among the younger men" in the law schools. For this reason he has asserted that legal realism needs "scarcely to be called a movement any more." [10]

At the same time, it would be mistaken to assume that the critique of the realists has been universally accepted. Their victory may now be taken for granted among the younger men in the law schools. Yet, what is true of some or most of the younger men is not true of all. Also, what is true of the younger men is not necessarily true of the older men. Moreover, the triumph of the legal realists has not been as great outside as inside the law schools. Their views are far from being universally accepted by the bar or bench. The classical theory of the judicial process has been

[10] Margaret E. Hall (ed.), *The Selected Writings of Benjamin Nathan Cardozo* (New York: Fallon Publications, 1947), p. 10; Yntema, "American Legal Realism in Retrospect," *Vand. L. Rev.*, XIV (1960), 325; Gilmore, "Legal Realism: Its Cause and Cure," *Yale L. J.*, LXX (1961), 1048; David Riesman, "Law and Sociology: Recruitment, Training, and Colleagueship," *Law and Sociology: Exploratory Essays*, ed. William M. Evan (New York: Free Press of Glencoe, 1962), p. 33.

generally discredited, and in that sense the skepticism of the realists has done its work. Still, many of those who reject the older notions have not completely accepted the ideas of the legal realists. Rather, a good many lawyers have adopted a point of view midway between traditional legal formalism and rule-skepticism. At least a survey of the relevant literature indicates that many take a more conservative view than that of the legal realists.[11] For these jurists, in many, indeed probably the majority, of all cases,

[11] Typical is the statement that "no one advocates abandonment of the rule [of *stare decisis*] for the great majority of cases; the only dispute focuses on how often the rule should be disregarded and the factors that make departure justifiable." "Hospital Liability in the New York Court of Appeals: A Study of Judicial Methodology," *Colum. L. Rev.*, LXI (1961), 897. Also, see Paul J. Mishkin, "The High Court, The Great Writ, and the Due Process of Time and Law," *Harv. L. Rev.*, LXXIX (1965), 56. According to Mishkin, "While the Blackstonian conception is not entirely valid, neither is it wholly wrong. For it is certainly true that courts in general handle the vast bulk of cases by application of preexisting law." *Ibid.*, 60. For Mishkin the declaratory theory "embodies substantial elements of truth. This is most evident in the context of routine judicial operation in the minerun of cases." *Ibid.*, 63. Additional bibliographical data may be found in Rumble, "Rule-Skepticism and the Role of the Judge: A Study of American Legal Realism," *J. Pub. L.*, XV (1966), p. 258, n. 32. Some jurists, of course, take a view much more in accord with that of the realists. Three outstanding examples are: Edward H. Levi, *An Introduction to Legal Reasoning* (Chicago: University of Chicago Press, 1948); Julius Stone, *Legal System and Lawyers' Reasoning* (Stanford, Calif.: Stanford University Press, 1964); and Alf Ross, *On Law and Justice* (Berkeley: University of California Press, 1959). For Ross the "doctrine of *stare decisis* is in reality only an illusion. It is an ideology upheld for certain reasons in order to conceal from its supporters and others the free, law-creative function of the judge, and to convey the delusive impression that he applies only already existing law which can be settled by virtue of a set of objective rules as indicated in *stare decisis*." *Ibid.*, p. 88.

the application of antecedent rules to the facts of concrete cases has been an effective means to achieve legal certainty. They feel, too, that this ought to remain the standard method by which decisions are reached.

The existence of such views means that an analysis of rule-skepticism is not of historical significance only; it also has contemporary relevance. Such an analysis is an essay in legal history; but it is an essay of very current significance. In any case, the interpretation advanced here should not obscure the variations in the views of the realists. The reasons for their distrust of established rules varied, as did their estimates of the precise impact of such rules. Nonetheless, they shared at least one very important and distinctive attitude. The reasons for and degree of rule-skepticism may have varied, but distrust of established rules as the most basic determinants of concrete decisions is widespread. Nine factors seem to account for its pervasiveness in the realist movement.

The Multiplicity of Precedents

The first and most obvious influence is the growth of precedents. As Cardozo pointed out in 1932, "a good many causes have conspired to induce the change of pose. For the lawyer and the judge, a driving force at all times has been the avalanche of precedents. Battered and pelted, we grope for a principle of order that will compose the jarring atoms, or at least permit us to forget them and ignore their oppositions." [12] These "jarring atoms" and "oppositions" may have been forgotten by some. But they were very close to the hearts of the legal realists, who pointed out again and again that "there are usually plenty of

[12] *Selected Writings,* ed. Hall, p. 8.

precedents to go around; and with the accumulation of decisions, it is no great problem for the lawyer to find legal authority for most propositions." [13] If some lawyers were reluctant to avow that "you will almost always find plenty of cases to cite in your favor," [14] the same cannot be said of the legal realists. They felt no compunctions in announcing that "out of the numerous competing theories, doctrines, formulas, and rules at hand in every case [the judge] . . . can always find those that fully justify the policies which to him seem dominant." [15] Indeed, Felix Cohen was so impressed by the range of competing precedents that he felt "no judge could possibly hand down a decision in any case for which a commentator could not find a precedent, even if the judge himself failed to find one. To say that a decision is unprecedented is to say either (1) that we do not agree with the use it makes of the precedents, or (2) that we do not know the precedents that might be cited in its support." [16] Most of the realists did not go quite this far. Virtually all of them were agreed, however, that the precedents are too conflicting to compel any specific decision in a litigated case. The range

[13] William O. Douglas, "Stare Decisis," *Essays in Jurisprudence from the Columbia Law Review* (New York: Columbia University Press, 1963), p. 19. For a study of the relationship between Douglas and the realist movement, see John W. Hopkirk, "The Influence of Legal Realism on William O. Douglas," *Essays on the American Constitution,* ed. Gottfried Dietze (Englewood Cliffs, N.J.: Prentice-Hall, 1964).

[14] S. S. Gregory, as cited by Jerome N. Frank, *Law and the Modern Mind* (Garden City, N.Y.: Doubleday, 1963), p. 111, n. 2.

[15] Leon Green, "Recent Steps in Law Administration," *J. A. Jud. Soc'y,* XIV (1930), 115.

[16] Lucy Kramer Cohen (ed.), *The Legal Conscience: Selected Papers of Felix S. Cohen* (New Haven: Yale University Press, 1960), p. 129.

of choice which confronts the judge "disposes of all question of 'control' or 'dictation' by precedent." [17]

The Multiplicity of Precedent Techniques

Awareness of the "avalanche of precedents" pervades the realist movement. One of the unique achievements of the late Karl Nickerson Llewellyn was to insist that the range of techniques for the *interpretation* of precedents is equally wide. The particular object of his keen critical mind was the traditional assumption that each litigated case has a *ratio decidendi* which controls future decisions. He began from a perspective typical of the legal realists: "For, whereas much or most of what is commonly written about precedent takes as its raw material what judges have *said* about precedent, I propose to take as mine, not so much what they have said as what they have *done* about it." [18] He reached the conclusion that what has been said obscures certain key realities. In particular, it conceals the fact that the techniques actually used by courts to determine the *ratio decidendi* of prior cases are many and competing. "The going ways of case law" are "multiple and conflicting." If one investigates "our case law system as it lives and moves," then one must see that "the relation between the rule and the cases may move all the way from copying any words printed by anybody in a 'law' book to meticulous reexamination of precise facts, issues, and holdings, in total disregard of any prior language whatsoever." Moreover, "any degree or kind of operation within that lordly range is correct, doctrinally, if doctrine

[17] Llewellyn, *The Common Law Tradition: Deciding Appeals* (Boston: Little, Brown, 1960), p. 76.

[18] Llewellyn, *The Bramble Bush: On Our Law and Its Study* (New York: Oceana, 1960), p. 64.

be taken to a description of what authoritative courts are doing with and to cases and rules, and doing with effective authority." [19]

In *The Bramble Bush*, Llewellyn singled out for special emphasis two kinds of "operations." One is the "strict" or "orthodox" method. It is the practice of claiming that the *ratio decidendi* as stated by the court went beyond the precise issues involved in the case. A judge can,

through examination of the facts or of the procedural issue, narrow the picture of what was actually before the court and can hold that the ruling made requires to be understood as thus restricted. In the extreme form this results in what is known as expressly "confining the case to its particular facts." This rule holds only of redheaded Walpoles in pale magenta Buick cars.

The major function of this technique is to provide courts with a perfectly respectable means of evading the apparent implications of prior rules. "It is in practice the dogma which is applied to *unwelcome* precedents. It is the recognized, legitimate, honorable technique for whittling precedents away, for making the lawyer, in his argument, and the court, in its decision, free of them. It is a surgeon's knife." Using as a standard the actual operations of the courts, however, a totally different practice is at least as common and legitimate. This is the "loose view of precedent." It means that

a court has decided, and decided authoritatively, *any* point or all points on which it chose to rest a case, or on which it chose, after due argument, to pass. No matter how broad the statement, no matter how unnecessary on the facts or the proce-

[19] Llewellyn, "The Rule of Law in Our Case-Law of Contract," *Yale L. J.*, XLVII (1938), pp. 1246, 1246–1247.

dural issues, if that was the rule the court laid down, then that the court has held. Indeed, this view carries over often into dicta, and even into dicta which are grandly obiter. In its extreme form this results in thinking and arguing exclusively from *language* that is found in past opinions, and in citing and working with that language wholly without reference to the facts of the case which called the language forth.

The function served by this method is, moreover, the exact opposite of the strict method. "This is a device not for cutting past opinions away from judges' feet, but for using them as a springboard when they are found convenient. This is a device for *capitalizing welcome precedents.*" Since both methods are normally available to courts, "the doctrine of precedent . . . is two-headed. It is Janus-faced . . . it is not one doctrine, nor one line of doctrine, but two, and two which, *applied at the same time to the same precedent, are contradictory of each other.*" [20]

In *The Common Law Tradition* Llewellyn expanded this type of analysis. There he listed sixty-four "available impeccable precedent techniques."

To the judge or court each individual precedent technique speaks thus: As you search for the right rule of law to govern the case in hand, I am *one* of the things which, respectably, honorably, and in full accordance with the common law tradition . . . you are *formally* entitled in and by your office to do to and with any prior relevant judicial language or holding as it comes before you.

The existence and use of so many different techniques reveals once more the vast range of choice in the interpretation of precedents. They indicate the different outcomes which are possible "if the varying procedures should be

[20] Llewellyn, *The Bramble Bush,* pp. 66–67, 67, 67–68, 68.

applied to the same precedent on the same point in any single pending case." The multiplicity of competing precedent techniques reveals that *stare decisis* "has in the past been, now is, and must continue to be, a norm of change, and a means of change, as well as a norm of staying put, and a means of staying put. *The growth of the past has been achieved by 'standing on' the decided cases;* rarely by overturning them."

Still further, what is true of techniques for the interpretation of precedents is also true of techniques for the interpretation of statutes. "Again and again," Llewellyn once wrote, "I have had to insist that the *range* of techniques correctly available in dealing with statutes is roughly equivalent to the range correctly available in dealing with case law materials." To be sure, "the accepted convention still, unhappily, requires discussion as if only one single correct meaning [of a statute] could exist." Nonetheless, the rules of construction actually used by judges and lawyers are multiple and conflicting. "There are two opposing canons on almost every point." [21]

Logical Indeterminacy of Established Rules

Another factor which impressed some of the realists is the logical indeterminacy of established rules. The specific decisions of prior cases, so the argument runs, do not necessarily imply any particular rule. "The periodic attempts of students of the common law to put forward logical formulae for discovering 'the rule of a case' all

[21] Llewellyn, *The Common Law Tradition*, p. 76; *Jurisprudence,* p. 71; *The Common Law Tradition,* pp. 371, 521. For a list of the competing canons of statutory construction, see *The Common Law Tradition,* pp. 522–525.

betray an elementary ignorance of the logical fact that no particular proposition can imply a general proposition."

Elementary logic teaches us that every legal decision and every finite set of decisions can be subsumed under an infinite number of different general rules, just as an infinite number of different curves may be traced through any point or finite collection of points. Every decision is a choice between different rules which logically fit all past decisions but logically dictate conflicting results in the instant case. Logic provides the springboard, but it does not guarantee the success of any particular dive.[22]

Consequently, Felix Cohen concluded, "the search for a logical formula that will determine precisely what rule each decision implies is a wild goose chase starting from a logical confusion." "No one of these rules [of prior cases] has any logical priority; courts and lawyers choose among competing propositions on extra-logical grounds." [23]

Herman Oliphant advanced a similar argument. His celebrated and frequently misunderstood Presidential address to the Association of American Law Schools in 1927 is a good example. In it he contended that there "can be erected upon the action taken by a court in any case . . . a gradation of generalizations. . . . Sometimes it is built up to dizzy heights by the court itself and at times, by law teachers and writers, it is reared to those lofty summits of the absolute and the infinite." What is more, there "stretches up and away from every single case in the books, not one possible gradation of widening generalizations,

---

[22] Felix S. Cohen, *Ethical Systems and Legal Ideals: An Essay on the Foundations of Legal Criticism* (Ithaca, N.Y.: Cornell University Press, 1959), pp. 34 (n. 47), 35.

[23] *The Legal Conscience*, p. 88; Cohen, *Ethical Systems and Legal Ideals*, p. 36, n. 47.

but many. Multitudes of radii shoot out from it, each pair enclosing one of an indefinite number of these gradations of broader and broader generalizations." [24]

An example used by Oliphant illustrates his point. A's father persuades her not to marry B, as she had promised to do. B sued for damages. A's father was held not to be liable. Around that decision rings of ever-widening generalizations can be built. Various rules can be adduced as the *ratio decidendi*. Among them are the norms that (1) fathers are privileged to induce daughters to break promises to marry; (2) parents are so privileged; (3) parents are so privileged as to both daughters and sons; (4) all persons are so privileged as to promises to marry; (5) parents are so privileged as to all promises made by their children; (6) all persons are so privileged as to all promises made by anyone. None of these rules is the necessary logical implication of the decision. The conclusion that A's father was not liable to B could be subsumed under each.

The significance of this fact is the range of choice which it discloses in the *interpretation* of precedents. No inexorable logic dictates any particular choice. A student

is told to seek the 'doctrine' or 'principle' of a case, but which of its welter of stairs shall he ascend and how high up shall he go? Is there some one step on some one stair which is *the* decision of the case within the meaning of the mandate stare decisis? . . . Each precedent considered by a judge and each case studied by a student rests at the center of a vast and empty stadium. The angle and distance from which that case is to be viewed involves the choice of a seat. Which shall be chosen?

[24] Herman Oliphant, "A Return to Stare Decisis," *A. B. A. J.,* XIV (1928), 73.

Neither judge nor student can escape the fact that he can and must choose.[25]

Once more, this does *not* mean that judicial decisions are totally unpredictable. It does mean that "the predictable element in it all is what courts have done in response to the stimuli of the facts of the concrete cases before them." [26]

Ambiguity of Legal Language

One of the influential currents of modern thought has been an increased awareness of the ambiguity of ordinary language. It is a current which had some impact upon the realists. What is true of ordinary language is, they insisted, equally true of legal language. As Jerome Frank pointed out in 1941, "In the last ten years or so, Leon Green, Walter Cook, Thurman Arnold, and others of us, inspired by Holmes, undertook the dissection of legal terminology. We skinned the peel off much legal jargon; many law-words (not all, of course) then proved to be like onions—you peeled and peeled and there was nothing left." [27] Some realists contended, indeed, that legal language is even more ambiguous than ordinary language. Fred Rodell's analysis is illustrative.

Almost all legal sentences, whether they appear in judges' opinions, written statutes, or ordinary bills of sale, have a way of reading as though they had been translated from the German by someone with a rather meagre knowledge of English.

[25] *Ibid.* For an excellent analysis and survey of formulas for the determination of the *ratio decidendi* of a case, as well as criticisms of them, see Stone, *Legal System and Lawyers' Reasonings*, pp. 267–300.

[26] Oliphant, *op. cit.*, p. 159.

[27] "A Lawyer Looks at Language," *Language in Action*, ed. S. I. Hayakawa (New York: Harcourt, Brace, 1941), p. 329.

Invariably they are long. Invariably they are awkward. Invariably and inevitably they make plentiful use of the abstract, fuzzy, clumsy words which are so essential to the solemn hocus-pocus of The Law. . . . And no segment of the English language in use today is so muddy, so confusing, so hard to pin down to its supposed meaning, as the language of The Law. It ranges only from the ambiguous to the completely incomprehensible.

For Rodell, legal language is "jargon which completely baffles and befoozles the ordinary literate man." Its " 'willfullys' and 'maliciouslys' . . . cannot possibly be pinned down to a precise meaning." Moreover, legal words are "so treacherous of meaning that the same principle can often be used on both sides of the same dispute." [28]

The majority of legal realists stated their views in somewhat more restrained fashion. Nonetheless, they insisted that lawyers often use "what the layman describes as 'weasel words,' so-called 'safety-valve concepts,' such as 'prudent,' 'negligence,' 'freedom of contract,' 'good faith,' 'ought to know,' 'due care,' 'due process'—terms with the vaguest meaning—as if these vague words had a precise and clear definition." [29] Moreover, the same vagueness characterizes statutory language. Typical is the assertion of Max Radin that "a statute is a general statement. It describes a general situation. It is a picture of which the outline is not solid steel, but rubber, or . . . a wreath of smoke. It can be extended pretty widely and contracted pretty narrowly. And if you are a little clever, it will catch or let out the situation you are deciding." The view of

[28] Rodell, *Woe Unto You, Lawyers!* (2d ed.; New York: Pageant Press, 1957), pp. 124–125, 10, 13, 112.

[29] Frank, *Law and the Modern Mind*, p. 30.

Joseph Walter Bingham is also representative. For him, "legislative expression often does not indicate clearly and certainly the intended effects upon concrete events. Not uncommonly it is very vague. Sometimes it amounts to only a bare declaration of general policy. Sometimes it is awkward, defective, or even misleading." [30]

If many legal rules are too vague to prescribe a clear answer for a concrete problem, then what is their function? According to some of the legal realists, it is either to express or to evoke certain emotions. "Many abstract terms, which once had content, but now have little of substance, acquire an intense 'emotive value'; they stimulate not intellection but strong feelings. They acquire an 'affective resonance' and represent 'emotional abstractions.' " [31] The "man of ordinary prudence" is an excellent example. To be sure, "he looks like a real fellow, the model of mankind. He is generally so considered. He is called the 'objective' as opposed to the 'subjective' standard. But all of this is due to vivid language. He is a mere figure of speech." In fact, this "abstraction"

is a mere caution, pointing the jury in as dramatic a way as possible the directions their deliberations should take. . . . The formula is as much for controlling the jury's deliberations as for measuring the party's conduct. . . . It does exactly what

[30] Radin, "The Theory of Judicial Decision: Or How Judges Think," *A. B. A. J.,* XI (1925), 360–361; Bingham, "What is the Law?" *Mich. L. Rev.,* XI (1912), 24–25. Also, see the following articles by Radin: "Statutory Interpretation," *Harv. L. Rev.,* XLIII (1930), 863; "Realism in Statutory Interpretation and Elsewhere," *Calif. L. Rev.,* XXIII (1935), 156; and "A Short Way with Statutes," *Harv. L. Rev.,* LVI (1942), 388. For an interesting criticism of Radin's views, see James M. Landis, "A Note on 'Statutory Interpretation,' " *Harv. L. Rev.,* XLIII (1930), 886.

[31] Frank, *Law and the Modern Mind,* p. 66.

any good ritual is designed to do; its function is psychological. It serves as a prophylaxis.[32]

Rituals have, of course, value. But their use often creates an "appearance of continuity, uniformity and definiteness which does not in fact exist." Vague language cannot interpret and apply itself. "The serpent in the imagined garden of Eden is the irrepressible semantic problem." [33]

Social and Economic Change

One of the "facts of life" which impressed itself most indelibly upon the minds of the legal realists is the celerity and pervasiveness of social change. When Herman Oliphant wrote that "we in the field of law are far from having finished drawing all the implications of the fact that the last two hundred years have brought more changes in the circumstances of men living together than the previous two thousand years had done," he articulated a sentiment which virtually all of the legal realists shared.[34] One of its implications is the inability of old rules to provide clear guidance for the unprecedented situations characteristic of a world in flux.

Even in a relatively static society, men have never been able to construct a comprehensive, eternized set of rules anticipating all possible legal disputes and settling them in advance. Even in such a social order no one can foresee all the future permu-

[32] Leon Green, *Judge and Jury* (Kansas City, Mo.: Vernon Law Book Co., 1930) , pp. 162–63, 174. For other examples, see Green, "The Individual's Protection under Negligence Law: Risk Sharing," *Nw. U. L. Rev.*, XLVII (1953) , 767–768.

[33] Frank, *Law and the Modern Mind*, p. 30; *Courts on Trial: Myth and Reality in American Justice* (Princeton: Princeton University Press, 1950) , p. 299.

[34] Oliphant, *op. cit.*, p. 74.

tations and combinations of events; situations are bound to occur which were never contemplated when the original rules were made. How much less is such a frozen legal system possible in modern times. New instruments of production, new modes of travel and of dwelling, new credit and ownership devices, new concentrations of capital, new social customs, habits, aims and ideals—all these factors of innovation make vain the hope that definitive legal rules can be drafted that will forever after solve all legal problems.[35]

Needless to say, these factors also make vain any hope that the application of old rules to unforeseen situations can be an effective means to dictate specific decisions.

The Uniqueness of the Factual Situations

Another factor upon which some of the legal realists placed considerable weight is the uniqueness of the factual situations involved in each litigated case. According to Rodell, for instance, this is indeed the "joker" in the classical theory of judicial decision-making. It presupposes that "problems and fact situations, by reason of their similarity or dissimilarity, fall naturally into groups." It also assumes that most new cases or problems that come up are "enough like some batch of cases and problems that have come up before to be controlled by the same principle that controlled them."[36] Yet no "two, much less twenty, fact

[35] Frank, *Law and the Modern Mind,* p. 6.

[36] Rodell, *Woe Unto You, Lawyers!* pp. 114–115, 115. The views of Eugene Wambaugh, a Professor at Harvard Law School at the turn of the century, offer an excellent example. In a classic explanation of how the *ratio decidendi* of a case is to be determined, he fully admitted that the circumstances of two cases are never precisely identical, and that this seems to negate the control which precedents can exert over future decisions. As he once wrote, it "seems to follow that the decision establishes no rule save that in an exactly identical case the rights of the parties will be precisely what the rights are

situations or legal problems can ever be sufficiently alike to fall naturally—that is, without being pushed—into the same category. The very existence of two situations or problems means that there are differences between them."

As with the two automobile accidents, so with any two legal disputes that ever have come up or could come up—except that most legal disputes are far more complicated, involve many more facts and types of facts, consequently present the judges with a far wider selection from which to choose the "essential" facts, and so open up a much greater range of legal principles which may be applied or not applied. And since no *two* cases ever fall "naturally" into the same category so that they can be automatically subjected to the same rules of Law, the notion that twenty or thirty or a hundred cases can gather themselves, unshoved, under the wing of one "controlling" principle is nothing short of absurd.[37]

Finally, any decision that the facts of the instant case are similar *enough* to those of prior cases to warrant the same classification is a value-judgment. As such, it cannot be made without recourse to extra-legal considerations. As Felix Cohen put it, "What facts in a case are important when the case is being decided, and what facts are important after the case has been decided and when it is cited as a precedent, these are questions that cannot be answered

decided to be in the reported case. If this conclusion be correct, it seems to follow that in practice no decision has value as a precedent. No two cases are precisely alike." *The Study of Cases: A Course of Instruction* (Boston: Little, Brown, 1894), p. 14. He resolved this problem by contending that "as to this difficulty the obvious suggestion is that the differences may be immaterial." *Ibid.*

[37] Rodell, *Woe Unto You, Lawyers!* pp. 115–116, 118–119. For further illustrations and analysis of this point, see Levi, *op. cit.*

without criteria of importance. And every judgment of importance implies a judgment of value or public policy." [38]

The unique character of the facts in a case is important, too, because it gives judges an opportunity to reach a number of competing decisions *without* outright reversal of established rules. To be sure, in a limited number of cases the facts may be standardized. Then they must be classified as stipulated by antecedent rules, or these rules must be candidly overruled. As Jerome Frank once wrote, "Of course there are cases where the facts are so simple and undisputed and stereotyped that the judge must either apply a settled rule or frankly over-rule the precedents." Nevertheless, such cases are fewer "than most persons assume"; "cases unequivocally calling for the routine application of such rules seldom come into court"; "the facts of all but the simplest controversies are complicated and unlike those of any other controversies"; and *"in a profound sense the unique circumstances of almost any case make it an 'unprovided case' where no well-established rule 'authoritatively' compels a given result."* [39]

Impact of Psychology

No explanation of the widespread acceptance by the realists of rule-skepticism would be complete without some mention of the impact of psychological theories. A noted social historian has written that the prestige of science was "colossal" in the 1920's. He has gone on to say that "of all the sciences it was the youngest and least

[38] "Field Theory and Judicial Logic," *Yale L. J.,* LIX (1950), 260.
[39] Frank, *Law and the Modern Mind,* pp. 162 (n. 3), 288 (n. 7), 162.

scientific which most captivated the general public. . . . Psychology was king. Freud, Adler, Jung, and Watson had their tens of thousands of votaries." [40] The influence of psychology was not confined to the general public. It also had a very strong impact upon a number of different academic disciplines, including the law. Few lawyers were as heavily influenced as the legal realists. The mark of Freud upon Jerome Frank is clear. The same can be said of the impact of John Watson upon Underhill Moore and Herman Oliphant.

The influence of a Watson is, of course, different from that of a Freud. Behaviorism is one thing, psychoanalysis another. Nonetheless, both approaches tend to minimize the role of conscious, rational, articulated "reasons" in the process by which decisions are reached. It is this breeze in the new climate of opinion which affected the views of the legal realists. The interpretation of decision-making developed by Frank in *Law and the Modern Mind* is typical. As he wrote, "The process of judging, *so the psychologists tell us,* seldom begins with a premise from which a conclusion is subsequently worked out. Judging begins rather the other way around—with a conclusion more or less vaguely formed; a man ordinarily starts with such a conclusion and afterwards tries to find premises which will substantiate it." The judge is no exception.

Now, since the judge is a human being and since no human being in his normal thinking processes arrives at decisions (except in dealing with a limited number of simple situations) by the route of . . . syllogistic reasoning, it is fair to assume that the judge, merely by putting on the judicial ermine, will not acquire so artificial a method of reasoning.

[40] Frederick Lewis Allen, *Only Yesterday* (New York: Bantam Books, 1959), p. 140.

Judicial judgments, like other judgments, doubtless, in most cases, are worked out backward from conclusions tentatively formulated.[41]

Most of the legal realists did not go beyond this point in their analysis of the psychological roots of decisions. An article written by a then little known federal district judge was, though, frequently quoted in the literature of the new jurisprudence. In 1929 Joseph C. Hutcheson wrote that judicial decisions result from a feeling or "hunch— that intuitive flash of understanding which makes the jump spark connection between question and decision, and at the point where the path is darkest for the judicial feet, sheds its light along the way." According to Judge Hutcheson, "the judge really decides by feeling, and not by judgment; by 'hunching' and not by ratiocination." "The vital, motivating impulse for the decision is an intuitive sense of what is right or wrong for that cause." [42]

It is this denial of the causal role of formal, deductive, syllogistic reasoning in the decision-making process which links together rule-skepticism and psychological theory. At the same time, the impact of the latter can be exaggerated. The realists' interpretation of judicial decision-making is not primarily the attempt to apply to the subject matter of one discipline theories borrowed from another. New psychological theories were part of the climate of advanced opinion in the 1920's and 1930's, and this climate affected the realists as it did other intelligent, educated men and women. It strengthened their conviction that judicial decisions are not a response to formal, articulated rules. Nev-

[41] Frank, *Law and the Modern Mind*, pp. 108 (italics mine), 109.
[42] Hutcheson, "The Judgment Intuitive: The Function of the Hunch in Judicial Decision," ed. M. R. Cohen and Felix S. Cohen, *Readings in Jurisprudence*, pp. 469, 471.

ertheless, factors internal to the judicial process itself were just as important, and probably more important. The legal realists were not psychologists, and there is little evidence that most of them extensively read the literature of the new science. The realists were lawyers. As such, their interpretation of judicial decision-making probably reflects their experience with analysis of case reports more than the impact of non-legal literature.

A Pragmatic View of Logic

In his pioneering appeal for the "next step" in the development of a "realistic jurisprudence," Llewellyn wrote that the movement "fits into the pragmatic and instrumental developments in logic." He went on to state that "the only novel feature is the application to that most conventionalized and fiction-ridden of disciplines, the law." [43] This last statement is much too modest. The realist movement has an original sparkle of its own. Nonetheless, the pragmatic developments in logic did have an impact upon rule-skepticism. In particular, the version of this logic formulated by the late John Dewey played an important role. His views probably had a greater impact upon the realists than those of any other professional philosopher.

In 1924 Dewey wrote an article entitled "Logical Method and Law." In it he distinguished between two basic types of human conduct. One consists of action "with a minimum of foresight, without examination of what they [human beings] are doing and of probable consequences. They act not upon deliberation but from routine, instinct, the direct pressure of appetite, or a blind 'hunch.'" The other kind of behavior is that in which

[43] Llewellyn, *Jurisprudence*, p. 28.

"action follows upon a decision, and the decision is the outcome of inquiry, comparison of alternatives, weighing of facts; deliberation or thinking has intervened." Dewey defined logical theory as "an account of the procedures followed in reaching decisions of the second type, in those cases in which subsequent experience shows that they were the best which could have been used under the conditions." The significance of such a definition is the secondary role to which it relegates the syllogism. As Dewey put it, "the trouble is that while the syllogism sets forth the *results* of thinking, it has nothing to do with the *operation* of thinking. . . . No concrete proposition, that is to say, one with material dated in time and placed in space, follows from any general statements or from any connection between them." For,

as a matter of fact, men do not begin thinking with premises. They begin with some complicated and confused case, apparently admitting of alternative modes of treatment and solution. Premises only gradually emerge from analysis of the total situation. The problem is not to draw a conclusion from given premises. . . . The problem is to *find* statements, of general principles and of a particular fact, which are worthy to serve as premises.[44]

The major sign of the impact of this line of thought upon the rule-skepticism of the legal realists is their spirited critique of deductive logic. They did not deny its utility for certain purposes.[45] They did insist that the use of the syllogism tends to obscure how judges reach deci-

---

[44] John Dewey, "Logical Method and Law," *Landmarks of Law: Highlights of Legal Opinion,* ed. Ray D. Henson (New York: Harper, 1960) , pp. 117, 117–118, 118, 122.

[45] See Frank, *Law and the Modern Mind,* p. 74, n. 2.

sions—tends to obscure, that is, the operation of thinking.

The court can decide one way or the other and in either case can make its reasoning appear equally flawless. Formal logic is what its name indicates; it deals with form and not with substance. The syllogism will not supply either the major premise or the minor premise. The "joker" is to be found in the selection of these premises. In the great run of cases which come before the courts, the selection of principles, and the determination of whether the facts are to be stated in terms of one or another minor premise, are the chief tasks to be performed.[46]

The Need for Change

At the outset, it must be admitted that the link between rule-skepticism and the realists' felt need for legal change cannot be demonstrated. They neither said nor wrote that their analysis is a useful means to develop more liberal judicial attitudes. Moreover, from a logical point of view there is no link. Rule-skepticism can logically be maintained by liberals or conservatives, radicals or reactionaries. It is a factual interpretation of judicial decision-making. As such, it is logically independent of any particular scale of social or political values. Nevertheless, there is a strong historical connection between rule-skepticism and liberalism. The reason for the nexus stems from the particular uses to which rule-formalism had generally been put, up to the time when the realist movement emerged. For the most part, it served as a very convenient rationale for refusing to adapt law to new social conditions. The arguments that the judge had no choice but to reach a particular decision, that he was coerced by factors beyond his

[46] *Ibid.*, p. 72.

control, and that change is for legislatures rather than courts are examples. These are the specific reasons which the judicial conservatives of the modern era have so frequently adduced for their decisions. But if rule-skepticism is valid, then these particular arguments are invalid as a justification for any particular course of judicial action. If the realists are right, then the judge usually has a number of different choices. Each could be reconciled with established rules. Conservatism could, of course, still be justified. The appeal must be, however, to its fruits. The inexorable dictates of antecedent law no longer suffice. For, as Llewellyn wrote in 1931, one of the consequences of rule-skepticism is "that peculiar one of the ways of working with precedent which consists in blinding the eyes to policy loses the fictitious sanctity with which it is now enveloped *some of the time:* to wit, whenever judges for any reason do not wish to look at policy." [47]

It is impossible to provide conclusive evidence that the desire to unmask this "fictitious sanctity" was *one* factor responsible for rule-skepticism. Some evidence does exist to suggest that this desire did play *a* role. In the first place, the legal realists were convinced that law had lagged behind the times. Indeed, Llewellyn wrote in 1931 that one of their common points of departure is "the conception of society in flux, and in flux typically faster than the law, so that the probability is always given that any portion of law needs reëxamination to determine how far it fits the society it purports to serve." He pointed out, too, that the realists' divorce "of Is and Ought for purposes of study" is "temporary," because "to men who begin with a suspicion that change is needed, a permanent divorce would be

---

[47] Llewellyn, *Jurisprudence*, p. 71.

impossible." [48] In the second place, the sympathy of the legal realists for, and their participation in, the New Deal reveals the general direction of the changes which they felt to be necessary. In 1934 Jerome Frank wrote that "in many ways those who sympathize . . . with experimental jurisprudence have found it easy to work for the new deal." [49] Easy or not, many of the exponents of "realism" were active in the administrations of F. D. R. The list includes Mr. Justice Douglas, Thurman Arnold, Herman Oliphant, Felix Cohen, and, of course, Frank himself.[50]

[48] *Ibid.*, pp. 55, 55–56.

[49] Jerome N. Frank, "Experimental Jurisprudence and the New Deal," U.S., *Congressional Record*, 1934, LXXVIII, p. 12413. According to Frank, "one of the most interesting facts some of us lawyers encountered in the early days of the whirl of the new deal . . . was this: there were two kinds of lawyers working on the new deal. The first were admirably adapted to aid in setting up new government experiments. . . . They could work 16 hours . . . every day in the week. The other group of lawyers . . . were confused and soon became weary. . . . The first group, on the whole, were those who, consciously or unconsciously, share that point of view toward legal techniques . . . known as 'realistic jurisprudence.'" *Ibid.*, 12412. Frank went on to point out that "the experimentalist has learned from experience that usually—of course, not always, but in most cases, if he starts with his conclusion, he can find satisfactory premises. There are . . . plenty of vacant premises, or at any rate, premises which can be sufficiently repaired or remodeled. Notably is this true in the field of . . . 'constitutional law.' Often . . . the same is true in the interpretation of highly ambiguous or highly generalized statutes." *Ibid.*, 12413.

[50] William O. Douglas was appointed to the Securities and Exchange Commission in 1936. He served as Chairman from September 1937, until April 1939, at which time he was appointed to the Supreme Court. Frank's *If Men Were Angels: Some Aspects of Government in a Democracy* (New York: Harper, 1942) was dedicated to "Mr. Justice William O. Douglas who, while Chairman of the Securities and Exchange Commission, superlatively demonstrated that effective administration can be made an important instrument

Still further, many of the legal realists who were not employed by the federal government in this era voiced their sympathies for its programs. More than one advocate of realistic jurisprudence, for example, testified in defense of President Roosevelt's controversial "court-packing" plan. The statement by Llewellyn that *"whatever bill comes out of committee backed by the President needs fighting support"* is typical.[51] The bluntness of Leon Green is less representative. For him, "the opposition is political. . . . Those who talk as though the court system is not a political matter talk nonsense. As long as the courts play their role in our government they will be and should be at the very heart of our political order." [52]

In light of evidence such as this, it is difficult not to infer that the political values of the realists had some impact on their rule-skepticism. At the same time, it would definitely be mistaken to interpret it as nothing more than a juristic

---

of true democracy." Frank held a variety of positions in the New Deal. For an interesting description of his role in some of them, see Arthur Schlesinger, Jr., *The Age of Roosevelt: The Coming of the New Deal* (Boston: Houghton Mifflin, 1959), II, esp. pp. 16 *et seq.* Frank was appointed to the Securities and Exchange Commission in 1937 and succeeded Douglas as Chairman in 1939. He was appointed to the Second Circuit Court of Appeals in 1941 and served on it until his death in 1957. Thurman Arnold was an Assistant Attorney General in charge of the Anti-Trust Division of the Department of Justice from 1938 to 1943. According to one historian he "turned out to be the most vigorous trust-buster in history." William Leuchtenburg, *Franklin D. Roosevelt and the New Deal: 1932–1940* (New York: Harper and Row, 1963), p. 259. Herman Oliphant was General Counsel for the Department of Treasury from 1934 until his death in 1939. Felix Cohen was an Assistant Solicitor in the Department of Interior from 1933 to 1948.

[51] Llewellyn, "A United Front on the Court," *Nation,* CXLIV (1937), 289.

[52] Green, "Unpacking the Court," *New Republic,* XC (1937), 67.

rationale for liberal change. The politics of the realists cannot be ignored, yet should not be overemphasized, either. The currents of thought which produced rule-skepticism did not flow from any one spring.

Implications of Rule-Skepticism

Two implications of rule-skepticism are of special importance. The first is that in any litigated and contested case courts must choose between conflicting premises for their decisions, and that this choice must be made on extralegal grounds. In any case doubtful enough to be litigated, competing legal authorities can be found to justify conflicting decisions. Then "the available authoritative premises—i.e., premises legitimate and impeccable under the traditional legal techniques—are at least two." More important, "The two are mutually contradictory as applied to the case in hand." [53] Finally, choice between the two can only be made and justified in terms of extralegal values. It can only be made, that is, in terms of the policies furthered by, or the *social* consequences of, alternative decisions.

If deduction does not solve cases, but only shows the effect of a given premise; and if there is available a competing but equally authoritative premise that leads to a different conclusion—then there is a choice in the case; a choice to be justified; a choice which *can* be justified only as a question of policy —for the authoritative tradition speaks with a forked tongue.[54]

The other inference concerns the kinds of considerations which must be taken into account for predictive purposes. Once it is realized that established rules do not and cannot determine specific decisions, then it must also

[53] Llewellyn, *Jurisprudence*, p. 58.   [54] *Ibid.*, p. 70.

be realized that these rules "are none too good as bases of prediction." [55] For this reason, it was argued, *"the particular kind of certainty* that men have thus far thought to find in law is in good measure an illusion." [56] The application of established rules to the facts of particular cases has not been an effective means to achieve uniformity of decisions. To be sure, judicial decision-making is not without patterns of uniformity. But this uniformity is not due to the impact of established rules. Prediction must be based, therefore, on factors "in good measure outside these . . . traditional rules." [57] It must be rooted, in other words, in the attitudes or values of the judge. As Llewellyn once put it, not "until you see this double aspect of the doctrine-in-action, do you appreciate how little, in detail, you can predict *out of the rules alone;* how much you must turn, for purposes of prediction, to the reactions of the judges to the facts and to the life around them." [58]

The significance of both of these inferences cannot be exaggerated. They are largely responsible for two central themes in the literature of the legal realists. The first is the recommendation of new methods for reaching decisions. The second is the development of more adequate techniques for the prediction of decisions. These are two of the most distinctive lines of analysis pursued by the legal realists. Each stems from rule-skepticism. The nature of each will be analyzed in detail in subsequent chapters.

Opinion-Skepticism

Closely related to rule-skepticism is opinion-skepticism. This last phrase is not used by the legal realists, but is

[55] Frank, *Law and the Modern Mind,* p. 163.
[56] Llewellyn, *Jurisprudence,* p. 61 (italics mine) .   [57] *Ibid.*
[58] *The Bramble Bush,* p. 68.

nevertheless a useful label for an important idea in their literature. It is an idea which probably reflects more markedly than any other single theme in their movement the impact of psychological theories. We have seen that such theories had some impact on the realists' explanation of how decisions are *reached;* psychological doctrine had a greater influence on their interpretation of how decisions have traditionally been *justified.*

One of the best descriptions of opinion-skepticism was given by Llewellyn in 1931. He wrote that one of the distinctive marks of the realist movement is "the tentative adoption of the theory of rationalization for . . . the study of opinions."

An early and fruitful line of attack borrowed from psychology the concept of *rationalization.* . . . To recanvass the opinions, viewing them no longer as mirroring the process of deciding cases, but rather as trained lawyers' arguments made by the judges (after the decision has been reached), intended to make the decision seem plausible, legally decent, legally right, to make it seem, indeed, legally inevitable—this was to open up new vision.[59]

The pervasiveness of this vision among the legal realists cannot be doubted. In 1933 Felix Cohen wrote that " 'realistic jurisprudence' has sprung in great measure from the recognition that principles enunciated by courts as grounds of decision often represent nothing more objective than a resolution to use sanctified words wherever specified results are dictated by undisclosed determinants." [60] In language which was to raise the hair of their more traditional brethren, the realists assailed the conven-

---

[59] Llewellyn, *Jurisprudence*, pp. 56, 58.
[60] Cohen, *Ethical Systems and Legal Ideals*, p. 237.

tional reasoning of judicial opinions as "window dress-
ing," as "the formal clothes in which he [the judge] dresses
up his thoughts," as "devices for concealing rather than
disclosing what the law is." [61] We "delude ourselves and
likewise . . . others by insisting that those delightful word
jousts we call opinions are dependable guides to the workings of the judicial process." [62]

Two factors account for this interpretation of judicial
opinions. The first and most dramatic is the impact of
Freudian psychology. Harold Lasswell has written that the
1920's were "the high tide of psychoanalytic receptivity." [63]
The legal realists did not remain unwashed. A book
published by the historian James Harvey Robinson—*The
Mind in the Making*—seems to have been of particular
importance. For Robinson, *"Most of our so-called reasoning consists in finding arguments for going on believing as
we already do."* He went on to argue that "almost all that
had passed for social science, political economy, politics,
and ethics in the past may be brushed aside by future
generations as mainly rationalizing." [64] The influence of
this book, particularly, has been attested to by Llewellyn.
In 1960 he wrote that "in 1920, *as a result of* James
Harvey Robinson's *Mind in the Making,* a Freudian interpretation of judicial opinions broke upon the little
world of legal scholarship." [65]

---

[61] Frank, *Law and the Modern Mind,* pp. 141, 140.

[62] Green, *Judge and Jury,* p. 53.

[63] Lasswell, "The Impact of Psychoanalytical Thinking on the
Social Sciences," *Psychoanalysis and Social Science,* ed. Hendrik M.
Ruitenbeek (New York: Dutton, 1962), p. 6.

[64] Robinson, *The Mind in the Making: The Relation of Intelligence to Social Reform* (New York: Harper, 1921), pp. 41, 47.

[65] Llewellyn, *The Common Law Tradition,* p. 12 (italics mine).
In so far as the law is concerned, the concept of rationalization had

The other factor is less dramatic but probably of equal significance. It is simply the experience of extensive case analysis. Opinion-skepticism is, in part, a result of "perceiving case after case in which the opinion is clearly almost valueless as an indication of how that case came to decision." [66] The most detailed non-Freudian explanation of this phenomenon in the literature of the realists came from the pen of Joseph Walter Bingham.

In the first place, the opinion is generally written after the judgment has been determined upon. In the second place, often it is the opinion of only one of the judges of the court. The reasons of the different judges who concur in the decision may vary widely. . . . Thirdly, it is often a difficult task for a man to comprehend clearly and accurately the real motives which have led to his decision. In many cases it requires powers of insight into one's personal mental and psychological machinery, conscious and subconscious, and analytical ability which are possessed by only a small portion of humanity. Fourthly, accurate generalization and expression is a difficult task in which few are adepts, and are not essential to the functions of the judge.[67]

---

been applied three years before the publication of Robinson's book. See Theodore Schroeder, "The Psychologic Study of Judicial Opinions," *Calif. L. Rev.*, VI (1918), 89. For Schroeder, "The written opinion is little more than a special plea made in defense of impulses which are largely unconscious." "According to the old manner of appraising judicial opinions, we accepted at their face value the reasons assigned by the judge, just as though they were an adequate explanation of his decision. Soon it will be different." *Ibid.*, pp. 95, 94. Schroeder proved to be an apt prophet.

[66] Llewellyn, *Jurisprudence*, p. 58. For some examples, see Arthur C. Bachrach, "Reflections on Brief Writing," *N.Y. L. J.*, LXXXIX (1933), 366, 390.

[67] See Bingham, "What is the Law?" *Mich. L. Rev.*, XI (1912), 21–22; Bingham, "Legal Philosophy and the Law," *Ill. L. Rev.*, IX (1909), 116.

The frequency of such interpretations is the major reason why it would be mistaken to attach too much significance to psychological theory as an explanation of opinion-skepticism. Obviously such theory had a very important impact upon the views of the realists. The concept of rationalization was in the air. The advocates of "realistic jurisprudence" used it for their own purposes. Still, their experience with reading, analyzing, and explaining judicial opinions is probably of equal significance.

The Rival Views of Pound and Cardozo

At the outset of this chapter the point was made that rule-skepticism is a distinctive product of the realist movement. It is now possible to validate this interpretation by contrasting the views of the realists with those of their progressive predecessors. Roscoe Pound and Benjamin N. Cardozo are two excellent examples. They were certainly among the most influential leaders of progressive American jurisprudence at the point in time at which the realist movement emerged. Each was critical of the classical view of the judicial process. But the criticisms of each were more conservative than those of the legal realists. Moreover, this fact is one reason why both Pound and Cardozo were critical of the exponents of realism, and vice versa.[68]

---

[68] See Rumble, "Legal Realism, Sociological Jurisprudence, and Mr. Justice Holmes," *Journal of the History of Ideas*, XXVI (1965), 547; Corbin, "Judicial Process," *Conn. B. J.*, XXXIII (1959), 285; Corbin, "Introduction; A Symposium in Honor of the Fortieth Anniversary of the Publication of Mr. Justice Cardozo's Storrs Lectures," *Yale L. J.*, LXXI (1961), 199; Llewellyn, *The Common Law Tradition*, pp. 99, 117, 190, 430–435; Frank, *Law and the Modern Mind*, pp. 252–258; Frank, "Cardozo and the Upper-Court Myth,"

No one needs to be informed of the role of Pound in the revolt against the mechanical theory of the judicial process. In 1922 he delivered the Storrs Lectures at the Yale Law School. They were later published as *An Introduction to the Philosophy of Law*. Again and again he insisted on the fallacies of the classical view of judicial decision-making. Nonetheless, his criticisms stopped far short of the point reached by the legal realists. The most convincing evidence of that is his solution for "the basic problem of jurisprudence." This is the problem of "rule and discretion, of administration of justice by law and administration of justice by the more or less trained intuition of experienced magistrates." His solution was to "partition" the field of law between the two. One part would consist of those areas in which individualization in the application of law has developed. These are the areas "that almost without exception . . . have to do with cases involving the moral quality of individual conduct or of the conduct of enterprises." Examples are equity, torts, the law of public utilities, the law of fiduciary relations, the law of domestic relations, criminal procedure, the informal methods of petty courts, and the practices of administrative tribunals. In each of these areas a large measure of discretion in the application of law is inevitable, and all attempts to "cut down this margin have proved futile." Here, "complete justice is not to be attained by the mechanical application of fixed rules," and "we resort to standards." Moreover, "the sacrifice in certainty in so doing is more apparent than actual. For the certainty attained by mechanical application of fixed rules to human conduct has always been illusory."

Law & Contem. Prob., XIII (1948) , 369; Cardozo, *Selected Writings*, ed. Hall, pp. 7–46; and the articles cited *supra*, p. 29, n. 53.

This is not true, however, of other fields of law. Examples are "inheritance and succession, definition of interests in property and the conveyance thereof, matters of commercial law and the creation, incidents, and transfer of obligations." These areas have proved to be "a fruitful field for legislation" or codification. The reason is that "every promissory note is like every other. Every fee simple is like every other. Every distribution of assets repeats the conditions that have recurred since the Statute of Distributions." Moreover, wherever legislation is effective, then "mechanical application is effective and desirable" as a means to insure legal certainty.[69]

Like Pound, Cardozo was critical of the classical theory of the judicial process. Thus, he confessed, "I take judge-made law as one of the existing realities of life." Also, he insisted that "hardly a rule of today" exists "but may be matched by its opposite of yesterday," and admitted that "for every tendency one seems to see a counter-tendency; for every rule its antonym. Nothing is stable. Nothing absolute." And he agreed that "as the years have gone by . . . I have become reconciled to the uncertainty, because I have grown to see it as inevitable." [70] Like Pound, however, Cardozo stopped short of the point reached by the legal realists. Even in his first and greatest

[69] Pound, *An Introduction to the Philosophy of Law* (rev. ed.; New Haven: Yale University Press, 1954), pp. 54, 68, 70, 71, 69, 70–71, 69. See the following articles by Pound: "Mechanical Jurisprudence," *Colum. L. Rev.*, VII (1908), 605; "The Need of a Sociological Jurisprudence," *Green Bag*, XIX (1907), 107; "Law in Books and Law in Action," *Am. L. Rev.*, XLIV (1910), 12; "Liberty of Contract," *Yale L. J.*, XVIII (1909), 454; and "Justice according to Law," *Essays in Jurisprudence from the Columbia Law Review* (New York: Columbia University Press, 1963).

[70] Cardozo, *The Nature of the Judicial Process* (New Haven: Yale University Press, 1921), pp. 10, 26, 28, 166.

book—*The Nature of the Judicial Process*—he circled such statements as I have quoted with one qualification after another. They are qualifications which clearly reveal the far more conservative character of his outlook. Thus he insisted that the freedom of judicial choice operated only in a sharply limited number of cases. He was careful to point out that his concern in the bulk of the book "with the creative or dynamic element" in the judicial process "is likely to give a false impression, an over-colored picture, of uncertainty in the law and of free discretion in the judge." For the "merely static" precedents outnumber the "creative or dynamic" precedents "many times." "In countless litigations, the law is so clear that the judges have no discretion." His own experience as a judge seemed to confirm this. "Of the cases that come before the court in which I sit a majority . . . could not, with semblance of reason, be decided in any way but one. The law and its application alike are plain." In a later book, he expanded the number of such cases from a majority to "nine-tenths" of those that "come before a court." [71] Still further, he also claimed that the vast majority of decisions not only are, but ought to be, reached in this way. "I think adherence to precedent should be the rule and not the exception." [72] His reasons are virtually identical with those of the advocates of the orthodox doctrine of legal certainty.

As this brief outline indicates, opinion-skepticism is virtually absent from the literature of either Pound or Cardozo. Also, their rule-skepticism is not nearly as radical as that of the realists. Neither emphasized as much the multiplicity of precedents or techniques for their interpretation,

[71] *Ibid.,* pp. 164, 129, 164; Cardozo, *Selected Writings,* ed. Hall, pp. 212–213.
[72] Cardozo, *The Nature of the Judicial Process,* p. 149.

the logical indeterminacy of established rules, the ambiguity of legal language, the rapidity and pervasiveness of social change, and the uniqueness of the factual configurations in litigated and contested cases. Both felt that prior rules are a much more effective means to determine specific decisions than did the realists. Moreover, neither Pound nor Cardozo had the same view as the realists of the nature of the judicial choice. Both tended to interpret the alternative which confronts judges as either reversal or affirmation of prior rules. Both minimized the number of competing decisions which are possible without outright reversal of established rules. Neither insisted that "beneath what looks on the page as 'mere' following, . . . there swirls a constant current of creation." [73] As Llewellyn once wrote:

Yet the particular symbol "precedent" or "stare decisis" calls up (even to Cardozo) chiefly connotations of standing pat upon the past, of refusing to open up the policy questions in the new case. . . . *Change,* on the other hand, calls up connotations of upsetting traditional technique, upsetting expectations, endangering stability. This is as regrettable as it is misleading. It confines the NAME *stare decisis* to a single one among the many phases that doctrine takes in action. In fact our case law is, and has always been, in constant process of change. *And in fact the change has been brought about . . . by the process known as "standing" on precedent, stare decisis.* You must know where you want to go in the case in hand before you *can* utilize the precedents effectively. They can limit you, before you decide, but they cannot deprive you of choice. A decision on policy remains inescapable, because the precedents are multiform, ambiguous, *never* fixed; and because the tradition-hallowed techniques for dealing with them *(wholly within the "principle" of stare decisis)* permit you to

[73] Llewellyn, *The Common Law Tradition,* p. 116.

squeeze out of the same set of precedents any one of a dozen *different* conclusions or rules.[74]

Similar criticisms were advanced against Dean Pound.[75]

In light of these differences, it is not surprising that neither Pound nor Cardozo drew the same inferences from their analysis of the judicial process as did the realists. The latter felt the need to formulate new methods for reaching decisions to be much more imperative than either Pound or Cardozo. The same can be said of the dire urge of the realists to develop new techniques for the prediction of decisions. Both the need and the urge stem from a skepticism toward established rules as means to compel particular decisions which is more radical than that of their predecessors.

Criticisms of Rule-Skepticism

The legal realists have been subject, from the outset of their movement, to a variety of criticisms. The focus, nature, and intensity of the reaction has varied, but the stream of criticism has flowed on. Moreover, none of the themes in the realist movement has evoked a more spirited critique than those explained in the foregoing pages of this chapter. No account of rule-skepticism would be complete without some examination of this reaction. Only then can the views of the realists be placed in perspective and evaluated dispassionately.

One of the first criticisms is that the advocates of "realistic jurisprudence" exaggerated the irrational character of judicial decision-making. A whole school of thought has contended that their critique "smacks of the race track,

[74] Llewellyn, *Jurisprudence*, p. 91, n. 8.

[75] For a good illustration, see Frank, *Law and the Modern Mind*, pp. 151–152, 221–231, 312–326.

the tout, and the lady with hat pin suspended above her program ready to prick out the 'winner' by a lusty jab at the entries with her eyes closed." [76] The point of view of the realists "repudiates and renounces all the efforts man has made through the ages to bring order out of disorder by something man has persistently . . . believed in but is now asked to deride: his reason." [77] Realism's "psychologism . . . pure or diluted . . . reduces man (and judge) to the level of a human machine, ousts intellect as the governing force in the fabrication of judicial opinions, unseats reason." [78] It rejects "the mental capacity of judges to decide the issues before them fairly and impartially according to traditional law." [79] The vital issue between realists and nonrealists is, thus, "the contest between the force and validity of principles, precedents, reason, free will, and impartial justice on the one hand, and the impact of emotion, irrationalism, bias, environment, and juristic skepticism in the legal order." [80]

Most of these statements are from the pens of the natural law critics of the realists. The alleged irrationalism of the latter was attacked, however, by those who cannot unequivocally be identified with this tradition. Pound is an excellent example. In his mind, the "new realists of today" assume "that psychology has overthrown the whole

---

[76] Kennedy, "To Hunch or not to Hunch," *N.Y. L. J.*, LXXXIX (1933), 742.

[77] Philip Mechem, "The Jurisprudence of Despair," *Iowa L. Rev.*, XXI (1936), 674.

[78] Kennedy, "Psychologism in the Law," *Geo. L. J.*, XXIX (1940), 149.

[79] Kennedy, "My Philosophy of Law," *My Philosophy of Law: Credos of Sixteen American Scholars* (Boston: Boston Law Book Co., 1941), p. 154.

[80] *Ibid.*, p. 157.

science of jurisprudence"; contend that reason and the existence of rules of law are an "illusion"; maintain that "brutality" is a "test of actuality"; and regard the attempt to hold down the individual judge to prescribed paths of action as futile. For these reasons, he contended, "the term 'realism' . . . is a mere boast." Its advocates have exaggerated "the alogical and irrational features of the judicial process." For these reasons, also,

too much has been claimed . . . for [Holmes] . . . as a skeptical realist. . . . He did not seek an easy retreat from the hard work of the judicial office by way of a theory of the psychologically inevitable judicial impotence to reach an impersonal result. He did not regard law or laws or legal technique as masks to cover individual items of judicial behavior each on its own basis of individual psychology or prejudice or unguided intuition.[81]

A second line of criticism is that the realists underestimated the degree of legal certainty, and misunderstood the reasons for its existence. For this reason, it has been argued, the "new skeptics" are "disappointed absolutists." Rejecting the "clock-work logic" of traditional legal determinism, the realists "react into an opposite extreme of naive unwillingness to recognize the less absolute, but none the less relatively effective, way in which legal rules do their work." Holding an impossibly exalted view of certainty, "they insist on all or none." Moreover, the realists have forgotten that "the decisional behavior of past judges . . . is for the most part dependable . . . only to the extent that judges follow rules and precedents, or in

81 Pound, "Fifty Years of Jurisprudence," *Harv. L. Rev.*, LI (1938), 786; Pound, "The Call for a Realistic Jurisprudence," *ibid.*, XLIV (1931), 698; Pound, "Fifty Years of Jurisprudence," *ibid.*, LI (1938), 795–796, 800, 792.

other words make a deliberate effort to imitate their predecessors." For, the only "practical way" to secure uniformity is "for different judges to recognize and abide by an obligation to bring their decisions into unison by giving effect in those decisions to the same legal formulas or rules." [82]

A third recurring criticism is that the realists exaggerated the range of "creative choice" available to the judge. The views of Cardozo are illustrative. He was not wholly unsympathetic to the realist movement. The tone of his address to the New York Bar Association in 1932 is moderate and understanding. He admitted that

the teachings of the neo-realists were and still are of great value to jurisprudence in ridding *stare decisis* of something of its petrifying rigidity, in warning us that in many instances the principles and rules and concepts of our own creation are merely *apercus* and glimpses of reality, and in reminding us of the need of reformulating them or at times abandoning them altogether when they stand condemned as mischievous in the social consciousness of the hour, the social consciousness which it is our business as judges to interpret as best we can.

Moreover, Cardozo also recognized that in some kinds of cases the choice which confronts the judge is of the character described by the realists. These are the "exceptional cases . . . where the creative function is at its highest. These are the cases that have a maximum of interest for the student of legal methods. These are the cases in which neo-realism . . . has its maximum of truth and also its maximum of utility." Nonetheless, Cardozo insisted that the realists "placed the creative potency of the judgment

[82] John Dickinson, "Legal Rules: Their Function in the Process of Decision," *U. Pa. L. Rev.*, LXXIX (1931), 835, 835–836, 840, 845.

too far into the foreground, and cast too far into the background the significance of words." Next to the exceptional cases stand the run-of-the-mill variety. They constitute "nine-tenths, perhaps more, of the cases that come before a court." The results of such cases "are predetermined . . . in the sense that they are predestined—their fate preestablished by inevitable laws that follow them from birth to death." Thus "the range of free activity is relatively small." [83]

A fourth and related criticism has been that the realists exaggerated the ambiguity of legal language. According to John Dickinson, for example,

Legal terms like "negligence," "cruelty," "reasonable rate," "restraint of trade," which form the component elements of so many rules of law, are not peculiar or different from other terms of ordinary discourse in having a central core of habitually established content surrounded by a penumbra of doubtful border-line cases.[84]

More recently, H. L. A. Hart has echoed a similar theme. He has claimed that rule-skepticism is inconsistent with the fact that "there will indeed be plain cases constantly recurring in similar contexts to which general expressions are clearly applicable"; that "there is general agreement in judgments as to the applicability of the classifying terms"; and that "general terms would be useless to us as a medium of communication unless there were such familiar, generally unchallenged cases." [85]

A fifth criticism has been developed recently by Edward

[83] *Selected Writings,* ed. Hall, pp. 13, 20, 13, 212, 213.

[84] Dickinson, "Legal Rules: Their Application and Elaboration," *U. Pa. L. Rev.,* LXXIX (1931), 1085.

[85] Hart, *The Concept of Law* (Oxford: Clarendon Press, 1961), p. 123.

RULE-SKEPTICISM

J. Blaustein. It is directed against the emphasis of the realists upon the logically indeterminate character of established rules. According to Blaustein, "the fundamental error of the Realists is that they confuse a *logical reason* with a *logically necessary reason*. They suppose that to be a reason at all means to be a logically necessary reason." This assumption is fallacious because "the fact is . . . that our legal reasoning, like our reasoning about matter of fact, is not of the same character as our reasoning in mathematics and to measure the two sorts of reasoning by the same standards invites confusion." Such measurement obscures the fact that in many cases decisions which are logically possible "are legally impossible, because they fly in the face of well-established legal principles or precedents." As a result,

frustrated in their attempts to find logically necessary precedents, the Legal Realists overreacted by virtually abandoning, at least in theoretical terms, the system of precedent itself. If a precedent was not a logically conclusive determinant for the decision of a case, it could not serve as a logical reason for the decision at all.[86]

Oddly enough, opinion-skepticism has not been subject to nearly as much critical attention as rule-skepticism. Perhaps its most significant critique has come from Edward Stevens Robinson. His views merit special attention for a number of reasons. He was, for one thing, a professional psychologist. In addition, he was a visiting lecturer at the Yale Law School in the heyday of the realist movement. In this capacity he taught a seminar with Thurman Arnold on the social psychology of judicial institutions.

[86] Edward J. Blaustein, "Logic and Legal Realism: The Realist as Frustrated Idealist," *Cornell L. Q.*, L (1964), 29, 31, 32.

The two also collaborated on a course in legal ethics. Finally, Robinson was generally sympathetic to the views of the realists. Thus he described his major juristic work as "part of the realistic movement in American jurisprudence." In other words, he was an "insider" who did not share the visceral reaction to legal realism so common among its early critics.

The major object of Robinson's critique is the concept of rationalization. In his mind, it has "too often . . . furnished justification for careless or prejudiced generalization rather than instruments for rigorous analysis." The mere failure by a judge to mention a particular factor does not necessarily mean that it had "functional importance." For this reason "the search for unconscious factors in judicial behavior can never be a fool-proof procedure and it is always in danger of suffering as much from the unconscious wishes of the analyst as from those of the judge." Also, the fact that the judge mentioned certain factors in his opinion endows them with psychological importance. "The mere fact that a man attributes to himself certain *reasons* for his conduct makes those reasons themselves psychologically important." What is more, stated reasons may in fact function as actual or potential motives for decisions. "When men rationalize their actions they are nearly always striving to do more than hide their real motives. They are expressing their ideals of what the motives of such actions ought to be." If such expressions are "not motives when they first arise, their mere repetition is likely to establish them as such." Finally, the stated reasons for decisions may be "to a degree at least indicative of the impulses that actually did play a part in reaching that decision." Indeed, "in many instances these reasons are more than reliable symptoms of previous thinking. They may give a psychological analysis of that thinking which could not have been found in the thinking itself. Much of what goes on in private deliberation is not only dim and fragmentary to the thinker himself; much of it must be interpreted before it can be intelligibly described."

The general conclusions which Robinson reached in light of such an analysis are of particular interest. Needless to say, he did not deny that judicial opinions may be rationalizations which distort the "real" reasons for decisions. He did insist that "what is required as a basis for a naturalistic jurisprudence is a psychology capable of seeing that legal doctrines which are not to be taken literally are yet to be taken seriously." More important, he contended that the efficacy of "stated" reasons "is always a problem as to their actual effectiveness at a given time, a given place, and in a given individual." The problem of their efficacy is, in short, one which only empirical analysis of concrete cases can establish.

Whether, in his explicit statement of his reasons for concluding thus and so, a man gives a largely accurate or a largely fictitious account of himself is another one of those matters of fact. They are not always easy to settle, but certainly they can never be settled by the loose, lazy, and frequently cynical use of such terms as *unconscious complexes* and *rationalization*.[87]

Evaluation of the Criticisms

At the outset, some of the criticisms can only be described as hyperbolical. None of the realists repudiated or renounced reason. None reduced man or judge to the level of a machine. Some of their books and articles could be

[87] Edward Stevens Robinson, *Law and the Lawyers* (New York: Macmillan, 1935), pp. vii, 139, 144, 145, 147, 173, 147, 146–147, 174.

made, it is true, to appear in this light. The chief examples are Frank's *Law and the Modern Mind,* Arnold's *The Symbols of Government,* and the latter's *The Folklore of Capitalism.* These are the books, naturally, which most irritated the early critics of the realists. Still, none of these works *if read carefully* is guilty of all the sins ascribed to it. Moreover, the critics have often unjustly assumed that valid criticisms which can be fairly advanced against some statements of Arnold and Frank apply with equal validity to all of the realists. Such an assumption cannot be reconciled with the facts. Most of the realists did not deny that legal rules existed, or that judicial decision-making was marked by significant patterns of regularity. Also, the impact of psychological theory varied immensely. Even those realists whose views were most heavily influenced did not deny that the role of reason or the degree of judicial self-consciousness could be increased.[88] Still further, many of the critics simply failed to come to grips with the major arguments in terms of which rule-skepticism was *justified.* From the perspective of the present, this is surely one of the most striking characteristics of the reactions to the realist movement. The realists' analysis of precedents, legal language, social change, logic, or the facts may not be beyond criticism. Nonetheless, the kind of appraisal which it has induced has all too frequently been superficial.

Most important of all, the critics have tended to overlook one crucial characteristic of rule-skepticism. They have ignored the fact that it is intended to apply only to the interpretation or application of established rules in litigated, contested, and appealed cases. One or two of the advocates of "realistic jurisprudence" did, to be sure,

[88] See *infra,* pp. 193–198.

96

argue that what is true of rules involved in such litigation is also true of other rules.[89] The majority of legal realists did not, however, share this view. The point which they wished to emphasize was that *"in any case doubtful enough to make litigation respectable* the available authoritative premises . . . are at least two, and . . . two . . . mutually contradictory as applied to the case at hand."* [90]

The failure to recognize this fact is unfortunate for several reasons. To begin with, it has induced critics to attack the realists for views which are erroneous, but which most of them did not hold. It is a mistake to deny the existence of rules "the application of which individuals can see for themselves in case after case, without further recourse to official direction or discretion." [91] Such a denial is inconsistent with the crucial function of legal rules as directives for human behavior. Most of the legal realists did not deny, however, that some rules perform this function meaningfully. Their point is that such rules are usually not the focus of controversies in cases which are doubtful enough to be litigated, contested, and appealed.

The tendency to ignore this point is also unfortunate because it has obstructed full recognition of one of the realists' greatest contributions. This is their illumination and explanation of the nature of the choice which confronts judges. Preceding jurists had interpreted this choice to be either confirmation or reversal, application or nonapplication, of established rules. The great achievement of the legal realists is to demonstrate that the matter is far

---

[89] See Rodell, *Woe Unto You, Lawyers!* pp. 120–122.

[90] Llewellyn, *Jurisprudence,* p. 58 (italics mine).

[91] Hart, *Concept of Law,* p. 133.

more complicated. In a vast number of cases the choice is not *whether* but *how* to apply *which* rules. The difficult task which confronts judges is to choose between competing decisions, authority for each of which can usually be found in the established rules. If the implications of prior rules were not in this respect uncertain, then the case would usually not be litigated or, at least, appealed. In Frank's words:

Each week the courts decide hundreds of cases which purport to turn not on disputed "questions of fact" but solely on "points of law." If the law is unambiguous and predictable, what excuses can be made by the lawyers who lose these cases? They should know in advance of the decisions that the rules of law are adverse to their contentions. Why, then, are these suits brought or defended? In some few instances, doubtless, because of ignorance or cupidity or an effort to procure delay, or because a stubbornly litigious client insists. But in many cases, honest and intelligent counsel on both sides of such controversies can conscientiously advise their respective clients to engage in the contest . . . because, prior to the decision, the law is sufficiently in doubt to justify such advice.[92]

As Frank has indicated, some cases are litigated even though the outcome of the application of established rules to the facts is clear. Such litigation generally stems from ignorance, cupidity, an effort to procure delay, the insistence of a stubbornly litigious client, or a desperate though improbable hope. In other cases which are litigated the major issues concern questions of fact. The application of antecedent rules is clear. What is in doubt is what in fact happened. In each of these circumstances, however, the case is likely either not to be litigated, or contested, or if litigated and contested, appealed. If it is doubtful enough

[92] *Law and the Modern Mind,* p. 9.

to be appealed, then the interpretation and application of the relevant rules is probably not clear.

The point to be emphasized is, thus, that the very fact of litigation and appeal usually indicates the existence of alternative premises. Each could be used to justify conflicting decisions. Once that stage is reached, either the finding, interpretation, or application of the rules by means of which the facts will be classified opens up a wide range of choice. If the drama of the appellate courtroom has begun, then "either interpretation of language or the sizing up of the facts, or the choice open as among available divergent premises or tendencies in our multiwayed legal scheme, or the like, will allow a fair technical case to be made either way or a third or fourth other way, *if one looks at the authorities taken alone.*"[93] Moreover, the choice to use one rule rather than another as the premise for the decision cannot logically be made on the basis of the relevant authorities. The choice between rule A and rule B logically implies the existence of some extralegal standard on the basis of which the choice is made. It implies, that is, a judgment about the desirability of some *social* value to be advanced by the decision.

To say all of this is not to suggest that rule-skepticism is exempt from legitimate criticism. What is true of most cases which are doubtful enough to be litigated, contested, and appealed is not true of all. Moreover, some of the realists did tend too dogmatically to generalize on the basis of insufficient evidence. Their research is impressive. In particular, this is true of their studies of constitutional law, torts, and contracts.[94] The evidence which was accu-

---

[93] Llewellyn, *The Common Law Tradition*, p. 21.

[94] See Llewellyn, "The Rule of Law in our Case Law of Contract," *Yale L. J.*, XLVII (1938), 1245; Llewellyn, "The Constitution as an Institution," *Colum. L. Rev.*, XXXIV (1934), 1; Llewellyn, "Behind

mulated in these areas about the range of choice available to the judge in the interpretation and application of established rules is vast. Moreover, the fact that the existence of this range of choice has been confirmed by Llewellyn's random sample of cases cannot be ignored. This is the technique which he employed in *The Common Law Tradition*. In his words,

A feature of the book which is unique and which goes to the essence is that demonstrations will be undertaken not on cases carefully selected to convenience, nor yet on cases of high importance, nor on cases of particular subject-matter, but on mine-run stuff as it comes unselected from the mine: the cases in sequence as they stand in the reports, often enough the cases of a single opinion-day . . . the *demonstrations* which clinch the vital points are done on stuff from the daily grist which is like your tomorrow's case and mine.[95]

---

the Law of Divorce: I," *Colum. L. Rev.*, XXXII (1932), 1281; *ibid.*, II, XXXIII (1933), 244; Llewellyn, "On Warranty of Quality and Society: I," *Colum. L. Rev.*, XXXVI (1936), 699; *ibid.*, II, XXXVII (1937), 341; Cook, "The Logical and Legal Basis of the Conflict of Laws," *Ill. L. Rev.*, XXXI (1936), 143; Cook, "Substance and Procedure in the Conflict of Laws," *Yale L. J.*, XLII (1933), p. 333; Douglas, "Vicarious Liability and Administration of Risk: I," *Yale L. J.*, XXXVIII (1929), 584; *ibid.*, II, XXXVIII (1929), 720; Douglas, "Some Functional Aspects of Bankruptcy," *Yale L. J.*, XLI (1932), 329; Green, *Judge and Jury* (Kansas City, Missouri: Vernon Law Book Co., 1930); Green, *The Rationale of Proximate Cause* (Kansas City, Mo.: Vernon Law Book Co., 1927); Green, *Traffic Victims: Tort Law and Liability* (Evanston: Northwestern University Press, 1958); Rodell, *Nine Men: A Political History of the Supreme Court from 1790 to 1955* (New York: Random House, 1955); and Corbin, *Corbin on Contracts: A Comprehensive Treatise on the Rules of Contract Law* (8 vols.; St. Paul: West Publishing Co., 1950). For additional bibliographical data, see Llewellyn, *Jurisprudence*, pp. 74–76.

[95] Llewellyn, *The Common Law Tradition*, p. 6.

Nonetheless, the research of the legal realists is probably not fully representative or widespread enough to warrant the inference that their conclusions are universally valid for all litigated, contested, and appealed cases.

Finally, the evidence adduced by the exponents of realism does not warrant the inference that established rules *could* not have determined *any* past decision. Their analysis does justify, to be sure, two very important inferences about *most* litigated, contested, and appealed cases. One is that competing decisions can usually be reached without outright reversal of established rules. The other is that these rules were *probably* not the decisive factor inducing the decision reached. What is *probably* true of decisions in most cases is not *necessarily* true, however, of decisions in all cases. Even in some cases doubtful enough to be litigated, contested, and appealed it is always possible that the impact of established rules has been decisive. The judge may not have been aware, for example, of the alternatives available to him. Llewellyn once pointed out:

Often the prior cases push so strongly toward one line-up that he will not even see the chance we here point out to line them up differently. Then, unless the result raises the hair (*his* hair, not yours!), and forces a different outcome so to speak at the muzzle of a gun, the judge will never get as far as inquiring into justice. He will decide "by law" and let it go at that. Particularly . . . will this be true of the weaker, the less skillful judge. Advance upon him with a ladder sound in logic, and he grows uncomfortable: his duty calls for application of the law; his skill does not suffice to find the alternative ladder which a more able or sophisticated mind might find.[96]

Unfortunately, it is difficult to tell how many decisions are reached for this reason. The evidence adduced by the

[96] Llewellyn, *The Bramble Bush,* pp. 73–74.

realists does justify skepticism toward the assumption that the number is large. It seems unreasonable to suppose that judges have not been aware in most cases of the "alternative ladders" open to them. Nonetheless, it is also unreasonable to deny that in some cases judges may have felt compelled by established rules to reach one decision.

Insofar as opinion-skepticism is concerned, it is difficult not to sympathize with the knowledgeable and reasoned critique of the late Edward S. Robinson. The efficacy of stated reasons in the decision-making process is a problem of a given time, place, and individual. The determination of whether a particular explanation of a specific decision is fictitious or accurate is a nice question of fact. The loose, lazy, and frequently cynical use of such terms as "unconscious complexes" and "rationalization" cannot settle the matter. Some of the realists did too enthusiastically assume that

the deductive logic of opinions need by no means be either a *description* of the process of decision, or an *explanation* of how the decision had been reached. Indeed over-enthusiasm has at times assumed that the logic of the opinion *could* be neither; and similar over-enthusiasm . . . has worked at times almost as if the opinion were equally valueless in predicting what a later court will do.[97]

[97] Llewellyn, *Jurisprudence*, p. 58. A statement by the authors of a recent study of the jury is of relevance in this connection: "For the largest part the hidden reasons of the jury are reasons which can stand public scrutiny; not infrequently the jury's rule turns out to be the law in another jurisdiction. The realist emphasis seemed often to lend itself to a kind of inside dopester jurisprudence in which the real reasons for decisions would be very different from the surface reasons, and probably rather nasty. In so far as this study can be said to be a venture in realism, it suggests that the ideas embodied in the formal rules and doctrines of law are close to the policies that actually motivate decision-makers in the real world." Harry Kalven,

A justified enthusiasm and an unwarranted overenthusiasm are, however, two different things. The critique of the realists was not only inspired by psychological theory. It was, in addition, a reflection of case analysis. Such analysis reveals that the opinion frequently is almost valueless as an indication of how the decision was reached. Many judges are reluctant to discuss the "real" reasons for, or at least the policies advanced by, their decisions. They frequently do not indicate the values or social objectives which they wished to achieve. The question of why they interpreted or applied established rules in one way rather than another equally possible way remains unanswered.

No general statement can be made as to how often this reluctance appears. This is a problem which only empirical studies of the judicial process can resolve. At the same time, the existence of some reluctance is clear. Moreover, a case can be made for the view that judges are *more* reluctant than other officials to discuss the policy reasons for their decisions. The impact of the traditional judicial norm that considerations of policy are not the business of a court has been marked. One sign of its influence has been a reluctance on the part of judges to discuss in their opinions the pragmatic reasons for one decision rather than another.[98]

Unresolved Problems

This sympathetic evaluation is not intended to imply that the views of the realists constitute a wholly adequate interpretation of judicial behavior. Two problems, in par-

---

Jr., and Hans Zeisel, *The American Jury* (Boston: Little, Brown, 1966) , p. 497.

[98] For further discussion of this point, see *infra,* pp. 206–215.

ticular, still remain to be solved. The first is the determination of the actual impact of established rules. The great achievement of the realists has been to establish a justified skepticism toward the theory that such rules have been decisive. But they did not indicate what precise role antecedent rules have in fact played, or how their effect can be determined. In his first article Joseph W. Bingham wrote that "it is difficult to generalize satisfactorily concerning the exact measure of the influence which precedents exert on judicial decisions." [99] In 1931 Jerome Frank pointed out that "how much influence the general propositions called 'legal rules' actually have on judges we seldom if ever know." [100] Both of these statements are no doubt true. A generation of legal realists has not, unfortunately, done much to remedy the situation. [101]

The other major problem is the nature of the extralegal factors which have in fact determined most decisions in cases doubtful enough to be litigated, contested, and appealed. One achievement of the realists has been to point out the relevance of such factors. But they were not agreed on what extralegal values were most important, or *why* judges developed different views of public policy. Put differently, no psychological or sociological *theory* of decision-making was widely accepted. More important, the

[99] "What Is the Law?" *Mich. L. Rev.,* XI (1912), 111.

[100] "Are Judges Human?" *U. Pa. L. Rev.,* LXXX (1931), 44.

[101] For a notable exception, see Underhill Moore and Charles C. Callahan, "Law and Learning Theory: A Study in Legal Control," *Yale L. J.,* LIII (1943), 1. The purpose of this very behavioral study was not, however, to determine the impact of established rules upon judges. Rather, it was to measure the effects of parking signs, of the tagging of automobiles, and of traffic regulations on the behavior of automobile drivers. For an interesting analysis of the study, see Hessel Yntema, " 'Law and Learning Theory' through the Looking Glass of Legal Theory," *Yale L. J.,* LIII (1944), 338.

advocates of "realistic jurisprudence" did not develop an analytical framework in terms of which hypotheses could be tested.[102] There are, to be sure, exceptions to this generalization. The efforts of the realists to develop new techniques for the prediction of decisions did result in the formulation of some important models of decision-making. For the most part, however, the movement did not develop what today would be regarded as a very sophisticated science of decision-making. This is the gap which the judicial behavioralists have, in part, tried to fill. Their success will be appraised subsequently.

Conclusion

Rule-skepticism is not, then, the be-all and end-all. It is, however, the begin-all, if the nature of judicial decision-making is to be fully understood. Moreover, it has two important and more general implications. One is as a means to understand the actual *human* meaning of any legal system. If the critique is warranted, then no legal

---

[102] See Theodore L. Becker, *Political Behavioralism and Modern Jurisprudence: A Working Theory and Study in Judicial Decision-Making* (Chicago: Rand McNally, 1964). According to Becker, "Legal academicians and appellate judges-jurisprudents have produced some broad, theoretical material which could lay a basic framework for much intensive, behaviorally-based research. But they have not designed nor conducted any empirical research which could yield any quantifiable information about the possible peculiar nature of the appellate decision-making process. There has been no work accomplished that would avail us of empirically verified, motivationally-oriented propositions that are the *sine qua non* for constructing hard theory on the nature of that process." *Ibid.*, pp. 64–65. Becker's book is an interesting and significant effort to fill this gap by wedding "the best of the two approaches, i.e., that of the political behavioralists and that of the legal scholars, in an attempt to advance toward a sound, empirically verifiable theory of judicial decision-making." *Ibid.*, p. 4.

order can be fully or even adequately understood until the actual interpretation, application, and enforcement of its general norms are known. Only with such knowledge can, to borrow a phrase from William James, its "cash value" be discovered. For until general rules are interpreted and applied their actual meaning for and bearing upon concrete situations cannot be fully ascertained.

The other important implication of rule-skepticism is for the panoply of social organizations in addition to those which are part of the legal system of the modern state. The use of rules as a means to reach and to justify decisions extends to virtually all human institutions. This includes even such a basic unit of society as the family. An interpretation of the impact of established rules upon decision-makers in these institutions which is very similar to that of traditional jurisprudence is far from uncommon. Assertions are frequent that those in authority had no choice but to reach one decision, or that they were coerced by rules which they were powerless to modify. The human condition is apparently such that the existence of competing decisions, each of which can be reconciled with established rules, is often not admitted. The burden of freedom in this sense is frequently too great for most of us to acknowledge. One of the greatest contributions of the legal realists is, nonetheless, to have pointed out *that* and *why* it exists. It is a contribution which illuminates not only the judicial institutions of the nation state, but decision-making in all human organizations.

III

Fact-Skepticism

The realist movement, it has been emphasized, was a revolt against the classical theory of judicial decision-making. The critique which was advanced has two major thrusts. One is rule-skepticism. All of the realists contributed to its development. The other is fact-skepticism, and it is the special creation of the late Judge Jerome N. Frank. Indeed, in the latter stages of his life Frank vigorously criticized most of his fellow realists for their indifference to the process and liabilities of fact-finding. In the words of Edmond Cahn, Frank

believed that realists like Karl Llewellyn and Felix Cohen were fighting the battle of the 1920's long after the adversary had left the field and that their continued preoccupation with rule-skepticism was not only redundant but actually dangerous. For while theorists kept their eyes glued on the permutations of legal rules, no one was doing anything about the law's seriously defective machinery for finding the *facts*. As he saw them, his fellow realists were defaulting in their obligation to shift the campaign from rule-skepticism to fact-skepticism.[1]

What is fact-skepticism? What accounts for it? What can be done to reduce it? How valid is it? The purpose of this chapter is to attempt to answer these questions. No account of the realist movement would be complete without such an effort. After the great and glorious days of the 1930's Frank developed a line of thought which is relatively unique. He continued, however, to regard himself as a realist. Moreover, the train of thought which he created

[1] "Introduction," *A Man's Reach: The Philosophy of Judge Jerome Frank*, ed. Barbara Frank Kristein (New York: Macmillan, 1965), pp. xii–xiii. It should also be pointed out that *after* his full-fledged commitment to fact-skepticism Frank sometimes seriously modified his rule-skepticism. The vast majority of legal realists did not deny, it has been demonstrated, a significant degree of regularity in the decisions of appellate courts. They did insist, however, that this regularity is not most basically due to the impact of established rules. *These* "paper" rules, or rules "on the books," do not provide a reliable basis for prediction of future decisions. In *Law and the Modern Mind* Frank's belief in this point of view is clear. Later in his career, though, he sometimes insisted not only that upper-court decisions are predictable, but predictable *on the basis of* and *because of* established rules and principles. Typical is his statement that "in most cases, if the trial court decisions are appealed, prediction of the upper court decision is easy; Those courts will foreseeably apply a precise rule to facts which are . . . for those courts, virtually the same as stipulated facts. Neither the facts nor the legal rules being in doubt, the outcome is obvious." " 'Short of Sickness and Death': A Study of Moral Responsibility in Legal Criticism," *N.Y.U. L. Rev.*, XXVI (1951), 588. Cf.: "Courts are constantly determining which of several rival rules to apply. Is it any the less true of the choice of rules than of the choice of theories that 'the choice is not foreclosed by anything entitled to be called authority'? And do not rules, like legal theories, serve chiefly to 'explain a result after it has been reached,' and are not rules, like legal theories, usually 'useless beforehand as a guide for reaching' the result?" Frank, *Law and the Modern Mind* (Garden City, N.Y.: Doubleday, 1963), pp. 287–288.

constitutes a distinctive contribution to the jurisprudence of this century.

Definition of Fact-Skepticism

No comprehensive definition of fact-skepticism can be found in Frank's books and articles. Some of the students of his thought have interpreted its meaning very broadly. For them fact-skepticism is identifiable with the whole range of ideas which Frank developed most notably in books such as *Courts on Trial*. The late Edmond Cahn is an example.[2] It seems more useful, however, to define fact-skepticism less inclusively. The major advantage of such a procedure is that it distinguishes more clearly than otherwise is possible between different elements in Frank's thought.

Interpreted narrowly, fact-skepticism has two related but not identical meanings. The first is the likelihood that

[2] See *Confronting Injustice: The Edmond Cahn Reader,* ed. Lenore L. Cahn (Boston: Little, Brown, 1966), esp. pp. 265–324 (which reprint Professor Cahn's articles on Frank and fact-skepticism). According to Cahn, fact-skepticism involves "five more or less distinguishable stages: (1) a demonstration that the law's fact-finding process is uncertain, seriously fallible, and largely unpredictable; (2) a set of proposed reforms . . . to the end of reducing the incidence of fact-finding errors; (3) a set of proposed changes in the education of lawyers and the equipment of judges, in order to increase their professional competence and reduce their biases; (4) an agenda of substantive reforms, such as abolition of capital punishment, in order to mitigate the harms resulting from erroneous fact-finding; and (5) an all-pervading search for enlightenment . . . and for humility and compassion." *Ibid.,* pp. 321–322. For a somewhat different *definition* of fact-skepticism, see Cahn, "Introduction," in Jerome Frank, *Courts on Trial: Myth and Reality in American Justice* (New York: Atheneum, 1963), p. ix. Also, see Julius Paul, *The Legal Realism of Jerome N. Frank: A Study of Fact-Skepticism and the Judicial Process* (The Hague: Nijhoff, 1959).

the facts as found by judge or jury do not correspond to the actual facts. This is a central theme, for example, of *Courts on Trial*. There Frank criticized the classical theory of judicial decision-making, schematically represented as R (rules) $\times$ F (facts) = D (decision). A key chapter is entitled "Facts Are Guesses." The title reflects a basic idea elaborated upon in the chapter. The following passage is typical:

What is the F? Is it what actually happened between Sensible and Smart? Most emphatically not. At best, it is only what the trial court—the trial judge or jury—thinks happened. What the trial court thinks happened may, however, be hopelessly incorrect. But that does not matter—legally speaking. For court purposes, what the court thinks about the facts is all that matters. The actual events, the real objective acts and words of Sensible and Smart, happened in the past. They do not walk into court. The court usually learns about these real, objective, past facts only through the oral testimony of fallible witnesses. Accordingly, the court, from hearing the testimony, must guess at the actual, past facts. Judicially, the facts consist of the reaction of the judge or jury to the testimony. The F is merely a guess about the actual facts. There can be no assurance that that F, that guess, will coincide with those actual, past facts.[3]

Not only is there no assurance that these guesses coincide with the actual facts, but the chances are high that they will not. "The reactions of trial judges or juries to the testimony are shot through with subjectivity." Also, no objective tests exist through which the extent to which these reactions coincide with what actually happened can be measured.[4]

[3] Jerome N. Frank, *Courts on Trial: Myth and Reality in American Justice* (Princeton: Princeton University Press, 1949), pp. 15–16.
[4] *Ibid.*, pp. 22, 49–50.

The second meaning of fact-skepticism is that the reactions of the judge or jury to the facts are inherently unpredictable. "The chief obstacle to prophesying a trial-court decision is . . . the inability . . . to foresee what a particular trial judge or jury will believe to be the facts." "It is impossible, and will always be impossible, because of the elusiveness of the facts on which decisions turn, to predict future decisions in most (not all) lawsuits, not yet begun or not yet tried." Moreover, this obstacle constitutes the major source of legal uncertainty. "The major cause of legal uncertainty is fact-uncertainty—the unknowability, before the decision, of what the trial court will 'find' as the facts, and the unknowability after the decision of the way in which it 'found' those facts."

For Frank, the great defect of all previous accounts of the judicial process is the failure to pay sufficient attention to fact-skepticism in both of these senses. The gulf between traditional assumptions and the realities of the matter is so vast, indeed, that it can only be explained as a form of "modern legal magic." One of the most interesting facets of Frank's work is his attempt to apply psychological and anthropological theories to law. In his first major work he relied heavily on psychoanalytical concepts to explain what he then regarded as "the basic legal myth." This is the view that "law either is or can be made approximately stationary and certain." Significantly, in *Law and the Modern Mind* he dismissed any attempt to explain this "myth" by interpreting the facts as "the scape-goat." Nonetheless, he tried to account for the pervasive drive for certainty in psychoanalytical terms. It stems from the fact that men "have not yet relinquished the childish need for an authoritative father and unconsciously have tried to find in the law a substitute for those attributes of firmness, sureness, certainty and infallibility ascribed in childhood to the father." [5]

In *Courts on Trial,* Frank had reached the conclusion that the chief source of unpredictability is fact-uncertainty. He persevered, however, in his use of nonlegal concepts as explanatory devices. One of them is the concept of magic developed by anthropologists. For Frank, "magic is stereotyped, wishful thinking applied to the overcoming of obstacles. It is the nonempirical, illusory, way of achieving practical aims. It is born of panic fear, of dread, of the felt need to believe that what is helpful can be and has been discovered, of driving, insistent, longings." This dread is evident in the rites and rituals of primitive societies. It is, for Frank, equally apparent in the universal tendency to ignore the significance of trial courts. Study of them reveals that "legal rights are . . . dependent on human guesses about the facts of cases." But

many lawyers . . . are reluctant to admit that state of affairs and its concomitant chanciness. Like "primitive" men, they consider that chanciness terrifying. "Primitive" man, to overcome his terror, used magic, openly and unashamed. Many modern lawyers use magic—without being aware of it. . . . In order to avoid facing up to disagreeable situations and difficulties in court-house government, they have contrived a description, and a theory, of its workings which do not jibe with its observable realities.[6]

Frank's ire was not confined only to traditional lawyers.[7] The views of some of the most advanced jurists of this century were also subject to militant criticism. His cri-

[5] Jerome N. Frank, *Law and the Modern Mind,* pp. xiii, xi, xiv, 13, 8, 22.

[6] Frank, *Courts on Trial* (1949), pp. 43-44, 50.

[7] See *ibid.,* p. 62.

tiques of Cardozo, Pound, Llewellyn, and Felix Cohen provide useful examples. They are illustrations which must be examined briefly in order to demonstrate the novelty of Frank's fact-skepticism.

In the closing pages of *The Nature of the Judicial Process,* Cardozo acknowledged that he had "thrown, perhaps too much, into the background and the shadow the cases where the controversy turns not upon the rule of law, but upon its application to the facts." He justified his procedure on the ground that such cases "leave jurisprudence where it stood before. As applied to such cases, the judicial process . . . is a process of search and comparison and little else." [8] No better grist could have been supplied for the always vigorous mills of Frank. In his mind Cardozo "suffered from a sort of occupational disease, appellate-court-itis." His "relatively placid" picture of the judicial process cannot be reconciled with, and indeed grossly distorts, the realities of trial-court fact-finding. His description, "superlative in respect of uppercourts, is bizarre if deemed to include an account of trial-court ways—as bizarre as would be an account of manners at Buckingham palace if taken as also a true portrayal of rush-hour behavior in the New York subways." [9]

Frank's denunciation of the views of Roscoe Pound is equally vivid. In his *Introduction to the Philosophy of Law,* the latter drew the distinctions outlined in the second chapter of this book. He argued that "mechanical application of law" is both "effective and desirable" with respect to property and commercial law. The major rea-

<hr />

[8] Benjamin N. Cardozo, *The Nature of the Judicial Process* (New Haven: Yale University Press, 1921), p. 163.

[9] Frank, *Law and the Modern Mind,* p. xxix. For Frank's most complete critique of Cardozo, see Frank, "Cardozo and the Upper-Court Myth," *Law & Contemp. Prob.,* XIII (1948), 369.

son for its effectiveness is the repetitive and similar characteristics of the factual configurations which arise. "Every promissory note is like every other. Every fee simple is like every other. Every distribution of assets repeats the conditions that have recurred since the Statute of Distributions." [10] Again, such statements ignited the combustible and potent critical fires of Frank. "The truth is that the talk about mechanical operation of rules in property, or commercial, or other cases is not at all a description of what really happens in courts in contested cases. It is a dogma based upon inadequate observation." It ignores the consequences which result if a question of fact is raised, contested, and tried before a jury. "Is it not absurd to say that the rules will then be mechanically applied? Anyone who has ever watched a jury trial knows the rules often become a mere subsidiary detail, part of a meaningless but dignified liturgy recited by the judge . . . to which the jury pays scant heed." Much the same is true if a question of fact is raised and contested before a judge. For

the "facts," it must never be overlooked, are not objective. They are what the judge thinks they are. And what he thinks they are depends on what he hears and sees as the witnesses testify—which may not be, and often is not, what another judge would hear and see. Assume ("fictionally") the most complete rigidity of the rules relating to commercial transactions. . . . Still, since the "facts" are only what the judge thinks they are, the decision will vary with the judge's apprehension of the facts.[11]

The third object of Frank's not inconsiderable critical zeal to be examined here is Karl N. Llewellyn. His great

[10] Pound, *An Introduction to the Philosophy of Law* (rev. ed.; New Haven: Yale University Press, 1954), pp. 70–71.

[11] Frank, *Law and the Modern Mind*, pp. xviii, xvii–xviii, xviii–xix.

sin, as is the case with Cardozo and Pound, is his failure to examine the trial-court process. Instead of observing the behavior of the Cheyenne Indians, Llewellyn should have focused on data closer to hand. "By spending a few nickels on subway-fares for short trips from Columbia Law School . . . to lower New York City, [he] could have studied in detail the trial courts of that metropolis. He could then have written a book on the anthropology of Tammany-Hall Indians, many of whom are first-rate trial judges." In a more serious vein, Frank contended that Llewellyn's description of the judicial process is, "concerning the bulk of it, seriously deficient anthropology, for he has obtained his information about our trial courts derivatively."[12] As a result, both he and the other realists "grossly exaggerate the extent of legal certainty, because their own writings deal only with the prediction of upper-court decisions. . . . [They are] but the left-wing adherents of a tradition."[13] As such, they are "magic addicts" who "manage to fool themselves" as much as did traditional jurists.[14]

Felix Cohen is the final case in point. He neglected as did most of the other realists the fact-finding process on the trial-court level. His attempt to predict decisions by study of the background factors of judges thus leaves out "the vast majority of decisions of cases in which social, economic, political and professional considerations are entirely, or almost entirely, absent, and where the rules are clear, the facts alone being in dispute."[15] This neglect has led to a vast exaggeration of the extent to which decisions can be predicted through the application of sociological techniques. Although such techniques are immensely use-

[12] Frank, *Courts on Trial* (1949), p. 77.
[13] Frank, *Law and the Modern Mind*, p. xii.
[14] Frank, *Courts on Trial* (1949), pp. 77, 68.   [15] *Ibid.*, p. 149.

ful in the study of appellate courts, the vast majority of cases occur on the trial-court level. Here sociological study is not a fruitful means to make predictions more accurate.

The influences operating on a particular trial judge, when he is listening to, and observing, witnesses, cannot be neatly caged within the categories of his fairly obvious social, economic and political views. Even the older psychology would suggest that these pigeon-holes are insufficient. . . . The "new psychology," Freudian or otherwise, properly emphasizes these peculiarly individual factors. These uniquely, highly individual, operative influences are far more subtle, far more difficult to get at. Many of them, without possible doubt, are unknown to anyone except the judge. Indeed, often the judge himself is unaware of them.[16]

The sociological approach ignores, in other words, the fact that judges with the same background will react differently to the facts. "It is very, very far from certain that the two judges would believe and disbelieve the same witnesses, and, consequently, that they would 'find' the 'facts' identically." Their fact-findings depend upon "undiscoverable personal quirks" which knock "galley west the hope of discovering that 'predictable uniformity in the behavior of courts' without which there can be no 'reasonably certain predictions' of decisions of most law-suits not yet commenced." [17]

Explanation of Fact-Skepticism

Fact-skepticism, in both of its meanings, has two major types of sources. One is the institutional process by which, in any contested case, the facts of a case are determined. The other is the subjective character of the reactions of

[16] *Ibid.,* p. 151.   [17] *Ibid.,* pp. 150, 149–150.

judges and jurors to the facts. The uncertainty spawned
by the first is to some degree eliminable, but that rooted in
the second is inevitable. Because it is, "the pursuit of
greatly increased legal certainty is, for the most part, futile." [18]

The trial process itself is a rich source of uncertainty for
a number of reasons. In the first place, the witnesses may
testify dishonestly. "We know, alas, that an immense
amount of testimony is deliberately and knowingly false.
Experienced lawyers say that, in large cities, scarcely a
trial occurs, in which some witness does not lie." In the
second place, the witnesses may testify honestly but incor-
rectly. Their observation of the past event may have been
erroneous, their recollection of even a correct original
observation may be faulty, their account in court of a
correct recollection may be in error, and their testimony
may be marred by "their prejudices for or against one of
the parties to the suit." In the third place, vital evidence
may no longer be available. With respect to a dead or
missing witness, "a crucial fact cannot be brought out, or
an important opposing witness cannot be successfully contradicted." Then, too, there is the missing or destroyed
letter, or receipt, or cancelled check. For all of these reasons, "the axiom or assumption that, in all or most trials,
the truth will out, ignores . . . the several elements of
subjectivity and chance." [19]

Some of this "subjectivity and chance" would exist in
any courtroom proceeding. In the American legal system
the likelihood of its presence is vastly increased by the
adversarial mode of trial. According to Frank, this method
is based on the "fight" theory. It derives from the origin of

[18] Frank, *Law and the Modern Mind,* p. xi.
[19] Frank, *Courts on Trial* (1949) , pp. 85, 19, 20.

trials as "substitutes for private out-of-court brawls." "Trial-by-battle" assumes that "the best way for a court to discover the facts in a suit is to have each side strive as hard as it can, in a keenly partisan spirit, to bring to the court's attention the evidence favorable to that side." This assumption is not totally without merit. "The zealously partisan lawyers sometimes do bring into court evidence which, in a dispassionate inquiry, might be overlooked." Also, "the opposed lawyers . . . illuminate for the court niceties of the legal rules which the judge might otherwise not perceive." Nonetheless, Frank claimed, the fighting spirit which the adversarial system promotes has become "dangerously excessive."

Evidence of this excessiveness is legion. For one thing, lawyers seek to discredit adverse witnesses regardless of the truth or falsity of their testimony.

As you may learn by reading any one of a dozen or more handbooks on how to try a law-suit, an experienced lawyer uses all sorts of strategems to minimize the effect on the judge or jury of testimony disadvantageous to his client, even when the lawyer has no doubt of the accuracy and honesty of that testimony. The lawyer considers it his duty to create a false impression, if he can, of any witness who gives such testimony. If such a witness happens to be timid, frightened by the unfamiliarity of court-room ways, the lawyer, in his cross-examination, plays on that weakness, in order to confuse the witness and make it appear that he is concealing significant facts.

For another thing, lawyers frequently seek to "hide the defects of witnesses who testify favorably to . . . [their] client. . . . In that way, the trial court is denied the benefit of observing the witness's actual normal demeanor, and thus prevented from sizing up the witness accurately." [20] Still further, lawyers try to conceal the existence of facts which they feel are detrimental to the interests of their client.

The partisanship of opposing lawyers is not the only unfortunate consequence of the adversarial system. Other odious effects are the reluctance of courts to render aid to victims of incompetent lawyers, the inability of impecunious litigants to finance the investigations necessary to reveal facts crucial to their case, and the use by prosecutors of unseemly methods in the interrogation of witnesses. The end result is that "our present trial method is . . . the equivalent of throwing pepper in the eyes of a surgeon when he is performing an operation." [21]

The second major seed of uncertainty is the subjective character of the reactions of judges and jurors to the facts. Frank singled out the jury system for special emphasis. In his mind, "a better instrument than the usual jury trial could scarcely be imagined for achieving uncertainty, capriciousness, lack of uniformity, disregard of the R's, and unpredictability of decisions." "More than anything else in the judicial system, the jury blocks the road to better ways of finding the facts." [22] "A wise lawyer will hesitate to guarantee, although he may venture to surmise, what decision will be rendered in a case heard and decided by a judge alone. Only a very foolish lawyer will dare guess the outcome of a jury trial." [23]

The reasons for the foolishness of such guesses are varied. An extremely important one is the fact that jurors are either unwilling or unable to apply the relevant legal rule to the facts. Their unwillingness is attested to by the com-

[20] *Ibid.*, pp. 80, 80–81, 81, 82, 83.   [21] *Ibid.*, p. 85.
[22] *Ibid.*, pp. 123, 138.
[23] Frank, *Law and the Modern Mind*, p. 186.

mon experience of jurors manipulating the facts in order to reach the desired result. They do not find the facts in accordance with the evidence. Rather, they "distort the facts and find them in such a manner that (by applying the rules of law laid down by the judge to the facts thus found) . . . [they] are able to produce the desired result." More important, jurors often do not understand the rules which they are supposed to apply to the facts. For Frank, indeed,

it is inconceivable that a body of twelve ordinary men, casually gathered together for a few days, could, merely from listening to the instructions of the judge, gain the knowledge necessary to grasp the true import of the judge's words, since these words have acquired their meaning often as the result of hundreds of years of professional disputation in the law courts. Inevitably, then, the jury cannot be equal to the task imposed upon them. At best, they bunglingly discharge their duty.

Nor should anyone be fooled by the elaborate instructions issued by the judge to the jury. They are nothing but "the talismanic words of Word-Magic," "debased or devitalized magic incantations." They are merely part of a complex ritual, "exercising phrases intended to drive out evil spirits . . . an inextricable part of a conventionalized system of observances." [24]

Another very significant factor is the inability of jurors to react objectively to the welter of testimony. They often cannot remember all of it. Their environment is unreal. They are selected, not for their impartiality, but for their likelihood to agree with the testimony favorable to one or another of the litigants. Often their deliberations are influenced more by the behavior of the lawyer than that of

[24] *Ibid.,* pp. 328, 195, 196, 198.

the witnesses. Balzac was right to define the jury as "twelve men chosen to decide who has the better lawyer." In short, their reactions are hopelessly subjective.

Many juries in reaching their verdicts act on their emotional responses to the lawyers and witnesses; they like or dislike, not any legal rule, but they do like an artful lawyer for the plaintiff, the poor widow, the brunette with the soulful eyes, and they do dislike the big corporation, the Italian with a thick, foreign accent.[25]

The end result is that jurors are notoriously poor fact-finders. For "adequate fact-finding . . . requires devoted attention, skill in analysis, and, above all, high powers of resistance to a multitude of personal biases. But these qualities are obviously not possessed by juries. They are notoriously gullible and impressionable."[26] Skillful fact-finding is difficult enough for experienced judges. It is well-nigh impossible for the untrained, inexperienced "man on the street."

In light of this, why has the jury system survived? According to Frank, none of the artful rationalizations adduced for it is persuasive. Jurors are not better fact-finders than judges, they are not skillful legislators, they do not provide an effective escape from corrupt or incompetent trial judges, they do not generate confidence in government, and they do not operate wisely in criminal cases. The survival of the jury system cannot be explained by any of these arguments. None is valid. Rather, trial by jury has persisted because "it serves two purposes: It preserves the basic legal dogma in appearance and at the same time (albeit crudely and bunglingly) circumvents it

---

[25] Frank, *Courts on Trial* (1949), pp. 122, 130.
[26] Frank, *Law and the Modern Mind,* p. 192.

in fact, to the end of permitting that pliancy and elasticity which is impossible according to the dogma, but which life demands." [27]

It will be pointed out subsequently that Frank regarded judges as much better fact-finders than jurors. Nonetheless, he insisted that fact-finding even by experienced, trained judges will forever be tarred by the brush of unpredictability. "Usually, then, it is all but impossible to predict how a particular trial judge will react to particular witnesses. In other words, a judge is not a mechanical comptometer. Prophecies of future trial-judge decisions cannot be worked out by the use of anything resembling a slide-rule." [28]

Two factors account for the inherent uncertainty of judicial reactions to conflicting testimony. The first is that the discretion which judges have in finding the facts is virtually uncontrollable. Much has been written in the American jurisprudence of this century about the existence of judicial discretion. One of Frank's many contributions is to indicate that this discretion applies as much or more to fact-finding than rule-applying.

When the oral testimony is in conflict as to a pivotal fact-issue, the trial judge is at liberty to choose to believe one witness rather than another. In other words, in most cases the trial judges have an amazingly wide "discretion" in finding the facts, a discretion with which upper-courts, on appeals, seldom interfere, so that, in most instances this "fact discretion" is almost boundless. And this is true regardless of the precision of the applicable legal rule.[29]

One important consequence of this is that the trial judge can " 'fudge' the facts he finds, and thus 'force the bal-

[27] *Ibid.*, p. 186.   [28] Frank, *Courts on Trial* (1949), p. 153.
[29] *Ibid.*, p. 57.

ance.' No one will ever be able to learn whether, in the interest of what he thought just, or for any other cause, he did thus misstate his belief." Frank cites a potent illustration. As a young lawyer, he had tried a case before an able trial judge without a jury. During the trial, the judge ruled in favor of Frank's adversary on every doubtful procedural question. To Frank's great surprise, the decision nonetheless was in favor of his client. A year later he met the judge, who recited this explanation of what he had done.

You see, on the first day of the trial, I made up my mind that the defendant, your client, was a fine, hard-working woman who oughtn't to lose all her property to the plaintiff, who had plenty of money. The plaintiff was urging a legal rule which you thought was wrong. I thought it was legally right, but very unjust, and I didn't want to apply it. So I made up my mind to lick the plaintiff on the facts. And by giving him every break on procedural points during the trial, and by using in my opinion the legal rule he urged, I made it impossible for him to reverse me on appeal, because, as the testimony was oral and in conflict, I knew the upper-court would never upset my findings of fact.[30]

The second factor is the subjectivity of the judge's reactions to the facts. Indeed, this is the most basic reason. It explains why no rules concerning the exercise of fact-discretion "have ever been or can ever be formulated." [31] Unfortunately, Frank never defined precisely what he meant by "subjective" in this context. The language of the following statements suggests, however, some of the varied

[30] *Ibid.,* p. 168.
[31] Frank, "Civil Law Influences on the Common Law—Some Reflections on 'Comparative' and 'Contrastive' Law," *U. Pa. L. Rev.,* CIV (1956), 900.

meanings which he attached to it. In his mind, "in the mine run of law suits—that is, the great bulk of law suits—the prejudices of judges and jurors . . . have no 'large scale social' character, and lack uniformity. They are distinctively individual, unconscious, un-get-at-able." They are "concealed, publicly unscrutinized, uncommunicated. . . . Secret, unconscious, private, idiosyncratic." [32] No pressures for uniformities can "penetrate deep enough to produce similarities in those unique, idiosyncratic, sub-threshold biases and predilections, of the divers individual trial judges . . . which terminate in fact-findings." [33] It would thus seem that Frank's use of "subjective" was intended to ascribe four basic characteristics to judicial reactions to the facts. They are idiosyncratic and lack uniformity; unconscious and unexplainable; irrational and biased; and private, uncommunicable.

That Frank ascribed these characteristics to most judicial reactions to the facts is clear; *why* he did is less certain. On the basis of the analysis which he advanced in his books and articles, two factors seem to have played an important role. The first was an extremely sensitive awareness of individual differences. Throughout his work the uniqueness of the personality of the judge is emphasized again and again.[34] Moreover, the "peculiarly individual traits" of judges are often "more important causes of judgments than anything which could be described as political, economic, or moral biases." [35] The other factor was the impact of psychological theory, which according to Frank

[32] Frank, " 'Short of Sickness and Death': A Study of Moral Responsibility in Legal Criticism," *N.Y.U. L. Rev.,* XXVI (1951), 573, 582.

[33] Frank, *Law and the Modern Mind,* pp. xxvi–xxvii.

[34] See *Courts on Trial* (1949), p. 153.

[35] *Law and the Modern Mind,* p. 114.

had produced the "best instruments now available for the study of human nature." [36] Throughout his life, he read widely in psychology. It profoundly affected his views of the judicial process.

Two schools of thought had a particularly noticeable impact upon Frank's view of judicial fact-finding. The first is Freudianism. The impact of its emphasis upon the unconscious and irrational roots of human thought is obvious. The second is Gestalt psychology. In *Law and the Modern Mind* the imprint of the first is most obvious, in *Courts on Trial* that of the second. Frank, it is true, cautioned against any whole-hog commitment to either school. Still, he felt that the emphasis in Gestalt psychology upon decisions as a response to the "whole" situation illuminated the thought processes of trial judges. "In particular, it sheds light on a trial judge's 'hunching.' The trial judge . . . experiences a gestalt. That is why he has difficulty in reporting his experience analytically. That is why, too, when he has heard oral testimony, his decision . . . may defy intelligent criticism." For his "decisional process, like the artistic process, involves feelings that words cannot ensnare. A large component of a trial judge's reaction is 'emotion.' . . . He cannot, with entire adequacy, formulate in logical, lingual, form, his reaction to the conflicting testimony at a trial." Thus the subjectivity of the trial judge's reactions to the facts is given an additional spark. "It inheres in his total reaction to the trial." [37]

This emphasis upon the subjective character of judicial fact-finding has been described in detail because it is probably the basic reason for Frank's fact-skepticism. It also

[36] *Ibid.,* p. 23.
[37] Frank, *Courts on Trial* (1949), pp. 171, 174, 176.

constitutes perhaps the basic explanation for his marked divergence from an otherwise pervasive theme in the realist movement. This is the attempt to increase the capacity to predict decisions, through the development of a "science" of law. According to Frank, such an endeavor is doomed to failure.

Since most persons consider that a true science makes predictions possible, we ought to put an end to notions of a "legal science" or a "science of law," unless we so define "legal" or "law" as to exclude much of what must be included in the judicial administration of justice, because no formula for predicting most trial-court decisions can be devised which does not contain hopelessly numerous variables that cannot be pinned down or correlated.

The insurmountable problem which thus confronts any attempt to develop a comprehensive predictive science of law is that trial courts must deal with many factors which are unique. This problem is insurmountable because a "science of the unique" is "self-contradictory, like a red-hot piece of ice or a live dead man." [38]

The Reduction of Fact-Uncertainty

No examination of Frank's fact-skepticism would be complete without some account of the measures which he advocated for the reform of the trial process. His goal is not simply to describe or to explain but to improve it. The objective of his exposé of legal myths and his revelations of "how court-house government actually operates" is to provoke "constructive skepticism." His aim is "to call attention to some court-house government activities which are less adequately performed than they could be," in order to encourage their "substantial betterment." Behind

[38] *Ibid.*, pp. 190, 191.

126

his tough-minded criticisms lurks, in other words, a very strong desire for reform. "I am—I make no secret of it—a reformer, one of those persons who . . . 'will not take evil good-naturedly.' " [39]

For present purposes, the most important manifestation of this proclivity is the attempt to reduce unnecessary fact-uncertainty. To be sure, "trial-court fact-finding can never be completely objective . . . unavoidably it involves conjectures . . . often it is but one element in a gestalt." Nevertheless, "all this does not at all compel the conclusion that the traditional fact-finding methods are not capable of marked improvement. . . . Everything feasible should be done so that the probability of accuracy in discovering the true facts of cases will be as high as is possible." To reject the possibility of reducing uncertainty because it cannot be completely obliterated is to take the unreasonable attitude of the man who turns "his back on all physicians merely because the flesh is heir to many diseases for which no cure has been, and in all likelihood will ever be, discovered by the medical profession." [40] Such an attitude is particularly reprehensible where the reduction of fact-uncertainty is concerned. The overwhelming majority of cases occur on the trial-court level. Only an exceedingly small proportion of these cases are ever appealed. The fact-finding errors which take place in even these cases are largely uncorrectible. The injustice which can result from these errors can be catastrophic. They generate inequality before the law, in that different rules may be applied to the same actions. Also, they cause the conviction of men for crimes which they did not commit.[41]

[39] *Ibid.*, p. 2.   [40] *Ibid.*, pp. 222, 425.

[41] See Jerome **Frank** and Barbara Frank, *Not Guilty* (Garden City, N.Y.: Doubleday, 1957).

The specific reforms which Frank advocated cannot be explained in detail here. They ranged over four areas. The first is legal education. Law schools should include on their faculty professors with from five to ten years of experience in actual legal practice. The casebooks used should contain the complete record of the whole case, from the court of first impression to the court of last resort. The students should observe at first hand the operations of trial and appellate courts. They should also frequently consult with and observe the out-of-court activities of lawyers. They should, too, observe the actions of legislatures and administrative agencies. Finally, the law schools ought to conduct legal clinics. They would be similar to the out-patient clinics run by medical schools. Then the human side of the administration of justice could be known as it actually works. The effect would be the conversion of the law schools from "library-law schools, book-law schools" into "lawyer-schools." The stultifying spirit of Christopher Columbus Langdell would be eliminated. Students would cease to be "like future horticulturists studying solely cut flowers; or like future architects studying merely pictures of buildings." They would no longer "resemble prospective dog-breeders who never see anything but stuffed dogs." [42] Roscoe Pound's felicitous phrase "law-in-action" would finally become a reality.

The second important institution in need of reform is the adversarial mode of trial. Frank did not recommend its abolition. He did suggest a number of modifications. Among the most important changes which he urged are: the creation of impartial governmental officials to dig up the facts which the parties to a case are either unable or unwilling to provide; the more liberal use in civil and

[42] Frank, *Courts on Trial* (1949), p. 227.

criminal cases of pretrial discovery practices, in order to fully acquaint both parties to the case with all the facts to be used; abolition of most of the exclusionary rules of evidence, rules which impede the discovery of relevant information; greater use of "testimonial experts" to testify about the credibility of witnesses; and more humane and intelligent examination of witnesses, to lessen the risk that the new, courtroom environment will foreclose effective and true testimony.[43]

A third area for reform is the training and practices of trial judges. The trial judge should be permitted to sit with the upper court if his case is appealed. He should not vote, but his presence would be useful. It would insure that the appellate judges fully understood what actually happened in the lower court. Also, the "cult of the robe" should be abandoned. For Frank, the robe is "an anachronistic remnant of ceremonial government."[44] It needlessly conceals from the public the actual character and mind of the judge. "A vital and developing America can risk full equality." Finally, the judge should undergo something close to psychoanalysis.

I say "something like," because the theory and techniques of the art of psychoanalysis are being constantly revised, and some adequate, less prolonged and complicated, substitute may soon appear. I do not believe that, through such self-study or otherwise, any judge will become aware of all his prejudices or always able to control those of which he is aware. But such self-knowledge . . . can be of immense help in reducing the consequences of judicial bias.[45]

The final object of Frank's unquenchable desire for reform is trial-by-jury. Ideally, he wanted "jury-less trials

---

[43] See *ibid.*, pp. 5–102.   [44] *Ibid.*, p. 260.   [45] *Ibid.*, p. 250.

before well trained, honest trial judges." [46] Practically, he realized that any such proposal faced insurmountable constitutional obstacles. He proposed, instead, a variety of "palliating reforms." One is the much wider use of special or fact verdicts, in order to insure as far as possible that juries do not twist the facts to fit the rule. Another is the expanded usage of special interrogatories by the judge to the jury, to achieve the same objective. Still a third is the creation of "special juries" of experts to advise the judge on matters which require special expertise. A fourth is the more widespread utilization of intermediate fact-finders to assist the judge. A fifth is the abandonment of most exclusionary rules of evidence. A sixth is the recording of "jury-room deliberations." A seventh is the initiation of special educational courses in the public schools in which the nature and purpose of the jury system will be fully explained.[47]

In fairness to Frank, his full awareness of the tentative character of any and all of these reforms should be pointed out. As he wrote in the last pages of *Courts on Trial*:

I suggest those reforms most tentatively. No one person, I least of all, has the competence to contrive sane, practical, solutions of the problems I have posed. Such solutions must come from the concerted efforts of many of our ablest minds, and not exclusively lawyers' minds. I hope that this book will stimulate sound thinking about those problems which, as I believe I have shown, have too long been disregarded.[48]

Evaluation of Fact-Skepticism

The sympathetic reaction which Frank's fact-skepticism has evoked among sophisticated and sensitive legal minds

[46] *Ibid.*, p. 145.   [47] See *ibid.*, pp. 108–145.   [48] *Ibid.*, p. 423.

is not surprising. His emphasis on the significance of trial courts is long overdue. They are the vehicle through which the legal rights and duties of the vast majority of litigants are practically determined. His insistence that facts are guesses, often of a chancy, unforseeable type, is perceptive. His contention that the unpredictability which *this* uncertainty breeds is a genuine source of legal uncertainty in any practical sense is also needed. It represents a welcome protest against a legal formalism which relegates trial-court practices to the back room of juristic inquiry. Finally, his proposals for the reduction of avoidable uncertainties merit careful consideration from relevant specialists. Nonetheless, his fact-skepticism is not incapable of criticism. Two questions, in particular, arise: (1) are the reactions of judges and jurors to the facts *as* unpredictable as Frank has claimed? (2) can these reactions be validly explained in terms of the factors upon which he has placed so much emphasis?

The significance of the first question stems from the rather impressionistic character of the evidence which Frank adduced. His experience cannot be ignored. Moreover, no one could deny that the reactions of judge or jury to the facts are often unpredictable. Still, Frank adduced little factual evidence to sustain his estimate of the very great degree of unpredictability. His estimate has not been universally accepted by trial judges of great experience. It has been denied, for example, by Charles E. Wyzanski. He has served as a United States District Judge in Massachusetts since 1942. According to Wyzanski, juries in his district "tend to act so uniformly that the court officers and attendants who have sat with hundreds of juries can make a substantially accurate prediction of how any given jury will act. Indeed, their prediction of jury action is much closer to the ultimate result than their prediction of judicial actions." [49] Wyzanski's view may be idiosyncratic. The point is that Frank cited few facts to support his estimate.

Moreover, recent empirical research probably justifies the inference that jury verdicts are not *as* unpredictable as Frank has suggested. The historic study published by Harry Kalven and Hans Zeisel is the major case in point. It is the most systematic empirical investigation of the jury system ever undertaken. One of the major themes of this work is the high coincidence between actual jury verdicts and the decision which the judge would have reached without a jury. In criminal cases "they agree to acquit in 13.4 per cent of all cases and to convict in 62.0 per cent of all cases, thus yielding a total agreement rate of 75.4 per cent." In civil cases judge and jury agree on the question of liability 78 per cent of the time. Thus "the over-all level of agreement between jury and judge is roughly the same whether the business is criminal or civil." For this reason the authors conclude that "in many ways our single most basic finding is that the jury, despite its autonomy, spins so close to the legal baseline." [50] It could be argued, of course, that the reactions of judges and jury whatever their similarities are still unpredictable. Reactions which manifest such a high degree of similarity would seem, however, to have at least a modicum of predictability.

The major question which can be raised about Frank's explanation of fact-skepticism is whether he ascribed too

[49] Wyzanski, "A Trial Judge's Freedom and Responsibility," *The Legal Process: An Introduction to Decision-Making by Judicial, Legislative, Executive, and Administrative Agencies,* ed. Carl A. Auerbach *et al.* (San Francisco: Chandler, 1961) , p. 266, n. 29.

[50] Harry Kalven, Jr., and Hans Zeisel, *The American Jury* (Boston: Little, Brown, 1966) , pp. 56, 64, 498.

much influence to idiosyncratic, arbitrary, and irrational factors. Any such question is most difficult to answer. It is relevant to point out, however, that the study by Kalven and Zeisel suggests that Frank's analysis is hyperbolical. In the first place, the high coincidence between verdicts of jurors and judges indicates a significant degree of uniformity in their reactions. In the second place, judges do not regard most of the verdicts of juries with which they disagree as arbitrary. Forty-six per cent of such verdicts are felt to be "tenable for a jury," and 24 per cent are regarded as those "which a judge might also come to." Only 30 per cent are classified by judges as "without merit." [51] In the third place, jurors seem to be reasonably competent fact-finders. In the words of Kalven and Zeisel,

We begin our inquiry into what the jury makes of the evidence by establishing two basic propositions. The first is simply that, contrary to an often voiced suspicion, the jury does by and large understand the facts and get the case straight. The second proposition is that the jury's decision by and large moves with the weight and direction of the evidence.[52]

Finally, jury "lawlessness" is often a rational quest for justice. "The upshot is that when the jury reaches a different conclusion from the judge on the same evidence, it does so not because it is a sloppy or inaccurate finder of facts, but because it gives recognition to values which fall outside the official rules." The jury, in short, "will move where the equities are." [53]

If this critique is valid, then the two questions raised at the outset of this section merit an affirmative answer. The reactions of judges and jurors to the facts are not *as* unpre-

---

[51] *Ibid.,* p. 430.   [52] *Ibid.,* p. 149.   [53] *Ibid.,* p. 495.

dictable as Frank has claimed. Also, his explanation of jury verdicts exaggerates the degree to which they are idiosyncratic, arbitrary, and irrational. Two factors perhaps best explain the reasons for these weaknesses in fact-skepticism. One is its author's tendency to generalize on the basis of insufficient evidence. What Lee Loevinger has written about *Courts on Trial* seems to apply to much of Frank's work: it "is filled with assumptions . . . which are obviously too broad to be supported by the personal observations of one man and yet are asserted without any apparent basis other than the author's opinion." [54] The other factor is the undue impact upon Frank of currents of psychoanalytical thought. Llewellyn advanced precisely this point in a review of *Law and the Modern Mind.* The particular object of his criticism is the explanation which Frank advanced of "the basic legal myth." Yet his strictures apply as well to Frank's more general use of psychoanalytical concepts.

How is it possible for the canny student who discriminates so skillfully the proved from the dubious when reading a legal writer to swallow at a gulp a yearning for pre-natal serenity which is not only unproved but unprovable? How can the same mind which cuts through rule and *legal* concept to bare decision accept as dogmatic . . . psychoanalytic concepts . . . accept them as applying not to *some* persons, but to almost all. The basic fallacy of whole-hog psychoanalytic theory is the assumption that what may well be possibly or even probably *often* true is always or almost always true. May be; but, pending proof, the man who has learned the unreliability of generalizations in the law can best remain skeptical.[55]

[54] Loevinger, Review of *Courts on Trial,* by Jerome N. Frank, *Etc.: A Review of General Semantics,* VIII (1950), 42.

[55] Karl N. Llewellyn, *Jurisprudence: Realism in Theory and Practice* (Chicago: University of Chicago Press, 1962), p. 105.

Conclusion

Even so, the value of Jerome Frank's fact-skepticism is considerable. He did pinpoint *one* source of legal uncertainty which prior jurists as well as most of his fellow realists tended to ignore. Moreover, he alerted juristic minds to the always present possibility that the facts as found by judge or jury do not correspond to the actual facts. In the process he pointed the way to reforms in an area of crucial *human* significance. As Julius Paul has pointed out,

his searching analysis of trial court activities exposed what was for him the soft underbelly of the judicial process, and brought home to the general public (though not always as successfully as he would have wished) the necessity for judicial reform.[56]

Still further, the value of Frank's insights is not confined to the judicial process. They illuminate all types of decision-making. The late Edmond Cahn has written that fact-skepticism is equally enlightening "whether applied to law or the social sciences, religion, philosophy, or our daily interpersonal relations." He has also asserted that it constitutes "an epoch-making contribution . . . to the understanding of the entire human condition." [57] This last statement may be somewhat too lyrical in its praise of fact-skepticism. Nonetheless, the insights of Judge Frank do illuminate the human condition. Virtually every institution eventually evolves established modes for resolving disputes or problems. The application of established rules

[56] Paul, *The Legal Realism of Jerome N. Frank*, p. 120.

[57] Cahn, "Introduction," *Courts on Trial* (New York: Atheneum, 1963), p. ix; Cahn, "Jerome Frank's Fact-Skepticism and Our Future," *Yale L. J.*, LXVI (1957), 824.

to the facts is characteristic of such procedures. In this process the danger constantly arises that the established rules, or the policies which are implemented through them, will be applied to an unreal state of affairs. That is, rules or policies will be used to reach decisions about events which did not in fact occur. When this takes place, the decision-maker reaches conclusions which are *in light of his own values* wrong. Also, from the point of view of the subject the decisions may be unjust. Viewed as a moral protest against this contingency, against sloppy or cavalier fact-finding, Frank's fact-skepticism constitutes a profound contribution both to jurisprudence and to human life.

IV

The Prediction of Decisions

In 1931 Llewellyn wrote that the "earliest lines of attack" pursued by the realists "converge to a single conclusion: *there is less possibility of accurate prediction of what courts will do than the traditional rules would lead us to suppose.*"[1] He did not specify the degree to which accurate prediction is possible. Nor did he indicate precisely how much less this possibility is than has traditionally been assumed. Vagueness on these points haunts the realist movement. Nonetheless, the vast majority of its participants did not deny that judicial behavior is to a significant degree predictable. Their most basic disagreement with traditional jurists is not, as it often seemed to be in the 1920's and 1930's, about the *existence* of legal certainty in this sense. The most fundamental sources of discord between the realists and their predecessors stem, rather, from conflicting answers to two other questions. The first is,

[1] Llewellyn, *Jurisprudence: Realism in Theory and Practice* (Chicago: University of Chicago Press, 1962), p. 60.

what *accounts for* or *explains* the judicial uniformities which make forecasts possible? The second is, *how* can prediction be made more accurate?

The first question has traditionally been answered by reference to the impact of pre-existing legal rules. The application by different judges of the same rule or principle to similar sets of fact is the major reason for uniformities in judicial behavior. If rule-skepticism is valid, then this *explanation* is erroneous. The *existence* of regularities in judicial decision-making is a fact. But it is a fact which has to be explained by the impact of factors "in good measure outside these same traditional rules." [2] The range of choice logically possible in the application and interpretation of established rules is too great. Their impact cannot explain *why* judges to some degree make the same choices.

The answer of traditional jurists to the second question is the logical implication of their response to the first. The major reason why decisions are not always predictable must be due to some degree of vagueness or conflict in established rules. The way to increase predictability is, therefore, to refine and reformulate these rules. As Felix Cohen put it: "The function of the jurist, upon this assumption . . . is to ferret out the gaps and inconsistencies in the given system, and to suggest new arrangements of axioms and theorems, new definitions, and new formulations." The majority of realists did not deny a certain utility to this approach. They would agree with Cohen that

when the systematic jurist has done his task he has done an important work. If he has done it with a mathematical impar-

[2] *Ibid.,* p. 61.

tiality towards the inconsistent rules he discovers, recognizing in them not a ground for rejecting an "incorrect" rule but only the mark of diversity in systems among which *a priori* choice is impossible, there will be none to dispute the scientific value of his contribution.[3]

Nonetheless, most of the realists also claimed that the method of the systematic jurist is not the most useful means to develop more valid forecasts of judicial decisions. The far better procedure is to try to discover the nature of the extralegal factors which are the actual determinants of judicial decisions. Only then will a truly scientific basis be provided for prediction.

The Idiosyncratic Position of Jerome N. Frank

Optimism that this goal can be achieved pervades the realist movement. The one outstanding exception is the late Jerome Frank. As far back as 1931 he was arguing that it is "improbable" that "further observation and description of what induces decisions will make future judicial decisions markedly more predictable." Even then he inclined "tentatively, to the belief that more accurate description of the judicial process will serve to show that efforts to procure such predictability (via anthropology, economics, sociology, statistics, or otherwise) are doomed to failure." [4] In *Courts on Trial*, which appeared in 1949, he was no longer tentatively, but forthrightly, committed to this view.

Frank's denial that accurate forecasts can ever be devel-

---

[3] Cohen, *Ethical Systems and Legal Ideals: An Essay on the Foundations of Legal Criticism* (Ithaca, N.Y.: Cornell University Press, 1959) , p. 236.

[4] Frank, *Law and the Modern Mind* (Garden City, N.Y.: Doubleday, 1963) , p. 399.

oped for most decisions stems from many factors. The most basic reason is, however, the "vagaries of trial-court fact-findings and gestalts." They

play havoc with the assumed correlations of (1) prelitigation, out-of-court, regularities with (2) in-court results. Once again, ability to predict the rules ("paper" or "real" rules) which a trial court will use in deciding a case, or which the upper court will use on an appeal from the trial court, does not mean ability to predict the decision when witness' credibility is crucial, as usually it is.

Thus, Frank went on to point out, it is not surprising that the most enthusiastic advocates of the predictive approach have been "men who know and care little about trials and trial courts. Consequently they have deceived themselves about these correlations." [5]

General Position of the Realists

Frank's pessimism on this score was not shared by the vast majority of realists. They were agreed that decisions could and should become more predictable. They were convinced, too, that the indispensable means to achieve this goal is the development of truly scientific approaches to the study of law. The "legal pseudo-analysis which results in a futile alleged science that might be denominated 'verbal jurisprudence' " [6] must be discarded. This "verbal jurisprudence," "pre-science of law," or "science of transcendental nonsense" has not produced "an ability

[5] Frank, *Courts on Trial: Myth and Reality in American Justice* (Princeton: Princeton University Press, 1949), p. 336.

[6] Joseph W. Bingham, "The Nature of Legal Rights and Duties," *Mich. L. Rev.*, XII (1913), 23–24, n. 23.

to predict that described effects will or will not follow from definite concrete conditions and forces." [7] Moreover, the traditional approaches have failed because "the application of truly scientific methods to the study of legal phenomena . . . has never yet been tried." [8] Much of the inspiration for the realist movement stemmed from the desire to correct this situation. In 1931, Walter Wheeler Cook pointed out that "for many years I have been asking myself the question: In what way or ways is it possible to study law scientifically?" [9] The same question was asked by all the advocates of "realistic jurisprudence."

Nevertheless, the fact that it was answered by different realists in varying ways cannot be ignored. The diversity in their viewpoints can be exaggerated; but it can also be underestimated. Insofar as the prediction of decisions is concerned, the diversity needs to be emphasized. In this respect realism is a "mass of trends" which "are centered in no man, in no coherent group. There is no leader. Spokesmen are self-appointed. They speak not for the whole but for the work each is himself concerned with." [10] What kind of approaches did the new movement produce? What response have they elicited, and what contribution have they made? The purpose of this chapter is to answer these questions. The essential place to begin the quest for an answer is by an explanation of the most important predictive models developed by individual realists.

[7] Bingham, "What Is the Law?" *Mich. L. Rev.*, XI (1912), 4.
[8] Cook, "Scientific Method and the Law," *A. B. A. J.*, XIII (1927), 303.
[9] Cook, "The Possibilities of Social Study as a Science," *Essays on Research in the Social Sciences* (Washington, D.C.: Brookings Institution, 1931), p. 27.
[10] Llewellyn, *Jurisprudence*, p. 69.

Fred Rodell's Approach

The writings of Fred Rodell extend back into the late 1930's. Still, his best outline of how to predict decisions was not published until 1962. He began from this premise.

Nor activism nor self-restraint nor federal-state relationships nor absolute constitutional commands lead a Sutherland to vote against the New Deal, a Brandeis for wage and hour laws, a Frankfurter against state right to counsel, a Black for freedom of assembly—nor do these easy abstract theories explain why each so voted. From John Jay on to Potter Stewart the vote of each Supreme Court Justice, however rationalized à la-mode, however fitted afterward into the pigeonhole of some pretty politico-juridical principle, has rather been the result of a vast complex of personal factors—temperament, background, education, economic status, pre-Court career—of whose influence on his thinking even the most sophisticated of Justices can never wholly be aware. . . . Only by examining the Justices individually as whole human beings, by probing beneath the protective shell of principles expressed in opinions, to try to find out what made or makes each Justice really tick, can past decisions be explained without constant contradiction and future decisions predicted with a surprising degree of accuracy.[11]

Thus, "a Justice's actual votes, regardless of his explicitly stated reasons, are rarely if ever primarily dictated by, or predictable in terms of, his firm belief or relative disbelief in judicial deferences." [12]

Rodell then briefly examined the voting records of Mr. Justice Black and Mr. Justice Frankfurter in order to

[11] Rodell, "For Every Justice, Judicial Deference Is a Sometime Thing," *Geo. L. J.,* L (1962), 700–701.

[12] *Ibid.,* p. 701.

illustrate this point. They have held and voiced strongly conflicting views on the question of judicial deference. In many cases, however, the actual votes of each Justice are difficult to deduce from this philosophy. For Black, "here the stark words of the Constitution, there an exegesis that puts words into the Constitution, here judicial deference, there judicial nondeference, are used as argumentative tools to make juridically respectable and intellectually compelling the results . . . [which he] wants to reach for essentially quite different reasons." Put more bluntly, these principles are rationalizations which tend to obscure the "real" reasons for the decisions. These reasons include Black's intense devotion to personal liberties, his strong sympathy for labor, his greater concern for the poor than the rich and for people rather than business organizations. His predilections in these directions and others "were all readily predictable when he came to the Court." They offer a much more solid basis for prediction than any of his attitudes towards judicial deference. Black's "votes on the Court . . . have been and remain predictable with far greater accuracy from his many-faceted evangelical yet practical humanitarianism, than from any complex of abstract jurisprudential principles." [13]

The same is true of Justice Frankfurter. His jurisprudential principles do not "constitute a reliable or revealing guide to analysis or prediction . . . in specific constitutional cases." His actual votes reveal that his deference is to "a nonexistent blueprint of the U.S. federal system . . . *as he would draft it;* to the precedent of past decisions, *as he considers them compelling;* and to the reasonable-or-unreasonable test, *as he applies it.*" This is revealed most clearly by the fact that Frankfurter is no more con-

[13] *Ibid.,* p. 703.

sistent than Black "in applying to issues right at hand his self-proclaimed rules for correct judicial conduct." With Frankfurter, as with Black, "motivations lie deeper" than articulated, systematic philosophies. The "real" reasons for Justice Frankfurter's decisions include his worship of the Court as an institution, his adulation for separation of powers, and his preoccupation with procedure rather than substance. As was also true of Black, Frankfurter's predilections in these directions "might easily have been predicted . . . from the formalistic nature of his early background, of his higher education, and of his professorial pre-Court career." Finally, the votes of Mr. Justice Frankfurter "have been and remain far more accurately predictable in light of his personal predilections . . . than in terms of the allegedly impersonal, objective, reasoned rules with which those votes are regularly rationalized." [14]

Perhaps the most dramatic feature of Rodell's article is his attempt to predict a specific decision of the Court. The landmark case of *Baker* v. *Carr* had been argued but not yet decided by the time his article was published. Rodell applied to the Court as a whole the same skepticism of stated principles and the same reliance on largely extra-legal factors which he had used to explain the decisions of Black and Frankfurter. The result was a prophecy of very high accuracy. Rodell predicted not only the decision, but the votes of seven out of eight Justices. He concluded his article with these words:

He who would analyze, predict or understand the Supreme Court's constitutional decisions will fare considerably better if he concentrates on that same infinite variety of human factors which make precise prediction impossible, than if he grants

[14] *Ibid.*, pp. 704, 706–707.

face value to such conditioned verbal behavior from the high bench as is illustrated by random and self-rationalizing balderdash about judicial deference to legislative will.[15]

The Method of Karl N. Llewellyn

A brief review of Llewellyn's interpretation of precedent is necessary if his recommendations for the prediction of decisions are to be fully understood. For him, *"every single precedent, according to what may be the attitude of future judges, is ambiguous,* is wide or narrow at need."[16] Precedents cannot, therefore, provide a meaningful basis for prediction.

Here . . . we have passed out of the realm of pure logic. We have indeed passed out of the realm of pure scientific observation and inference. Logic and science can tell us, and tell us with some certainty, what the doctrinal *possibilities* are. They can tell us whether without self-contradiction the results of the cases *can* be so settled as to stand together. They can even provide us with a tool for argument to a court that the cases *should* be made in this fashion to stand together. But they give us no certainty as to *whether* the possibility embodied in the argument will be adopted by a given court.[17]

Yet, throughout his life Llewellyn insisted that a significant degree of regularity does characterize judicial behavior, especially that of appellate court judges. Even in *The Bramble Bush* he contended that "the main thing is seeing what officials do . . . and seeing that there is a certain regularity in their doing—a regularity which makes possible prediction of what they and other officials are about to

[15] *Ibid.,* p. 708.

[16] Llewellyn, *The Bramble Bush: On Our Law and Its Study* (New York: Oceana, 1960) , p. 71.

[17] *Ibid.,* pp. 62–63.

do tomorrow." [18] In 1931 Llewellyn criticized the unpredictability which Jerome Frank so strongly emphasized in *Law and the Modern Mind*. "Law, in the sense of decision, is in fact much more predictable, and hence more certain, than his treatment would indicate." [19] In *The Common Law Tradition* the same theme was expanded upon. The work of appellate courts is reckonable "far beyond what any sane man has any business expecting from a machinery devoted to settling disputes self-selected for their toughness." [20] Indeed,

today, taking the close of the trial as a base line . . . a skilled man careful of the lines of factor here discussed ought even in the present state of our knowledge to average correct prediction of outcome eight times out of ten, and better than that if he knows the appeal counsel on both sides or sees the briefs.[21]

Statements such as these have sometimes been cited in order to demonstrate that Llewellyn's estimate of the predictability of judicial decisions changed radically. In the last years of his life, the argument runs, he regarded decisions as much more predictable than he did in the 1930's and 1940's. Some change of emphasis is surely discernible. Nevertheless, even in his early writings Llewellyn never denied that the regularity is there. The great problem is to tap its roots. Also, even in *The Common Law Tradition* Llewellyn is careful to point out that only "a skillful man careful of the lines of factor here sketched" is able to make reliable forecasts. This ability does not, in other words, belong to every student of law. Finally, Llewellyn insisted to the end that the regularity which makes forecasts possible is *not* primarily due to the impact of established rules.

[18] *Ibid.*, p. 13.　　[19] Llewellyn, *Jurisprudence*, p. 107.
[20] Llewellyn, *The Common Law Tradition: Deciding Appeals* (Boston: Little, Brown, 1960), p. 4.
[21] *Ibid.*, p. 45.

"Those aspects or factors which have achieved work-form as rules of law . . . give in themselves, *in general,* most inadequate guidance about how particular appeals are likely to come out." [22] The reason for this "inadequate guidance" is that established rules are not the most basic factors inducing decisions. On this point Llewellyn remained consistent throughout his life.[23]

Early Approach of Llewellyn

The difference in emphasis already noted is symbolic, however, of rather different approaches to the problem of

---

[22] *Ibid.,* p. 154.

[23] The spirit in which the point was articulated did undergo some change. In the text of *The Bramble Bush,* which was first published in 1930, Llewellyn wrote that *"rules,* in all of this, are important to you so far as they help you see or predict what judges will do or so far as they help you get judges to do something. That is their importance. That is all their importance, except as pretty playthings." *Ibid.,* p. 14. In the celebrated "foreword" to the reissue of this book in 1951 this radical skepticism toward the impact of established rules upon judges is somewhat modified. "For it is clear that one office of law [and of established rules] is to control officials in some part, and to guide them even in places where no thoroughgoing control is possible, or is desired." *Ibid.,* p. 9. Two points need to be emphasized in this connection. One is that Llewellyn's description of rules as "pretty playthings" signifies a degree of skepticism toward the impact of established rules which is not characteristic of his articles in the 1930's. Even in this early period he was careful, most of the time, to claim merely that they were not *the* decisive factor producing decisions. See, for example, his criticisms of Underhill Moore and Herman Oliphant in *Jurisprudence,* p. 60, n. 46. The second point is that this position is *not* abandoned by Llewellyn even in his *magnum opus.* The statement that "rules are not to control, but to guide decision" is typical. The same can be said of the proposition that one of the "basic facts" which has been made "clear" by the realist movement is that "the *rules of law, alone,* do not, because they cannot, decide any appealed case *which has been worth both an appeal and a response." The Common Law Tradition,* pp. 179, 189.

prediction developed by Llewellyn.[24] In his books and articles in the late 1920's and 1930's the general solution which he advocated was the development of a social science of law strongly behavioral in its orientation. Such an approach would be guided by four norms of inquiry. Each must be briefly examined if the character of Llewellyn's early work is to be fully revealed.

One norm is to focus study upon the behavior of judges. "One concerned with law as a social *science,* a science of observation, must center his thought on behavior." "It is *behavior* which must be the subject-matter of an observational science, of objective character, about things legal." [25] Unfortunately, behavior is precisely what the traditional approach to the study of law ignores. Such an approach is unfortunate because of the frequent gap between stated, articulated rules and the actual behavior of officials. The trouble stems from the fact that

if nothing be said about behavior, the *tacit* assumption is that the words do reflect behavior, and if they be the words of rules of law, do influence behavior, even influence behavior effectively and precisely to conform completely to those words. Here lies the key to the muddle. The "rules" are laid down; in the type-case they are "ought" rules, prescriptive rules: the writer's prescriptions, the writer's oughts, individually proclaimed oughts—the true rule is that judges should give judgment for the plaintiff on these facts. From this we jump without necessary notice into equivalent oughts as *accepted in*

[24] For development of this point, see Hayakawa, "Karl N. Llewellyn as a Lawman from Japan Sees Him," *Rutgers L. Rev.,* XVIII (1964), 717.

[25] Llewellyn, "Legal Tradition and Social Science Method—A Realist's Critique," *Essays on Research in the Social Sciences* (Washington, D.C.: Brookings Institution, 1931), pp. 99–100; Llewellyn, "The Theory of Legal 'Science,'" *N.C. L. Rev.,* XX (1941), 6.

the legal system under discussion: prevailing oughts—the authorities agree that judges should give judgment for the plaintiff on these facts. Here, again, without notice and without inquiry, we *assume* that *practice* of the judges conforms to the accepted oughts on the books; that the verbal formulations of oughts *describe* precisely the is-es of practice; that they *do* give such judgment on such facts. A toothed bird of a situation, in law or any other walk of life. Where is men's ideology about their doing, about what is good practice—where is that ideology or has it ever been an adequate description of their *working* practice? [26]

The second methodological norm is the careful distinction between "real" and "paper" rules and rights. The former are descriptive *of* the practices, the actions, and especially the remedies of courts. "They seek earnestly to go no whit, in their suggestions, beyond the remedy actually available." The test for the existence of a "real" rule or right is the fire of battle, what courts will do in fact. Paper rules are prescriptive in character. They are "the accepted *doctrine* of the time and place—what the books there say the law is." They are "the accepted patter of the law officials," the "official precept-on-the-books (statutes, doctrine laid down in the decision of a court, administrative regulation)," "rules of authoritative ought, addressed *to* officials, telling *officials* what the *officials* ought to do." [27] The great need for the distinction between the two types of rules stems from the possibility of divergence between stated doctrine and actual practice. Thus the law-man can "pay no heed at all," "listen partly," or "listen with all care," [28] to the paper rule. To be sure, the "paper" and the "real" rule for the situation may coin-

---

[26] Llewellyn, *Jurisprudence,* pp. 16–17.   [27] *Ibid.,* pp. 22, 23.
[28] *Ibid.,* p. 23.

cide. Nonetheless, the inspiration for the distinction is the likelihood that they will not.

The third norm was advanced in Llewellyn's second major interpretation of the realist movement. In 1940 he distinguished between two parts of the method which he described as the "essence of . . . the newer Jurisprudence." The first part is very similar to the approach in terms of which he attempted, in his Appendix to *The Common Law Tradition,* to define realism. Its *leitmotiv* is· the need to check constantly whether accepted doctrine can be squared with the totality of decisions. The jurist must "be content with no formulation which does not account for *all* of the results." The second part is directed to the situation which arises when the doctrines and the results cannot be squared. Its essence is to search for the "something else" which is at work helping the doctrine out, "for there is something else at work, helping all doctrines out." [29] The great necessity for either part of the method is the fact that "traditional prescriptive rule-formulations" may well not be the decisive factor producing the results.

The fourth norm is the attempt to eliminate some of the vagueness of traditional rules "by grouping the facts in new—and typically but not always narrower—categories . . . much narrower than the traditional classes." Such a procedure is not wholly novel. It is "in essence the orthodox technique of making distinctions, and reformulating." What is new is that the process of distinction is undertaken "systematically"; "exploited consciously, instead of being reserved until facts which refuse to be twisted by 'interpretations' force action"; and is based

[29] *Ibid.,* p. 135.

upon "distrust of, instead of search for, the widest sweep of generalization words permit." [30]

Later Approach of Llewellyn

In *The Common Law Tradition* the call for the creation of a science of law modeled along these lines is considerably muted, if it can be heard at all. Instead, two new themes are introduced. The first is the attempt to explain the patterns of uniformity in judicial decision-making by reference to fourteen "major steadying factors in our appellate courts." Supposedly, they furnish the basis upon which reliable predictions of future decisions can be made. The fourteen are the existence of "law-conditioned officials," personnel who are "all trained and in the main rather experienced lawyers"; the presence of "legal doctrine" and "known doctrinal techniques"; the responsibility of the judiciary for "justice"; the tradition of "one single right answer" for each case; the existence of written opinions "which tell any interested person what the cause is and why the decision—under the authorities—is right, and perhaps why it is wise," and which may also "show how like cases are properly to be decided in the future"; the existence of "a frozen record from below" and the fact that the issues before the court are "limited, sharpened, and phrased in advance"; the presentation, oral and written, of adversary argument by counsel; the practice of group decisions; the security for independent judgment which life tenure makes possible; a "known bench"; the "general period style and its Promise"; and, finally, "professional judicial office." [31] To be sure, "there is nei-

---

[30] *Ibid.*, pp. 59–60.
[31] See Llewellyn, *The Common Law Tradition*, pp. 19–51.

ther magic nor any assumption of the absolute in this 'fourteen.' " [32] Still, these are the "factors which if they have any power should be expected to produce a degree of depersonizing in the deciding far beyond that when such flywheel factors are not present." [33]

For Llewellyn, the most important of the fourteen factors is professional judicial office. "Office" means, essentially, the role which the judge is expected to play in our judicial system. No single word can precisely delineate the nature of this role.

The typical word, used as a sufficient word, is "impartial," which describes a condition: "not on either side, and without personal interest or desire re the outcome" is about as far as that word really takes you, though the dictionaries tend to add "just." But we mean when we use the word about a man in judicial *office* a great deal more. We mean, and definitely in addition, "upright." We also mean—and if we stop to think we know that we mean—not a passive but a positive and active attitude: the judge must be *seeking,* as best he can, to see the matter fairly, and with an eye not to the litigants merely, but to All-of-Us as well. We mean further, and importantly, still another attitude: "Open, truly open, to listen, to get informed, to be persuaded, to respond to good reason." Nay, more; we gather into this one weak, bleak word "impartial" a drive: an idea of effort, of self-denying labor, toward patience, toward understanding sympathy, toward quest for wisdom in the result.[34]

"Professional judicial office" is such an important factor because it is the major restraint upon the *use* of judicial freedom. The human element is not eliminated. "The factor of person is still important, even when we limit observation to that overwhelming bulk of the appellate

[32] *Ibid.,* p. 45 n. 41.   [33] *Ibid.,* p. 51.   [34] *Ibid.,* pp. 46–47.

judges to whom improper conduct in office would be un-thinkable." If this factor were not significant, then the existence of appeals or dissenting opinions could not be justified. The function of the judicial office is, instead, to create a tradition which "grips them [the judges], shapes them, limits them, guides them; not for nothing do we speak of *ingrained* ways of work or thought, of men *experienced* or case-hardened, of *habits* of mind." [35]

A second theme of *The Common Law Tradition* is the insistence that the judicial opinion, properly approached, is a useful tool for predictive purposes. The proper approach is to study opinions for what they reveal about the attitudes of judges, rather than legal doctrine only. This perspective involves, of course, some modification of the opinion-skepticism which characterized the realist movement in the 1930's. In *The Common Law Tradition* this modification is made explicit. Llewellyn's earlier point of view is not, it is true, completely abandoned. He still maintained that "only by happenstance will an opinion accurately report the process of deciding." Yet two new emphases do emerge. The first is the insistence that "such report is not really a function of the opinion at all." The second is the contention that, in spite of this, there is considerable "ore in the published opinion" which can be mined for predictive purposes. This can be seen in the fact that

by 1925 there had come to be a top bracket of the bar all over the country—not too many by percentage or even by nose count, but enough to be a bracket . . .—a top bracket who had begun to read any current case of interest not only for what it had laid down in words as doctrine or principle, nor only further (or in contrast) for what it had actually and narrowly decided, but for the "flavor" that could indicate how far that court, tomorrow, would stand to today's decision, or would expand it.

More important, this approach resulted in much greater predictability. It "proved to work out in the practical life of law. It made for safer counselling. It won cases on appeal. It brought its practitioners into the top bracket and it kept them there." Finally, this approach to judicial opinions *can be* turned into sustained and regular procedure for *anybody's* practice. For "the signs to be looked for, though wholly unstandardized, are nonetheless as gross and unmistakable as road signs, and . . . there are obvious and valuable procedures of interpretation and use which are well-nigh as simple and communicable as the driving of a nail." If the "average lawyer" will "shift his focus for a few hours from *'what* was held' in a series of opinions to what those opinions suggest or show about *what was bothering and what was helping the court* as it decided," then such a lawyer can "provide himself, and rather speedily, with the kit of coarse tools we have been discussing." [36]

The Functional Model of Felix Cohen

Like Llewellyn, Felix Cohen was very critical of the small minority of realists who denied the existence of significant uniformities in judicial behavior. He attacked specifically the views developed by Jerome Frank in *Law and the Modern Mind*. "If reasonably certain predictions . . . could never be made, as Jerome Frank at times seems to say, then all legal decisions would be simply noises, and no better grist for science than the magical phrases of

[36] *Ibid.,* pp. 56, 57–58, 58, 178.

transcendental jurisprudence." Such is not the case. "Actual experience does reveal a significant body of predictable uniformity in the behavior of courts. Law is not a mass of unrelated decisions nor a product of judicial belly-aches." "Large-scale social facts cannot be explained in terms of the atomic idiosyncrasies and personal prejudices of individuals. . . . That is why the 'belly-ache' theory of judicial decisions can never explain how any rule of law comes into being or changes in time."

At the same time, Cohen insisted that most traditional legal rules and concepts are futile for predictive purposes. Thus "a good many of the revered rules and principles of the law" turn out to be either "pious frauds, contradicted by the actual holdings in decided cases," or "so ambiguous that they have no predictive or scientific value," or mere "disguised tautologies." For this reason, traditional jurisprudence is but "a special branch of the science of transcendental nonsense." Its concepts "do not have a verifiable existence except to the eyes of faith," and its rules are "theorems in an independent system." To be sure, the language of this "science" is not completely useless. "The law is not a science but a practical activity, and myths may impress the imagination and memory where more exact discourse would leave minds cold." "Certain words and phrases are useful for the purpose of releasing pent-up emotions, or putting babies to sleep, or inducing certain emotions and attitudes in a political or judicial audience." Nonetheless, "valuable as is the language of transcendental nonsense for many practical legal purposes, it is entirely useless when we come to study, describe, predict, and criticize legal phenomena." [37]

[37] *The Legal Conscience: Selected Papers of Felix S. Cohen,* ed. Lucy Kramer Cohen (New Haven: Yale University Press, 1960), pp. 71, 70, 135, 46, 37.

Much the same kind of critique was advanced by Cohen against the attempt of the American Law Institute to reduce legal uncertainty. Its "Restatement of the Law" began in the early 1920's. A major consideration in the establishment of the Institute was the fact that "the law's uncertainties are very great." In the words of one of the architects of the Restatement, "the uncertainty, the confusion, was growing worse from year to year. . . . Whatever authority might be found for one view of the law upon any topic, other authorities could be found for a different view. . . . The law was becoming guesswork." [38] This diagnosis of the problem was shared by the legal realists. Nevertheless, most of them disagreed sharply with the remedy advocated by the Institute. The way to reduce uncertainty is not through the restatement of "the fundamental principles of the common law" which lie behind the "great swamp of decisions." [39] No one articulated this sentiment more sharply than Felix Cohen.

The age of the classical jurists is over. . . . The "Restatement of the Law" by the American Law Institute is the last long-drawn-out gasp of a dying tradition. The more intelligent of our younger law teachers and students are not interested in "restating" the dogmas of legal theology. . . . Creative legal thought will more and more look behind the pretty array of "correct" cases to the actual facts of judicial behavior, will make increasing use of statistical methods in the scientific description and prediction of judicial behavior, will more and more seek to map the hidden springs of judicial decision and to weigh the social forces which are represented on the bench.[40]

[38] *Proceedings of the American Law Institute,* I (1923), 48–49.
[39] *Ibid,* p. 52.
[40] Cohen, *The Legal Conscience,* pp. 59–60. For criticisms by other realists of the American Law Institute's Restatement of the Law, see

Instead of legal theology, Cohen advocated what he called "functionalism." As a scientific approach to the study of law, functionalism may be defined in terms of four postulates:

(1) The "definition of legal concepts, rules, and institutions in terms of judicial decisions or other acts of state-force. Whatever cannot be so translated is functionally meaningless."

(2) An ultimatum against all empirically unverifiable concepts, "all dogmas and devices that cannot be translated into terms of actual experience." "Any word that

---

Herman Oliphant, "The Problem of the Logical Method from the Lawyer's Point of View," *Proceedings of the Academy of Political Science,* X (1922–1924), 324; Bingham, "The American Law Institute vs. the Supreme Court; In the Matter of Haddock v. Haddock," *Cornell L. Q.,* XXI (1936), 393; Hessel Yntema, "What Should the American Law Institute Do?" *Mich. L. Rev.,* XXXIV (1936), 461; and Yntema, "What Would Law Teachers Like to See the Institute Do?" *Am. L. S. Rev.,* VIII (1936), 502. It should be emphasized that the criticisms voiced in these articles apply to the Restatement of the Law as originally conceived and first developed. They do not necessarily apply to the more recent restatements. Also, the realists were not unalterably opposed to all types of codification. For a good analysis of the limitations of codification, from the perspective of a "realistic" view of the judicial process, see Frank, *Law and the Modern Mind,* pp. 200–210, 336–338. Yet, even Frank stated that "a code deliberately devised with reference to the desirability of growth and stated in terms of general guiding and flexible principles may some day prove to be the way out of some of the difficulties of legal administration in America." *Ibid.,* p. 337. This sympathy toward certain kinds of codification is more clearly revealed by the efforts of the late Karl Llewellyn as the Chief Reporter of the Uniform Commercial Code, which has been adopted in forty-nine of the fifty states. For an interesting defense of the kind of codification reflected in the Uniform Commercial Code, see New York, Law Revision Commission: Study of Uniform Commercial Code, *General Statement to the Commission by Professor Karl N. Llewellyn,* Legislative Document N. 65 (A) (Albany: Williams Press, 1955).

cannot pay up in the currency of fact, upon demand, is to be declared bankrupt, and we are to have no further dealings with it."

(3) Examination of "unmentioned factors leading to a given decision. These factors may range from weakness of intellect or digestive disturbances to political beliefs or economic backgrounds." Special attention should be given to the values of the judge. Ultimately these determine his "selectivity patterns," the "grid" through which precedents and other rules are interpreted.

What is needed in law, if law is to become more scientific in the future than it has been in the past, is a body of learning from which we can predict that what looks like a straight story or a straight sale from one standpoint will look like a crooked story or a crooked sale from another, and from which we can predict the successive "distortions" that any observed social fact will undergo as it passes through different value-charged fields in the "world-line" of its history. . . .

We should be able to predict that what Justice X will view as "judicial protection of fundamental constitutional liberties" will be viewed by Justice Y as "federal interference with the constitutional freedoms of the states to experiment in the solution of their own social problems." [41]

(4) Exploitation of whatever concepts or methods the social sciences can provide for the study of judicial behavior. If "what a case 'stands for' " is "a problem not in logic but in judicial psychology," then the need to know the factors which condition "the habitual categories of thought of judges" becomes imperative. The need can only be fulfilled by "a systematic analysis of the economic and social background, the moral presuppositions, and the

[41] Cohen, *The Legal Conscience,* pp. 80, 47, 48, 82, 126–127.

psychological habits of thought of judges." [42] The development of such analysis demands the full utilization of whatever tools the social sciences can provide.

Only by probing behind the decision to the forces which it reflects, or projecting beyond the decision the lines of its force upon the future, do we come to an understanding of the meaning of the decision itself. The distinction between "holding" and "dictum" in any decision is not to be discovered by logical inspection of the opinion or by historical inquiry into the actual facts of the case. That distinction involves us in a prediction, a prophecy of the weight that courts will give to future citations of the decision rendered. This is a question not of pure logic but of human psychology, economics, and politics.[43]

The Behavioristic Model of Herman Oliphant

It has been pointed out throughout this study that the climate of opinion of the 1920's and 1930's had an important impact upon the realist movement. Behavioristic psychology constituted one of the vital new winds of doctrine. It was perhaps only natural that its approach should be applied to the study of law. The chief architect of this attempt among the legal realists was Herman Oliphant.

The major stimulus for his effort is the same as that of most of the other advocates of "realistic jurisprudence." It is the conviction that traditional legal rules and concepts are wholly inadequate as a basis for prediction of future decisions. Indeed, Oliphant's dissatisfaction was articulated in language more vivid than virtually any of the other realists. For him, the "patient particularism," the "Anglo-Saxon empiricism" of the "early common law"

---

[42] Cohen, *Ethical Systems and Legal Ideals*, pp. 244, 245, 238.
[43] Cohen, *The Legal Conscience*, p. 71.

had been replaced by "obscurant abstractions," an "orgy of overgeneralization," and "great cargoes of continental speculations." The result was that the study of law had been transformed into an "architecture of castles in the thin air of pure theory." The rigor of *stare decisis* has been replaced by "the current license of *stare dictis*"; "the student of law has turned from following decisions to following so-called principles." Our "categories of thought have become unreal by life having left them behind, and no alert sense of actuality checks our reveries in theory." We have become "intellectual infants with toothless gums too soft except for munching elastic generalities with sophomoric serenity."

Predictive problems stem, thus, from the elasticity of the generalities "munched" by judges and legal scholars. Still, judicial decision-making is characterized by patterns of regularity. The problem is how best to *explain* this uniformity, and thereby provide a reliable basis for the prediction of future decisions. The key method which Oliphant urged for this purpose is to shift attention from the "vocal" to the "nonvocal" behavior of judges. "A study with more emphasis on their *non-vocal behavior, i.e.,* what the judges actually do when stimulated by the facts of the case before them, is the approach indispensable to exploiting scientifically the wealth of material in the cases." Established rules or "prior rationalizations are rejected *for this purpose* because the facts prevail when they diverge from the prior generalizations and for each rationalization indicating one result, a contradictory one indicating the opposite result can usually be found." Still, there is a class of stimuli which can be scientifically studied. It is the facts. They are, indeed, "the only stimuli capable of scientific study as a basis for prediction."

The predictable element in it all is what courts have done in response to the stimuli of the facts of the concrete cases before them. Not the judges' opinions, but which way they decide cases will be the dominant subject-matter of any truly scientific study of law. . . . The response of their intuition of experience to the stimulus of human situations is the subject-matter having that constancy and objectivity necessary for truly scientific study.[44]

The Institutional Method of Underhill Moore

Moore's approach was more meticulously developed than that of any other realist. It is based upon a distinction between "institutional" and "legal" methods. The essence of the latter is the segregation "of 'the facts' and the decisions of courts in past cases . . . from the other factors constituting the litigation-situation and the attempt . . . to state propositions of 'law' which are the product of manipulation of these two factors alone." Such a method suffers from three major defects as an instrument of prediction. In the first place, it does not systematically consider the other relevant variables in the litigation situation. In the second place, any account of these other variables is haphazard. For example, judicial reference to the usual behavior of individuals is not uncommon. Still, the mention of such factors "is felt to be illicit and is accomplished with averted eyes. Consequently this factor is not adequately and systematically weighted." In the third place, the limited variables upon which traditional legal method focuses are not adequately investigated. Thus, the assumption is usually made that the facts of a case are those which appear in the opinion of the court.

[44] Oliphant, "A Return to Stare Decisis," *A. B. A. J.,* XIV (1928), pp. 74, 75, 160, 76, 161, 159 n. 5, 159.

The facts as they appear in the court records and briefs are ignored. This omission "must vitiate many of its results." Also, the legal categories and concepts used to classify the facts are most imprecise. They are "too inclusive to permit of adequate classification . . . too extended and elastic to permit of adequate manipulation of the data." The end-result is a method "hopelessly inadequate" for predictive purposes.[45]

The alternative approach which Moore recommended

[45] Underhill Moore and Gilbert Sussman, "Legal and Institutional Methods Applied to the Debiting of Direct Discounts—II. Institutional Method," *Yale L. J.*, XL (1931), 556, 558, 557, 559. For other studies by Moore, see Underhill Moore, "The Rational Basis of Legal Institutions," *Colum. L. Rev.*, XXIII (1923), 609; Moore and Gilbert Sussman, "The Lawyer's Law," *Yale L. J.*, XLI (1932), 566; Moore and Charles C. Callahan, "My Philosophy of Law," *My Philosophy of Law: Credos of Sixteen American Scholars* (Boston: Boston Law Book Co., 1941); Moore, Sussman, and C. E. Brand, "Legal and Institutional Methods Applied to Orders to Stop Payments of Checks," *Yale L. J.*, XLII (1933), 817, 1198; Moore and Callahan, "Law and Learning Theory: A Study in Legal Control," *ibid.*, LIII (1943), 1; and the studies cited *infra*, note 48. The fact that Moore's approach was more fully developed than that of any other realist was recognized by Karl Llewellyn. As he once wrote, "One or two [realists]—*perhaps for instance Underhill Moore*—may . . . have conceived and even put forward his thinking as sufficiently complete to deserve description as a philosophy, as expressing views on those phases of the institution of law which reach beyond description and the techniques of operation. I know of no other such, however, unless Jerome Frank's faith in the unreachability of facts be deemed of this nature." "I have never been able to make out whether it [Frank's faith] was." Llewellyn, *The Common Law Tradition*, pp. 510 (italics mine), 510, n. 3. For some interesting commentaries on Moore's work, see the memorial remarks of William O. Douglas, Carrol Shanks, and Charles E. Clark, as reprinted in *Yale L. J.*, LIX (1950), 187–195. Also, see F. S. C. Northrop, "Underhill Moore's Legal Science: Its Nature and Significance," *Yale L. J.*, LIX (1950), 196; Hessel E. Yntema, "Jurisprudence and Metaphysics: A Triangular Correspondence," *Yale L. J.*, LIX (1950), 275.

is the "institutional method." It is based upon the hypothesis

that the patterns to which the overt behavior in a locality more frequently conforms are among the cultural factors in a litigation-situation significantly connected with the decision, that the significance for prediction attributed in legal literature to past decisions is erroneously attributed, and that the semblance of likeness between decisions, when it does appear, does not indicate any predictive value in past decisions but rather a significant association of the decisions with another variable, i.e., the institutional patterns in the locality of the court. It is probable that the notion of a court as to the just, reasonable, fair, and convenient way . . . to behave and also as to the just, reasonable, fair, and convenient consequence which should be attached to the way the parties did behave is so associated with the more frequent and, therefore, regular overt behavior in such situations in the locality as to serve as an index useful in prediction.[46]

In particular, Moore felt that the degree of deviation in the behavior of the litigants from regular, overt, institutional behavior provides the crucial index in terms of which decisions could be predicted. The grosser the deviation, the more likely it is that the claims of the deviant litigant will not be judicially allowed. For this reason Moore insisted that the focus of scientific legal analysis should be the comparison of the behavior of the litigants with patterns of institutional behavior. Such a shift involves, it is true, the neglect of certain variables which may be significant. This is justified because "it would be absurd to attempt to state a litigation-situation in terms of

[46] Moore, Sussman, and C. E. Brand, "Legal and Institutional Methods Applied to Orders to Stop Payment of Checks—II. Institutional Method," *Yale L. J.,* XLII (1933), 1198–99.

all the variables in causal relation with the decision. The formulation of such an equation is a day-dream." Moreover, limitation of analysis to a few variables may result in predictions which are at least as certain as "the forecast of tomorrow's weather in New Haven." As Moore wrote,

The forecast of the course of decisions or even of a particular decision in some fields at least may perhaps be made as probable as the prediction of the meteorologist. The same course which was open to the weather prophet of the seventeenth century is open to the lawyer and the student of government today. The rigorous application of a defined method to measure defined variables in units as invariable as may be, and to state in terms of those units a relation between those variables is as available a procedure now as it was then. Is it not conceivable that the time will come when the lawyer in making his judgments will take into account the results of the methodical study of a few cultural and psychological factors as well as his law books and his intuitive valuations of such factors as he happens to think of just as today the American farmer in making his judgments takes into account the weather forecasts as well as the Farmers Almanac.[47]

Unlike many of the legal realists, however, Moore did not merely stipulate how decisions could be made more predictable: he also tried to test empirically the utility of his particular approach. One of the most interesting results of this facet of his work is the analysis of banker's set-off which he and Gilbert Sussman published in the *Yale Law Journal*.[48] The basic problem to which the articles are addressed is the effect of the arrival of the matu-

[47] Moore and Sussman, "Legal and Institutional Methods Applied to the Debiting of Direct Discounts—II. Institutional Method," *ibid.*, XL (1931), 560, 561–562.

[48] See *ibid.*, pp. 381, 555, 752, 928, 1055, 1219.

rity day of the customer's time note which had been discounted for him by his bank and credited to his account upon the bank's obligation to him to honor his checks. The technique used was to apply both "legal" and "institutional" methods to the study of the three principal cases. The cases were regarded as "peculiarly apt" because

they are the only decisions "in point." They are but three in number. As reported, and even as disclosed by the records, their "facts" are as much alike as the facts of distinct litigation-situations can be expected to be. Each case was decided by a different court and in a different state. In South Carolina the decision was for the customer; in New York and Pennsylvania, for the bank. The South Carolina decision was rendered in 1904; the others in 1920 and 1928 respectively.[49]

In the first article Moore and Sussman attempted to apply "legal method." The conclusion which they reached is that it is a method "so hopelessly inadequate to the purpose that the most generous rating of the article would class it among ingenuous post-rationalizations." For "the conclusion that the maturity of the customer's time note effected a reduction in the amount of the bank's obligation to honor his checks is an intuitive judgment based upon a composite of undisclosed and unanalyzed experience and evidence." Utilizing a variety of different methods for accumulating the relevant data, they then proceeded to apply their "institutional" method to the litigation-situations. The purpose was "to determine the type and degree of the deviation of the behavior of the litigants in each of the principal cases from the comparable sequences found to have been current in the jurisdiction at the time of the decision and to observe the correlation

[49] *Ibid.*, p. 564.

between the decision and the type and degree of deviation." [50]

The methods and specific conclusions reached about
each of the litigation situations were described in subsequent articles. In the final article the general inferences to
be drawn from the specific investigations of each of the
three cases were summarized. Two of the conclusions are
of particular importance. One is that the study confirmed
the hypothesis verification or invalidation of which had
been its purpose. Thus,

> in all three cases the second deviational transaction consisted
> of the dishonor of a check payable to a third person; in all, the
> comparable sequences were the same; and in all, the degrees of
> deviation were the same. In the *Callaham* case the first devia-
> tional transaction grossly deviated from its comparable se-
> quence and the judgment was for the customer; in the *Delano*
> and *Goldstein* cases the deviation of the first transaction was
> slight and the judgment was for the bank. . . . The study
> probably justifies the inference of a causal relation between
> three of the factors in a litigation-situation, viz., the behavior
> of the litigants, the institutional patterns of the jurisdiction,
> and the decision, which may be expressed in terms of the
> degree by which the behavior of the litigants deviates from
> the comparable sequences.[51]

The second conclusion concerned the theory of decision-
making evolved in light of these correlations. It is, in
essence, that the standard in fact used by the court is the
degree of deviation of the litigants from institutionalized

---

[50] *Ibid.*, pp. 559, 575.

[51] Moore and Sussman, "Legal and Institutional Methods Applied
to the Debiting of Direct Discounts—VI. The Decisions, the Institutions, and the Degree of Deviation," *Yale L. J.*, XL (1931), pp. 1249–
1250.

patterns of behavior. For example, in all three cases gross deviations from institutional patterns were "not accorded by the court a legal consequence conforming to the institutional consequence which would have followed had the standard device been used." In each of the three cases, also, slight deviations from institutional patterns were "accorded a legal consequence conforming to the institutional consequence which would have followed had the standard device been used." [52]

Criticisms: Traditional and Behavioral

The efforts of the realists to make the study of law more scientific have been subject to two very different kinds of criticisms. The first appeared mainly in the 1920's and 1930's. The basic form which it took is that the realists were too scientific, or "scientistic." The second criticism has only developed in the last decade. Its basic thrust is that the realists were not scientific enough. Both of the criticisms raise some issues which are beyond the scope of this chapter. Yet each must be briefly examined if the utility of the approaches outlined in the foregoing pages is to be evaluated.

In 1941 Moses Aronson advanced a typical example of the first kind of criticism. In a review of tendencies in American jurisprudence, he wrote that

realism represents a familiar stage in the development of jurisprudence which other disciplines have also traversed. It is the stage which in the history of thought is known as positivism . . . the essence of positivism consists in the belief that science alone is rational, and that in the application of the scientific

---

[52] *Ibid.*

technique lies the hope for the salvation of humanity. . . .
Realism is still in the early stages of that infantile disease of
adjustment to the scientific virus which all the disciplines,
physical as well as social, have experienced and outgrown.[53]

In other words, the realists placed too much faith in
science. Other critics elaborated upon this theme by arguing that the exponents of realism assumed "the infallibility of scientific methods," threatened "to sell the law
'down the river' to the social scientist," and ignored the
"wrangles, conflicts and confusions" in the disciplines the
concepts of which would be applied to law.[54] Still other
jurists pointed out that the enthusiasm of the realists for
science led to the error of defining law as a prediction
rather than a system of norms.[55]

From the perspective of the present the most notable
feature of this early reaction is its superficiality. The criticisms are not, to be sure, without their grain of truth.
Some realists did tend to ignore the problem which is
posed by disagreement among social scientists. Others did
confuse scientific rules *about* law with prescriptive rules *of*
law.[56] Neither of these criticisms is, however, a *fatal* obsta-

[53] Aronson, "Tendencies in American Jurisprudence," *U. Toronto
L. J.,* IV (1941), 102–103.

[54] Walter B. Kennedy, "The New Deal in the Law," *U.S. L. Rev.,*
XLVIII (1934), 63; Kennedy, "More Functional Nonsense—A
Reply to Felix S. Cohen," *Fordham L. Rev.,* VI (1937), 88.

[55] See Morris R. Cohen, *Law and the Social Order: Essays in Legal
Philosophy* (New York: Harcourt, Brace, 1933), p. 205.

[56] See Bingham, "What Is the Law?" *Mich. L. Rev.,* XI (1912), 22;
Frank, *Law and the Modern Mind,* pp. 46–52; Max Radin, Review
of *The Paradoxes of Legal Science,* by Benjamin N. Cardozo, *Calif.
L. Rev.,* XVII (1928), 75; James Allen (ed.), *Democracy and Fi-
nance: The Addresses and Public Statements of William O. Douglas*
(New Haven: Yale University Press, 1940); and Walter Wheeler

cle to the approaches which the realists urged for making predictions *more* reliable. Neither is *logically* inconsistent with the statement that these approaches can be useful for predictive purposes. In 1940 Llewellyn described the reaction to Jerome Frank's work as "a typical example of the cross-purposing of words in the Non-Joinder of Issues in Jurisprudence." [57] Much the same could be said of the early reaction to the efforts of the realists to devise better methods for predicting decisions.

The criticisms developed in the last ten years, especially by the judicial behavioralists, are a different kettle of fish. Their evaluation of the contribution of the realists has been more sympathetic. The criticisms of the behavioralists have also been more perceptive. The reaction of Glendon Schubert is a useful case in point. He is probably the most influential theoretician of judicial behavioralism. He has not denied the significance of the realists' endeavors. According to Schubert, they "raised important questions about judicial behavior." Also, they shifted "attention away from the manifest content of judicial opinions, and away from a concern for logical consistency among sets of legal norms. A knowledge of what judges do and say is important, but it is by no means enough; a realistic understanding of judicial decision-making demands that the acts of judges be examined like any other forms of social behavior." Finally, the realists reoriented "legal study in the spirit of the modern temper," and redefined

---

Cook, "The Logical and Legal Basis of the Conflict of Laws," *Yale L. J.*, XXXIII (1924), 476. The distinction between rules *about* law and rules *of* law was drawn, most of the time, by Llewellyn. See Llewellyn, *Jurisprudence*, pp. 56, 142, and Llewellyn, *The Bramble Bush*, p. 9.

[57] *Jurisprudence*, p. 150.

"its role as that of an applied social science." [58] Nonetheless, Schubert has been critical of the efforts of the advocates of "realistic jurisprudence" to develop a scientific approach to law.

The essence of his critique is that the achievements of the realists did not measure up to their pretensions. In a recent article, for example, he has argued that "legal research remains today at the primitive level of development, as a science, that generally characterized political science one or two generations ago. By and large, legal method is no more in phase with modern science than it was in the days of Austin . . . all of the talk about 'legal science' and computerized methods of retrieving legal data . . . notwithstanding." The legal realists are no exception, on the whole, to this generalization.

It might be objected that the legal realists of the 1920's and 1930's were—as many of them claimed to be—legal scientists; but such an objection misconceives both the requirements of science and the accomplishments of the realists. Science requires both theoretical models from which operationalized hypotheses can be inferred and methods for testing such hypotheses with data derived from empirical observations. The realists, with rare exceptions . . . had neither theory nor methods. . . . Lacking the technical training to do scientific research, they rarely followed through with the substantive findings to confirm (or refute) their often provocative, and sometimes brilliant, cues and hunches. Most of their work remained at the verbal level, in perfect harmony with the traditions of the profession of which they were a part.[59]

[58] Glendon Schubert (ed.), *Judicial Behavior: A Reader in Theory and Research* (Chicago: Rand McNally, 1964), pp. 2, 548–549, 549.

[59] Schubert, "The Future of Public Law," *Geo. Wash. L. Rev.,* XXXIV (1966), pp. 600, 600–601.

According to Schubert, thus, the legal realists went astray in at least two basic respects. In the first place, they failed to formulate theoretical models from which operationalized hypotheses can be inferred. In the second place, they did not devise methods for testing such hypotheses with data derived from empirical observations. The first charge is not wholly valid, insofar as the prediction of decisions is concerned. The legal realists did develop theoretical models from which operationalized hypotheses *can* be inferred. Some of the approaches examined in the foregoing pages are examples. Indeed, the behavioristic model of Oliphant is very similar to the "fact-model" of two distinguished behavioralists, Fred Kort and Reed Lawlor.[60] Each has attempted to correlate decisions with a very wide range of different possible combinations of factual situations. The purpose has been to indicate what combination of facts has in the past been associated with specific decisions, in order to provide a valid basis for prediction of future decisions. Such an approach is very similar to that of Oliphant.

It could be argued, of course, that the approaches of Rodell, Llewellyn, and Cohen are not fully developed. They do not specify *how* the personal predilections, values, and attitudes of the judge are to be either classified, measured, or tested empirically. In these respects far too much is left to the intuition of the skilled practitioner.[61] In these ways, too, the approach of the realists

[60] See Schubert (ed.), *Judicial Behavior,* pp. 477–505, and Schubert (ed.), *Judicial Decision-Making* (Glencoe, Ill.: Free Press, 1963), pp. 133–201.

[61] This criticism is advanced by Schubert against the approach of Fred Rodell. See *Judicial Behavior,* pp. 551–552. According to Schubert, "There would be little in the *substance* of Rodell's remarks to distinguish him from the judicial behavioralists with whom he ap-

does not go beyond, if it equals, the framework developed by Charles Grove Haines in 1922.[62] He provided at least a classification of the kinds of factors which influence judicial decisions, and by utilization of which empirical investigations could proceed. It is one thing to say, however, that some of the legal realists did not produce "models" for the prediction of decisions. It is another thing to contend that some of these models were not fully developed.

Schubert's second criticism has a higher degree of validity. It indicates the basic weakness in the approaches of the realists. They did not lack theoretical models from which operationalized hypotheses *could* have been inferred. The approaches urged by Llewellyn (in his articles of the 1930's) and Cohen are examples. Each of these men provided a framework in terms of which significant empirical investigations could have been undertaken. Indeed,

---

pears to find himself in fundamental disagreement. They too have debunked legal principles as factors controlling decisions; it is they, rather than he, who have attempted to undertake systematic investigations of the effect of background characteristics upon decisions. They also affirm the experimental method and the testing of hypotheses by making explicit predictions. . . . Therefore, not only would judicial behavioralists agree with the substance of most of Rodell's remarks; they would also have made precisely the same mistake in attempting to predict individual voting in *Baker*." The difference is that, for the behavioralists, "the question of methodology is not sublimated to the intuitional level; on the contrary, it is a critical consideration in any research design." *Ibid.*, p. 554.

[62] See Haines, "General Observations on the Effects of Personal, Political, and Economic Influences in the Decisions of Judges," *Ill. L. Rev.*, XVII (1922), 96. Haines classified the factors which are likely to influence judicial decisions into two basic types. One consists of remote or indirect influences, such as general and legal education, family and personal associations, wealth, and social position. The other consists of direct influences, such as legal-political experiences, political affiliations and temperament, and intellectual or temperamental traits.

the similarity between some of the cues which were suggested for this purpose and the approaches of the judicial behavioralists is striking. Nonetheless, most of the realists did not infer the kinds of hypotheses which are necessary. Certainly they infrequently developed methods for testing such hypotheses with data derived from empirical observations.

Llewellyn is a case in point. The model of legal science which he formulated in his early books and articles certainly provided a framework from which operationalized hypotheses could have been inferred and tested. To the best of my knowledge, however, the inferences were not drawn and the testing was not done. The formulation and verification of "real" rules remained an aspiration rather than a reality. Also, in *The Common Law Tradition* Llewellyn made little attempt to test empirically how the relative impact of any of his fourteen "steadying" factors could be ascertained. As Theodore Becker has pointed out,

Unfortunately . . . Professor Llewellyn jumps off in midstream and neglects to extrapolate upon the nature of the interrelationship between these factors, the extent and nature of overlap, the probable varying degrees of importance between the elements, as well as many other problems raised by a mere listing. Bare mention and a brief description of each element is deemed to be sufficient.[63]

[63] Theodore L. Becker, *Political Behavioralism and Modern Jurisprudence: A Working Theory and Study in Judicial Decision-Making* (Chicago: Rand McNally, 1964), pp. 63–64. Becker feels, however, that Llewellyn's list "is probably the most elaborate analysis of the nature of those discrete elements that substantially contribute to a constraint upon a judge (as contrasted with all other types of policy makers) in arriving at a choice between alternatives." *Ibid.*

Equally important, Llewellyn failed to indicate *how* the relative impact of the fourteen different factors could be assessed, and developed for predictive purposes. If these fourteen factors are the crucial determinants of judicial regularity, then they should provide a basis for prediction of decisions. Without knowing how to discover which is most important under what circumstances, their utility for this purpose is very limited.

What is true of Llewellyn is true, moreover, of Cohen and Oliphant. The models which each of them developed provided a base from which operationalized hypotheses could have been inferred and tested. Yet, the inferences were rarely drawn and the testings were seldom made. The same cannot be said, however, of Moore. He not only developed a theoretical model, but he also inferred hypotheses from it and devised methods for testing their validity. This very fact distinguishes his work from that of the other realists, as Moore himself was well-aware. Indeed, he once criticized "the signal failure of that group of brilliant intuitionists [the legal realists and their predecessors] who have focussed so long on current economic theories and social philosophies to do more than point out over and over again the very great probability of the very great significance of these factors." [64] In light of this, it is also not surprising to find that for Schubert,

Moore and Sussman . . . focus attention upon the critical test for any science; its capacity to increase the accuracy of predictions of future behavior, whether of particles or of people. Although they wrote over three decades ago, and Underhill Moore is considered to have been a leading realist, this article

[64] Moore and Sussman, "Legal and Institutional Methods Applied to the Debiting of Direct Discounts—II. Institutional Method," *Yale L. J.*, XL (1931), 563.

is . . . patently behavioral . . . it was Moore's fortune to be at least a quarter of a century ahead of his time, and to be writing for the wrong profession to boot.[65]

The major gap in the work of the realists is, thus, the failure to develop and to test empirically explanatory and predictive hypotheses about judicial behavior. They were not, to be sure, idle theorists who fiddled while Rome burned. The exponents of "realistic jurisprudence" did a considerable amount of research into various areas of law. The purpose of their research was not, however, to classify and to test empirically the various factors which may have determined specific decisions. In general, it was oriented along *more* traditional lines. Its purpose was to indicate, on the basis of analysis of judicial opinions, the "real" as distinct from "paper" rules which courts are in fact applying. The goal was to indicate what in this sense courts are actually doing, measured by the standards of their decisions rather than stated or formalized rules. More than this is required, however, if a valid explanatory theory is to be developed. Then the various factors which may be connected with judicial decisions must be classified, correlated, and tested. Only then will empirically valid knowledge of the relative weight to be attached to potentially influential factors be available.

Judicial Behavioralism and the Prediction of Decisions

The inevitable question to be asked in this context is whether and to what extent the judicial behavioralists have filled the gap left by the realists. An answer to this question is desirable for a number of reasons. In the first place, the advocates of behavioralism share the rule-

[65] Schubert (ed.), *Judicial Behavior*, p. 13.

skepticism of the legal realists. In the second place, the desire to study scientifically the decisions of judges is the *raison d'être* of the new movement. As Schubert has pointed out, it "represents the fusion of theories and methods developed in the various social sciences . . . in order to attempt to study scientifically how and why judges make the decisions that they do." [66] In the third place, this attempt constitutes the most significant effort of its kind by American scholars in the postwar era. Finally, the prediction of decisions has been of central concern to the exponents of the new approach.

Unfortunately, it is impossible in this book to develop a comprehensive answer to the question posed in the preceding paragraph. Schubert wrote in 1966 that "the behavioral approach to the field is scarcely a decade old." [67] In this relatively short span of time, however, the new movement has produced a voluminous literature. It is far too vast to examine systematically here. Nonetheless, a brief summary of the results of ten years of behaviorally oriented research is possible.

At the outset, a generally accepted and empirically confirmed theory by means of which judicial decisions can be *explained* has not yet emerged.[68] In this respect the gap left by the realists still remains to be filled. In other respects, however, the behavioralists have made signal advances. According to Schubert,

The specific accomplishments during the first decade related primarily to systematic examinations of judicial voting rec-

[66] *Ibid.,* p. 3.

[67] Schubert, "The Future of Public Law," *Geo. Wash. L. Rev.,* XXXIV (1966), 611.

[68] For a vigorous development of this point, see Becker, *Political Behaviorialism,* pp. 7–39.

ords, correlating such voting data with variables representing the political and economic attitudes of individual judges; their ethnic, socio-economic, and political background characteristics; the differentiation of subsets of judges (in appellate courts) into cohesive blocs; and leadership, influence, and bargaining processes in courts conceptualized as small groups.[69]

The accomplishments of the behavioralists also include the development and, in some instances, the application of useful methods for the prediction of decisions. No doubt, as of now most of the efforts have yielded only "postdictions." Still, it is important to remember that "if a method cannot postdict reasonably well, it is unlikely to predict reasonably well." Moreover, the percentage of successful postdictions has ranged significantly beyond mere chance. At the very least the conclusion is justified that "the use of quantitative prediction of court cases *plus* traditional prediction techniques is probably better than the use of the latter alone." [70] Precisely how much better is a question which only future research can answer. All in all, however, the judicial behavioralists seem to have advanced the cause of scientific progress beyond the point reached by the realists.

No simple explanation can be given of the failure of the realist movement to develop more in the directions taken

[69] Schubert, *Judicial Policy-Making: The Political Role of the Courts* (Chicago: Scott, Foresman, 1966), pp. 164–165.

[70] Stuart Nagel, "Predicting Court Cases Quantitatively," *Mich. L. Rev.*, LXIII (1965), 1422. For illustrations, see Schubert (ed.), *Judicial Decision-Making*, pp. 111–120, and Schubert (ed.), *Judicial Behavior*, pp. 433–588. For an interesting series of comments on the predictive efforts of the judicial behavioralists, see the articles in "A Symposium: Social Science Approaches to the Judicial Process," *Harv. L. Rev.*, LXXIX (1966), 1551.

by judicial behavioralism. The course of history, however, provided the behavioralists with at least two advantages not available to the realists. The first is the existence of a tradition of skepticism toward the impact of established rules. This tradition was the creation, in large part, of the legal realists. Its development, though, consumed their energies to a degree which was not necessary for the judicial behavioralists. The latter thus had an opportunity to explore the implications of this skepticism for the scientific study of law which was not present for the realists. The second advantage is the emergence of political behavioralism. This antedated judicial behavioralism and no doubt facilitated its development. As Schubert has pointed out,

Perhaps the major difference, which best explains why judicial behavioralism emerged among political scientists in the mid-fifties instead of among law professors in the twenties, is that the time was out of joint for the legal realists, who were not exposed to an influence comparable to the current of political behavioralism which political scientists might reject but could not ignore, during the past two decades.[71]

Two other factors cannot be ignored in any attempt to explain the somewhat different courses taken by legal realism and judicial behavioralism. One is that the behavioralists have been social scientists by profession, while most of the realists were lawyers. For this reason it was probably much easier for the former than the latter to exploit in practice the concepts and methods of the social sciences. The other factor is that the realists did not have as exclu-

[71] Schubert (ed.), *Judicial Behavior,* p. 3. For a study of the relationship between judicial behavioralism and legal realism, see David Ingersoll, "Karl Llewellyn, American Legal Realism, and Contemporary Legal Behavioralism," *Ethics,* LXXVI (1966), 253.

sive an interest in the scientific study of judicial decisions as do the behavioralists. The appeal for a value-free science of law can, to be sure, be found in the literature of the exponents of "realism." The appeal never submerged, however, their very keen interest in how decisions ought to be reached and justified. This interest may be a good thing; but it no doubt tended to divert energies from problems of greatest concern for the sociology of law.

The Contribution of the Realists

If it is true to say that, from a scientific point of view, the judicial behavioralists have progressed beyond the stage reached by the realists, then what is the contribution of the latter? To begin with, the exponents of "realistic jurisprudence" created a mood which probably facilitated the emergence of more scientific techniques. Judicial behavioralism might have developed without legal realism. The current of political behavioralism might have been in isolation enough to create it. The temper which the legal realists evolved, however, made the transition easier. They discredited legal formalism; they pointed out the need to search for the "something else" which is, in Llewellyn's words, "at work, helping all doctrine along"; they indicated the relevance of extralegal factors such as socioeconomic background to judicial decision-making; and they appealed for exploitation of the concepts and methods of the social sciences as aids in prediction. Still further, the realists formulated predictive models which still may be useful for sociologists of law. The best examples are the approaches urged by Oliphant and Moore, and by Llewellyn in his articles of the 1930's. Finally, the approaches of the other realists and the elder Llewellyn retain a certain practical utility which cannot be ignored. To suggest that the legal analyst should search out the personal predilections of the judge may not be the epitome of scientific sophistication. The same can be said of the proposal to examine judicial opinions for what they reveal about the values or attitudes of the judge. Yet, both of these cues are very useful for the average lawyer. They will help him in predicting how an actual court will react to his specific case. Reed Lawlor has written that

in the future, lawyers who consider the interest of their clients paramount will not hesitate to employ computers to aid them in solving the problems of their clients to the extent that computer techniques are applicable at the time. And judges who are called upon to decide important cases may raise their eyebrows at attorneys who do not make use of computer facilities in their review and analysis of the law.[72]

The point is that this future is still rather distant. Until it arrives, the average lawyer must do the best he can with tools which he understands and can use effectively. For this purpose the cues suggested by Llewellyn and Rodell are of great utility.

It could be argued, of course, that the average lawyer has long been aware of this. It could be contended, further, that his awareness antedated the realist movement. A generation of legal realists, it might be maintained, was not necessary to show the practicing lawyer the need to take into account personal predilections and individual attitudes. There is truth in such arguments. In a revealing passage, written in 1940, Llewellyn almost admitted as much. He asserted, at least, that

[72] "Stare Decisis and Electronic Computers," in Schubert (ed.), *Judicial Behavior*, p. 505.

indeed it is a fair generalization that almost nothing the newer Jurisprudence has yet found, and little that it seems likely to find within the next few decades, will prove in any manner *new*, to the *best* lawyers. It will be, as it has been, a putting together of different pieces of what the *best* lawyers know—different pieces which even the best lawyers do not commonly put together and *compare*—so as to make the resulting Whole give other lawyers, and especially new lawyers, a clearer and more usable picture of how the various crafts of the lawyer are best carried on.[73]

This interpretation of the realist movement is not, to be sure, wholly correct. Some of the recommendations of the "newer jurisprudence" for the prediction of decisions are new. The models developed by Oliphant, Moore, Cohen, and the younger Llewellyn constitute a rather sharp break with tradition. The application of these new methods requires the utilization of tools and concepts which are not the stock-in-trade of the lawyers' craft. In this respect the approaches represent a vision of the future which is more than a summary and comparison of what the best lawyers know. Nonetheless, the cues urged by many of the realists are justly subject to Llewellyn's interpretation.

To say this is not to minimize the contribution of even these realists. What is not new to the best lawyers may be new to other lawyers. Also, it is not unimportant to summarize and compare what the best lawyers know but do not summarize and compare. Judicial decisions can become more predictable if what is known to the best lawyers is articulated, systematized, and compared. The point of emphasis is simply that the plea for such an approach means that the actual break of many of the realists with

[73] Llewellyn, *Jurisprudence*, pp. 149–150.

tradition is less revolutionary than it has often seemed, either to them or their critics.[74]

[74] Llewellyn's reaction to the predictive efforts of Herman Oliphant and Underhill Moore is an interesting sign of this fact. His evaluation of their work was far from negative, but it reveals a rather different and more traditional perspective. Thus in 1931 Llewellyn wrote that "what one has gained by the new formulation, if it proves significant, seems to me to be a tool for clarifying the situation and the purposes; a means of bringing a hidden factor, perhaps *the* hidden factor in past uncertainty, into view; perhaps also a new insight into wise objectives, and so a key for reform." In 1940 Llewellyn wrote that the "behaviorist" may "gather twenty or two hundred cases on some situation, and try to play facts and issue straight against result. But if he succeeds, what he will bring out will be a *new and better rule or principle of case-law:* 'The factor which the judges have been feeling for, and responding to, in this situation, has not yet been clearly articulated in the rules in vogue. Here it is. It focuses the real issue; it lines up the cases; stating it this way helps you predict more accurately what will happen; it helps a judge see more clearly what to do, and why. It is *the true rule* of the situation.'" In the same year Llewellyn specifically evaluated the achievements of Moore and Oliphant in this fashion: "Moore had attempted study of the background of people's practices as a guide to decision of cases; the essential result on our question of certainty is that the technique attempted proves unworkable for the run of cases. Oliphant had attempted to correlate facts, issue, and results of cases independently of the reasoning of the opinions; the essential result from his work is that—as case-law history shows—this is frequently, but not always, an excellent road out of confusion, but that its effect is to give us new and clearer doctrine, to be dealt with still along the familiar case-law lines. And that on the grand scale of statistics, the method is impracticable." Llewellyn, *Jurisprudence,* pp. 60 (n. 46), 158, 159. This appraisal should be contrasted with that of Schubert, which is quoted in the text, *supra,* pp. 174–175.

V

Judicial Methodology

The realist movement has seldom been free from controversy. Nothing has engendered as much heat as the claim, and the denial, that the advocates of "realistic jurisprudence" were indifferent to "ought" questions. On the one hand, a generation of critics has identified the legal realists with the view that "there are not good decisions and bad decisions. There are just decisions. If goodness must be mentioned at all, then it is equivalent to what 'is' in law today." The charge has been common that "the Realists, by their own preference, bypassed the 'ought' of law as irrelevant to legal science"; ignored the problem of how judges "ought to decide to give effect to the purposes of the legal order"; and "continued, and even . . . reinforced, the positivistic bent which has restrained legal thinking in this country now for nearly a century." On the other hand, some jurists have vigorously rejected such criticisms. The essence of their response has been that

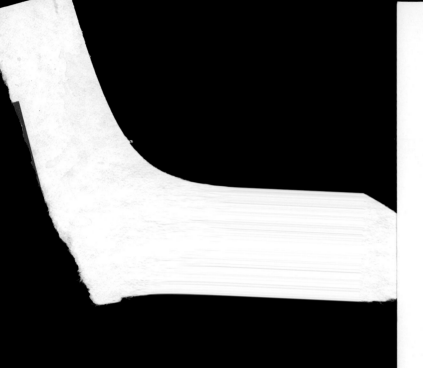

the image of the critics is of "a bogus American legal realism." [1]

How valid is this response? What norms, if any, did the realists recommend for decisions? How do these principles differ from those urged by the predecessors of "realistic jurisprudence"? What objections can be raised against the point of view of the realists? What contribution have they made? The purpose of this chapter is to answer these questions. Only then can the full dimensions of the realist movement be adequately understood.

Different Kinds of Normative Problems

It is necessary, at the outset, to distinguish between two basic forms of thought about what law ought to be. One is instrumental in character. Its purpose is to prescribe norms for procedures or ways of reaching and justifying decisions. The other is substantive. Normative thought in this second sense can again be of two types. One is analysis of the specific decisions which courts should reach. The other is prescription of general principles or theories by means of which specific decisions ought to be reached. It is this last kind of thought about what law ought to be which has traditionally preoccupied legal philosophers.

[1] Francis J. Lucey, "Natural Law and American Legal Realism: Their Respective Contributions to a Theory of Law in a Democratic Society," *Geo. L. J.,* XXX (1942), 506; Jerome Hall, "The Present Position of Jurisprudence in the United States," *Va. L. Rev.,* XLIV (1958), 323; Roscoe Pound, "Jurisprudence," *Encyclopedia of the Social Sciences,* VIII (1932), 485; Lon L. Fuller, *The Law in Quest of Itself* (Boston: Beacon Press, 1940), p. 61; Myres S. McDougal, "Fuller v. The American Legal Realists: An Intervention," *Yale L. J.,* L (1941), 834. Also, see Edwin N. Garlan, *Legal Realism and Justice* (New York: Columbia University Press, 1941), and Harry W. Jones, "Law and Morality in the Perspective of Legal Realism," *Colum. L. Rev.,* LXI (1961), 799.

On the basis of these distinctions it cannot be said that the realists were completely indifferent to "ought" questions about law. The late Edwin W. Patterson has stated, for example, that "having known personally nearly all of those who were . . . realists, the present writer can say that he has not known any group of men who were more earnestly concerned than they were for the discovery of the true and the good and for the development of means of promoting ultimately the welfare of their fellow men."[2] One sign of this concern is the effort of the legal realists to promote liberal statutes and judicial decisions. As Myres McDougal has pointed out, they

have been hard at work for the achievement of certain humanitarian and democratic ideals of intermediate or relatively low level abstraction, which most of us share today: civil liberties, social security, more goods to more people, healthful housing, conservation and full utilization of resources, collective bargaining, farm security, socialized medicine . . . better administration of justice, and so on.[3]

In addition to this, some of the legal realists were vitally interested in the prescription of certain instrumental norms. They were most anxious to revise traditional methods for reaching and justifying decisions. Indeed, the revisions which they recommended constitute one of their major contributions to American jurisprudence.

At the same time, the charge that the exponents of "realism" were indifferent to "ought" questions about law has a degree of validity. In the first place, the interest in such questions *expressed in their published writings* is not as

[2] *Jurisprudence: Men and Ideas of the Law* (Brooklyn: Foundation Press, 1953), p. 552.
[3] McDougal, *op. cit.*, pp. 835–836.

great as their interest in other legal problems. For this reason the interpretation of the realist movement advanced in this chapter is of necessity based upon a much smaller sampling of literature than is the case in other chapters. In the second place, the vast majority of realists were not themselves concerned with the prescription of general norms or principles by means of which specific decisions ought to be reached. Felix Cohen is, it is true, a notable exception to this generalization. The basic purpose of his first book was to formulate an ethical standard of legal criticism.[4] His task was to define the nature of the good and to indicate how it can be achieved through law. In these respects, however, his work differs sharply from that of the other realists.

To be sure, some of the major advocates of "realism" did not deny the importance of developing values or criteria by means of which decisions ought to be reached. Thus in his pioneering "call" for a "realistic jurisprudence" Llewellyn wrote that "there . . . remains, the inquiry into the purpose of what courts are doing, the criticism in terms of searching out purposes and criticising means. Here value judgments reenter the picture, and should." [5] One year later Jerome Frank asserted that "what the law ought to be constitutes, rightfully, no small part of the thinking of lawyers and judges. Such thinking should not be diminished, but augmented." [6] At the same time Llewellyn *stressed* the "temporary" character of the realists'

[4] See Felix S. Cohen, *Ethical Systems and Legal Ideals: An Essay on the Foundations of Legal Criticism* (Ithaca, N.Y.: Cornell University Press, 1933).

[5] "A Realistic Jurisprudence—The Next Step," *Colum. L. Rev.*, XXX (1930), 449.

[6] Frank, *Law and the Modern Mind* (Garden City, N.Y.: Doubleday, 1963), p. 181.

"divorce of Is and Ought for purposes of study." "To men who begin with a suspicion that change is needed, a permanent divorce would be impossible." [7] Four years later he wrote that "the fact is that any would-be innovator, or changer of things-as-they-are-at-the-moment, is of necessity interested in ideals and in ethical evaluations. In my own case, I think that demonstrable in every paper or book published, at least since 1925." [8] In 1940 he criticized the predictive theory of law precisely because it ignores the need to focus upon the "just" solution of cases. He went on to compliment Roscoe Pound for his consistent awareness of this fact.

For to Pound the heart and core of Jurisprudence is what the heart and core of Jurisprudence ought to be to any scholar: to wit, right guidance to the judge—or to the legislator—or to the administrator. And I for one am ready to do open penance for any part I may have played in giving occasion for the feeling that modern Jurisprudes or any of them had ever lost sight of this. I do not think any of them ever has. They seem to me to be singularly affected, one and all, with zeal for justice, and with zeal for improving the *legal* techniques for doing the law's business. But it is certainly in large part the result of Pound's indefatigable reaffirmance of the basic truth about the heart of Jurisprudence that the other moderns are taking pains these days to make sure that they get and keep these interests of theirs from being overlooked or misconceived.[9]

Moreover, it is precisely because of this recognition of the importance of "ought" questions of the substantive

[7] *Jurisprudence: Realism in Theory and Practice* (Chicago: University of Chicago Press, 1962), pp. 55, 56.

[8] Llewellyn, "On What Is Wrong with So-Called Legal Education," *Colum. L. Rev.,* XXXV (1935), 663, n. 5.

[9] Llewellyn, *Jurisprudence,* pp. 142, 152–153.

type that in 1939 Llewellyn appealed for the development of a *"lawyer's* Natural Law." In the last twenty years American jurisprudence has been characterized by the cry for a consciously value-oriented approach to the study of law. The need for such an approach was pointed out by Llewellyn before the last World War, for some of the same reasons that have influenced juristic developments in the past two decades. He was, it is true, critical of formulations of natural law which are "so broad as to require perplexing labor to give it any application concrete enough to be of service in practical legal work." Still, he vigorously asserted the need for what he called *"lawyer's* Natural Law," or "Natural Law in a *lawyer's* sense." This is the attempt "to bring the philosopher's Natural Law to bear in lawyerlike actual regulation of the multiple specific problems of human conduct." Such a *"lawyer's* Natural Law" is essential if the role of the judge is to be properly executed. The rules of this natural law "sit at the judge's side, and counsel steadily that all leeway properly entrusted to case-law judges be utilized to correct any incorrect positive rule-formulation so that it may more closely fit *the* correct rule-formulation." Thus "it is the aim and function of such Natural Law to be . . . drawn upon continually as a source of positive law." Finally, Llewellyn insisted that a lawyer's Natural Law

has a peculiarly fertile field wherever the precepts and concepts of positive law are malleable, are not caught into unchangeable authoritative words, and are subjected by the going tradition itself to constant reexamination and reformulation. It is thus peculiarly at home, it is indeed peculiarly needed, in a case-law system; for a case-law system places responsibility for day to day *reformulation* of rule and principle upon the bench. In a case-law system the verbal garb of rules is not fixed, and rephrasing to constantly and more closely approach a *righter* phrasing is not only proper, but is a bounden duty of scholar and judge.

For this reason he concluded that "it should occasion mild wonderment to find any Natural Law man and any so-called realist engaged in pegging brickbats at each other." [10]

It cannot be said, then, that the realists denied the importance of prescribing values or criteria in terms of which decisions should be reached. Nonetheless, most of them were not interested in this kind of prescriptive inquiry. As legal scholars, they were concerned with various other problems. One was the methods which courts should use in reaching and justifying decisions. The specific proposals which emerged from this interest must now be examined.

Realist Norms for Reaching Decisions

In 1940 Llewellyn wrote that "what the newer jurisprudes are worrying over is how to find a better, a more effective, a more reliable machinery for directing judges and other officials than the older rationale and doctrine have managed to give us." [11] One of the most basic reasons for the "worrying" was dissatisfaction with the traditional method by means of which, it has been felt, decisions ought to be reached. The essence of this method is the view that judges ought to reach the decision which is required by the application of established rules to the facts. The realists did not reject completely this basic article in the credo of the older "rationale and doctrine." In the first place, they were generally agreed that examina-

---

[10] *Ibid.*, pp. 111, 112, 113, 114, 115.   [11] *Ibid.*, p. 131.

tion of established rules or their application to concrete cases may provide the judge with valuable practical information. Prior cases

are not harmonious; in them can be found authority for both sides of almost any question. But they are instructive: they permit of a vast amount of comparison; they present material for testing a proposed rule by applying it to a great variety of cases . . . they supply arguments of learned and experienced men on both sides of vast numbers of questions. Surely only a vicious or a lazy judge would avoid such a field of instruction. . . . A judge who is ready to decide what is justice and for the public weal without any knowledge of history and precedent is an egotist and an ignoramus.[12]

In the second place, analysis of established rules can function as a desirable restraint.[13] The judge may wish to reach a decision for which no ground or authority can be found in prior rules. Under such circumstances the use of the traditional method should induce him to consider more carefully than he otherwise would whether his initial response is wise.

The theme of the legal realists is not, then, that courts ought to disregard established rules in the process of reaching decisions. The point which they wished to emphasize is, rather, that the consideration of such rules ought not to be the decisive method by which decisions are reached. Instead, it was felt that judges should consciously search *"within the limits laid down by precedent and statute"* for the decision which has the fairest, wisest, or most just outcome or result.[14] To define the method for

[12] Arthur L. Corbin, "The Law and the Judges," *Yale Review,* III (1914), 246–247.

[13] See Frank, *Law and the Modern Mind,* pp. 140–141.

[14] Llewellyn, *Jurisprudence,* p. 70.

decisions urged by the advocates of "realistic jurisprudence" in these terms is, to be sure, to give it the air of a truism. Who has ever denied that the judge should search for the just, wise, or fair decision? What jurist has recommended unjust, unwise, or unfair decisions? The answers to these questions are obvious. Nonetheless, the method urged by the realists is not a truism. It differs from that urged by traditional and, even, progressive legal theorists. Two of the differences are of special importance.

The first and most obvious difference is the more flexible attitude toward the use of established rules which is reflected in the realist method. The traditional point of view has been that judges should subordinate what they regard as the just, wise, or fair decision to that dictated by the application of antecedent rules to the facts. The rationale for this subordination has been varied. It has been justified as the indispensable means to achieve uniformity and predictability, to maintain equality before the law, to prevent arbitrary decisions, and to economize judicial labor. However the subordination is defended, the essential point urged is that judges should give first priority to the decision implied by established rules. According to the legal realists, however, the highest value should be given to the decision the outcome or result of which is pragmatically best.

Moreover, the attitude toward pre-existing rules advocated by the realists is more flexible than that urged even by their progressive predecessors. Pound and Cardozo once more provide useful examples of this point. Both of these distinguished jurists were, it is true, critical of the rigidity of the traditional method. Thus in *The Nature of the Judicial Process* Cardozo asserted that "the rule of adherence to precedent. . . . ought to be in some degree relaxed."

In its place he recommended what he called the method of sociology. By this he meant that the test for the use of a particular rule ought to be its "social value," the extent to which it contributes to "the welfare of society." In his mind, "not the origin, but the goal, is the main thing. . . . The teleological conception of his function must be ever in the judge's mind." [15] A somewhat similar view was advocated by Pound. In 1912 he listed as one of the six planks in the platform of sociological jurisprudence that of "equitable application of law." By this he meant that the legal rule should be viewed as a general guide to the judge, but not the ultimate basis for his decision. "Within wide limits he should be free to deal with the individual case, so as to meet the demands of justice between the parties and accord with the general reason of ordinary men." [16]

Nonetheless, neither Pound nor Cardozo were *as* critical of the traditional method as the legal realists. Also, neither urged the same *degree* of flexibility in the use of established rules as did the advocates of "realistic jurisprudence." Thus for Pound "equitable application" should be the norm for decisions only in those areas of law which concern the moral phases of individual or corporate conduct.[17] With respect to business or property transactions mechanical application should be the rule. Cardozo took a somewhat different stand, yet one which is much more

[15] Cardozo, *The Nature of the Judicial Process* (New Haven: Yale University Press, 1921), pp. 150, 66, 102.

[16] Pound, "The Scope and Purpose of Sociological Jurisprudence," *Harv. L. Rev.*, XXV (1912), 515.

[17] For the development of this distinction, see Pound, *An Introduction to the Philosophy of Law* (rev. ed.; New Haven: Yale University Press, 1954), pp. 48–72.

traditional than that of the legal realists. The sentiments which he articulated in *The Nature of the Judicial Process* provide the proof of the validity of this interpretation. There he not only contended that "adherence to precedent should be the rule and not the exception," but enumerated various reasons for this conviction. The most important of them are that it "will not do to decide the same question one way between one set of litigants and the opposite way between another"; that litigants must "have faith in the even-handed administration of justice in the courts"; and that "the labor of judges would be increased almost to the breaking point if every past decision could be reopened in every case." [18]

The second major difference between the realist and traditional methods for reaching decisions is the much greater emphasis in the former upon the value of self-consciousness. In his celebrated essay on the realist movement, Cardozo wrote that "we are talking about ourselves and looking into ourselves, subjecting our minds and our souls to a process of analysis and introspection with a freedom and in a measure that to . . . our predecessors would have been futile and meaningless or even downright unbecoming." [19] It is difficult to tell how widespread this analysis and introspection was, but the theme that it is desirable was reiterated constantly by the realists. The language of Oliphant appears again and again. For him, what is most needed is "complete and constant self-consciousness as to methods of thought and procedure." Indeed, the problem of substituting "a more conscious and

[18] Cardozo, *Nature of the Judicial Process*, pp. 149, 33, 34, 149.

[19] *Selected Writings of Benjamin Nathan Cardozo,* ed. Margaret E. Hall (New York: Fallon Publications, 1947) , p. 8.

methodical process" for an "intuitive empiricism . . . transcends in importance all other problems of legal education." [20]

Rationale of the Realists' Point of View

The method by means of which the realists felt decisions ought to be reached does differ, then, from the traditional method. Also, to some degree it differs from that of the progressive predecessors of the exponents of "realistic jurisprudence." Unfortunately, it is difficult to generalize accurately about the causes of these differences. Nonetheless, two factors appear to have had the greatest influence on the largest number of realists. One is the radical character of their skepticism toward the utility of established rules as means to reach specific decisions. The other is the intensity of their commitment to the value of judicial awareness of this fact.

If the rule-skepticism of the legal realists is valid, then the application of established rules to the facts of most cases cannot determine what decision a judge ought to reach. Use of this traditional method does not provide answers to the questions which must be answered before the decision can be reached. It does not inform the judge *which* among a number of competing rules he should select as the major premise; *how* he should interpret the rule which he does select; or *whether* the facts of the instant case are similar enough to those of prior cases to warrant the same classification. If conflicting major premises are available, then "there is a choice in the case; a choice to be justified; a choice which *can* be justified only as a question of policy—for the authoritative tradition

[20] Oliphant, "A Return to Stare Decisis," *A. B. A. J.,* XIV (1928), 161, 160.

speaks with a forked tongue." If the available leeway in the interpretation of established rules is "nothing less than huge," then "only policy considerations and the facing of policy considerations can justify 'interpreting' (making, shaping, drawing conclusions from) the relevant body of precedent in one way or in another." If in most cases the facts can be classified in conflicting ways, then "the way is open" to search "for the wise or fair outcome." [21]

A number of factors explain the very high value which was attached to judicial recognition of *how* open this way is. One of the most important is an intense awareness of the imperative need for the flexible use of established legal doctrine. The intensity of the awareness stems, in large part, from a most vivid impression of the rapidity of socioeconomic change. As Llewellyn pointed out in 1931, one of the characteristic marks of the realist movement is "the conception of society in flux, and in flux typically faster than the law, so that the probability is always given that any portion of law needs reexamination to determine how far it fits the society it purports to serve." [22] To be sure, Llewellyn went on to claim that this conception is not a distinctive characteristic of the legal realists. The existence of socioeconomic change had been recognized long before the 1920's and 1930's. Nevertheless, it made a more profound impression upon the realists than most of their predecessors. The chief evidence of this is the *more* flexible attitude toward the use of established rules urged by the proponents of "realistic jurisprudence." Only men profoundly disturbed by the gap between old rules and the new needs of a changing society could have so urgently advocated such a revision of traditional judicial methodology.

[21] Llewellyn, *Jurisprudence*, pp. 70, 71, 71–72.   [22] *Ibid.*, p. 55.

A second factor is the wisespread conviction that the "fictitious sanctity" of *stare decisis,* the "emotional compulsion of antequated legal doctrine," has needlessly impeded the process of change.[23] The doctrine of contributory negligence, as explained by Leon Green, is an excellent example. According to him, its application has had some notoriously undesirable consequences. Yet this "drama of injustice" has "not been due to any desire on the part of the judges of our courts to do injustice." Rather, it stems from "the exaggerated emphasis given the language of overcautious judges who . . . were seeking simple formulas. . . . These . . . became crystalized into doctrines which have strangled the thought processes of their successors for so long that they have atrophied." [24] What better way to eliminate this "atrophy" than to make judges fully conscious of the freedom actually available to them?

A third factor is the belief that the failure to recognize fully the limitations of established rules has made judicial decision-making less rational than it could be. As Frank once wrote, the "pretense" or "self-delusion" that when judges "are creating they are borrowing, when they are making something new they are merely applying the commands given them . . . cannot but diminish their efficiency." [25] Green's research in the area of negligence law once more provides insight into how the efficiency of judges has been diminished. For example:

The courts have insisted upon converting all manner of problems into those of causation. . . . It has been made to serve

[23] McDougal, *op. cit.,* p. 834.

[24] Green, "Illinois Negligence Law," *Ill. L. Rev.,* XXXIX (1944), 43.

[25] Frank, *Law and the Modern Mind,* p. 130.

such perverted uses until its meaning has been completely obscured. . . . The no mans-land of *remoteness* or *proximateness*—as the taste of the court requires—has proved an almost insuperable barrier to an attack upon the real issue involved in cases of this type. . . . The inquiry in such cases is, what is the right or interest sought to be vindicated and is the rule invoked therefor designed to protect it? [26]

The reality is that decisions do favor some interests and disfavor others. To shut our eyes to this fact or to resort to "doubtful formulas" does not mean that "judgment is escaped nor that it is an intelligent and acceptable judgment. It merely means that we have been saved the painful process of rational judging." [27]

A final factor is the faith that awareness of the range of choice open to judges will make their decisions less arbitrary. As Frank has written:

Every judge . . . unavoidably has many idiosyncratic "learnings of the mind," uniquely personal prejudices, which may interfere with his fairness at a trial. . . . Frankly to recognize the existence of such prejudices is the part of wisdom. The conscientious judge will, as far as possible, make himself aware of his biases of this character, and, by that very self-knowledge, nullify their effect. . . . The concealment of the human element in the judicial process allows that element to operate in an exaggerated manner: the sunlight of awareness has an antiseptic effect on prejudices.[28]

[26] Green, *The Rationale of Proximate Cause* (Kansas City, Mo.: Vernon Law Book Co., 1927), p. 122.

[27] *Ibid.,* p. 198. For an outstanding analysis of the whole problem of proximate cause and Dean Green's analysis of it, see Walter Probert, "Causation in the Negligence Jargon: A Plea for Balanced 'Realism,'" *U. Fla. L. Rev.,* XVIII (1965), 369.

[28] *In Re J. P. Linahan,* 138 F. 2d 652–653 (1943).

Indeed, Frank was so convinced of the antiseptic effect of the sunlight of awareness that he advocated "something like psychoanalysis" for each judge.[29] Most of the legal realists did not go this far. They were generally agreed, however, that complete and constant self-consciousness is a very good thing.

The Conflict between Frank and Llewellyn

One of the key issues which emerges from the method for reaching decisions advocated by the realists can be stated in this form: should the judge give first priority to the decision the results of which are best for the individual litigants involved in the case? Or should he attach highest value to the decision which reflects a rule of law which is best for the community at large, even if the application of this rule in the instant case results in injustice for the individual litigants? In some cases, of course, this conflict does not arise. A decision can be reached which is both just to the parties in the case, and which can be justified by a rule of law which is wise for the community at large. In other cases, however, the conflict between the two different kinds of results is genuine. Unfortunately, it is impossible to say how most of the realists felt this dilemma ought to be resolved. Frequently the problem was simply left unresolved, by a refusal to claim more than that the justice or wisdom or fairness of the outcome should be the objective. Nonetheless, the realist movement did produce outstanding advocates of the two basic alternatives sketched above. They are Frank and Llewellyn. The views of each must be analyzed in some detail, if the contributions of the realists to the problem are to be fully understood.

[29] Frank, *Courts on Trial: Myth and Reality in American Justice* (Princeton: Princeton University Press, 1949), p. 250.

Perhaps the best single statement of the procedure which Frank advocated is in *Law and the Modern Mind.*

We want judges who, thus viewing and *employing all rules as fictions,* will appreciate that, as rules are fictions "intended for the sake of justice," it is not to be endured that they shall work injustice in any particular case, and must be moulded in furtherance of those equitable objects to promote which they were designed.[30]

Two reasons seem to account for the high value Frank attached to this procedure. The first is the fact that the objective of any legal system is justice; and that "to be practically meaningful, judicial justice must be justice not merely in the abstract but in the concrete, in the court's decisions of the numerous, particular, concrete cases." [31] The second is that the facts of cases are never sufficiently alike to be classified in the same way without serious injustice to the parties involved.

The law is not a machine and the judges not machine-tenders. There never was and there never will be a body of fixed and predetermined rules alike for all. The acts of human beings are not identical mathematical entities; the individual cannot be eliminated as, in algebraic equations, equal quantities on the two sides can be cancelled. Life rebels against all efforts at legal over-simplification. New cases ever continue to present novel aspects. To do justice, to make any legal system acceptable to society, the abstract preestablished rules have to be adapted and adjusted, the static formulas made alive.[32]

It must be emphasized in this context that for Frank it is the individual judge's sense of what is just for the partic-

---

[30] Frank, *Law and the Modern Mind,* p. 180.

[31] Frank, "Civil Law Influences on the Common Law—Some Reflections on 'Comparative' and 'Contrastive' Law," *U. Pa. L. Rev.,* CIV (1956), 910.

[32] Frank, *Law and the Modern Mind,* p. 129.

ular case which should determine the decision to be reached. In this respect his views are very similar to, and may have been influenced by, those of the theoreticians of the *Freirechtslehre* which arose in Europe at the turn of the century.[33] In any case, he expressed agreement with their emphasis upon "the 'subjective sense of justice inherent in the judge'" as the decisive factor. Also, Frank admitted that the dimensions of this "sense of justice" varied greatly. He recognized that its fuller *conscious* exploitation in reaching decisions would make law even more unpredictable than it now is. Nonetheless, he still defended the desirability of such a decision-reaching procedure. Indeed, in one place Frank contended that the best way to get "stereotyped results" from judges is "to elect or appoint to the bench the most narrow-minded and bigoted members of the community, selected for their adherence to certain relatively fixed and simple prejudices." Such judges would be far more likely than "enlightened, sensitive, intelligent" individuals "to be and to remain ignorant of those niceties of difference between individuals the apprehension of which makes for justice."[34]

The model for decisions advocated by Llewellyn is best

[33] For a good selection of the writings of the leading advocates of the "free law" movement, see *Science of Legal Method: Select Essays by Various Authors,* trans. Ernest Brunchen and Layton B. Register ("Modern Legal Philosophy Series"; Boston: Boston Law Book Co., 1917). For expository and critical accounts, see Wolfgang Friedmann, *Legal Theory* (4th ed.; London: Stevens & Sons, 1960), and Julius Stone, *Legal System and Lawyers' Reasonings* (Stanford: Stanford University Press, 1964), pp. 227–229.

[34] Frank, *Law and the Modern Mind,* pp. 169 (n. 9), 143, 143–144. According to Frank, *"the question is not whether we shall adopt 'free legal decision' but whether we shall admit that we already have it." Ibid.,* p. 169, n. 9. See *ibid.,* pp. 201–206 for Frank's most complete analysis of the "free law" movement.

described in terms of his contrast between the "grand" and "formal" styles. Under the latter, judges *"sought* to do their deciding without reference to much except the rules, *sought* to eliminate the impact of sense, as an intrusion." As such, the Formal Style reflects the "orthodox ideology" against which "all modern thinking has played." The essence of this "ideology" is the view that "the rules of law are to decide the case; policy is for the legislature, not for the courts, and so is change even in pure common law." According to Llewellyn, this model dominated judicial thought from approximately 1870 until recent times. Moreover, "its image is with us still, distorting the common perception both of what our appellate courts are doing and of what they ought to do." [35]

The essence of the Grand Style is that "every current decision is to be tested against life-wisdom, and that the phrasing of the authorities which build our guiding structure of rules is to be tested and is at need to be vigorously recast in the new light of what each new case may suggest either about life-wisdom, or about a cleaner and more usable structure of doctrine." In the Grand Style " 'precedent' is carefully regarded, but if it does not make sense it is ordinarily re-explored; 'policy' is explicitly inquired into; alleged 'principle' must make for wisdom as well as for order if it is to qualify as such." According to Llewellyn, this style "prevailed in this country from Jefferson's Administration up roughly until Grant's." Moreover, it has begun vigorously to reappear of late in the work of appellate courts. Its recapture is not complete, yet "the phenomenon is . . . waxing steadily." Thus in 1960 Llewellyn wrote that the shift away from the Formal Style

[35] Llewellyn, *The Common Law Tradition: Deciding Appeals* (Boston: Little, Brown, 1960), pp. 5, 38, 6.

had become unmistakable by 1940. As of now the Grand Style is one of the dominant styles of judicial work.

Viewed as a model for how decisions ought to be reached, the Grand Style differs from Frank's norms in at least two respects. In the first place, more emphasis is placed upon the need for decisions to stay within the limits imposed by established rules. "The work of the job in hand, and even more of the job at large, must fit and fit into the body and the flavor of the law." This is the "law of fitness and flavor." In the second place, greater weight should be attached to "the facts of the situation taken as type" rather than the unique facts of the individual case. "The sense of the type-situation, where it can be tapped, outranks and outshines any 'fireside' stuff." "The wise place to search thoroughly for what is a right and fair solution is *the recurrent problem-situation* of which the instant case is *typical*." The major reason for the wisdom of such a procedure is that it will make judicial behavior more predictable.

It seems to me obvious at sight that this order of approach to the problem of deciding an appellate case *must* materially raise the level of reckonability, make results more even, make the operating factors easier to foresee and forefeel, make the ways of handling prior doctrine stand forth, make the new formulations so reached increase in adequacy both of content and of phrasing.[36]

At the same time, it would be misleading to imply that Llewellyn advocated this point of view with consistent clarity. On the one hand, at times his attitude seems to be that the judge should simply *consider* first the "facts of the

[36] Llewellyn, *Jurisprudence*, p. 217; Llewellyn, *The Common Law Tradition*, pp. 5, 149, 143, 159, 222, 245, 44.

situation taken as type." He should not necessarily, that is, subordinate the facts of the individual case to them.[37] On the other hand, at times Llewellyn takes a more conservative position. Sometimes he seems to suggest that, in general, the equities of the fireside should not be permitted to prevail. Typical of this strand in his thought is the statement that "the necessities of operation, the coarseness of our legal tools, as well as the needs of evenhandedness, are there to exact some human suffering as the price of any order in the kind of society we know. 'John Doe,' Pound writes and repeats, *in wisdom,* 'must sometimes suffer for the Commonwealth.' "[38]

In any case, the different kinds of results to which Frank and Llewellyn attached conflicting priorities reflect three still more basic points of disagreement. The first is in their somewhat different appraisals of the *value* of uniformity and predictability. Obviously each had a higher ranking in Llewellyn's hierarchy of values than in Frank's. The second is a somewhat different estimate of the *possibility* of uniformity and predictability. According to Frank,

we have sought to indicate that most specific decisions are not predictable and that there is little likelihood that they ever will be foretellable. . . . Wishes impossible of realization are frivolous. Whatever one may want the legal world to be, it is and will almost surely be uncertain. *And ethical attitudes towards law must conform to possibilities and feasibilities.* "Oughts" must be based upon "ises" and "cans."[39]

For Llewellyn, decisions are to a significant degree predictable. The third is a somewhat different *explanation* of why decisions are or are not foretellable. This difference

---

[37] See *The Common Law Tradition,* p. 270.

[38] *Ibid.,* p. 349 (italics mine).

[39] Frank, *Law and the Modern Mind,* p. 398.

ultimately reflects conflicting views of human nature. In Llewellyn's mind man is a creature who can be and is conditioned to respond uniformly to similar stimuli. The judge is no exception. Indeed, "the sustained and laudable pressures of our law-governmental institutions to condition the appellate judge *as if* he were in Pavlov's laboratory are amazingly effective in regard to his attitudes, his value-judgments, and his very intake of perceptions." [40] It is for this reason that Llewellyn could maintain, unlike Frank, that a conscious search for the wise, just, or fair outcome would not increase uncertainty. Judicial perceptions of what is wise, just, or fair are sufficiently similar to induce "reasonable regularity."

In any event, Llewellyn's view of how decisions ought to be reached is more conservative than that of Frank. Indeed, it could be argued that it is not very different from that urged by either Pound or Cardozo. Such an argument is not wholly specious. Like each of these men, Llewellyn placed considerable value on order and stability. Also, he seems at times to suggest that these values can be achieved by the application of established rules to the facts. Nonetheless, at least two important differences between the views of Llewellyn and either Pound or Cardozo can be found. One is that Llewellyn more consistently asserted that the wisdom, justice, or fairness of the result ought to be the ultimate standard for decisions. This view can be found in the writings of both Pound and Cardozo. Still, each man hedged it with more qualifications than Llewellyn added. The other difference is conflicting estimates of the limitation of established rules *as a means to dictate the specific decision in a concrete case.* Even in *The Common*

---

[40] Llewellyn, *The Common Law Tradition,* p. 204.

Law Tradition Llewellyn insisted time after time that their application does not answer the questions which must be answered before the decision can be reached. The existence of established rules does *limit* the range of competing decisions which are available to the judge. It does not *eliminate* the existence of competition. The need remains to choose between conflicting decisions, each of which can be reconciled with the authorities. Moreover, the need exists even in the average, run-of-the-mill case. It is not limited, as Cardozo felt it was, to that "percentage, not large indeed, and yet not so small as to be negligible, . . . where the creative element in the judicial process finds its opportunity and power." For Llewellyn,

the present material may make permanently untenable any notion that creativeness—choice or creation of effective policy by appellate judges—is limited to the crucial case, the unusual case . . . the tough and exhausting case, the case that calls for lasting, conscious worry. My material aims to put beyond challenge that such creativeness is instead every-day stuff, almost every-case stuff, and need not be conscious at all.[41]

In short, use of the traditional method cannot do what Cardozo and Pound thought it could do. "Our multi-wayed legal scheme . . . will allow a fair technical case to be made either way or a third or fourth other way, *if one looks at the authorities taken alone.*" [42] The problem arises from the fact that Llewellyn is somewhat less than consistent in the development of the prescriptive implications of this point.[43]

[41] Cardozo, *The Nature of the Judicial Process*, p. 165; Llewellyn, *The Common Law Tradition*, p. 190.

[42] *The Common Law Tradition*, p. 21.

[43] The most systematic analysis of the kind of issues which divided Frank and Llewellyn is to be found in Richard A. Wasserstrom, *The*

Norms for Opinions

The focus of the other basic reform in judicial methodology which can be found in the literature of the legal realists is the manner in which decisions are justified. The purpose of the change is to encourage judges to write opinions which furnish a more reliable basis for the prediction of future decisions. To be sure, recommendation of and interest in this reform is less widespread than advocacy of and concern with the method by which decisions ought to be reached. Nonetheless, the realist movement did produce two outstanding reformers of judicial opinions. They are Frank and Llewellyn. The specific changes

---

Judicial Decision: Toward a Theory of Legal Justification (Stanford: Stanford University Press, 1961). Wasserstrom does not consider in detail the views of either Frank or Llewellyn. He does analyze in depth, however, decision-making procedures which are similar to those advocated by these two legal realists. One is an "equitable decision procedure," which has as its "rule of decision the rule which prescribes that a decision is justifiable if and only if the consequences of that decision to the litigants are found to be more desirable, on balance, than the consequences of any other decision." This procedure for reaching and justifying decisions is very similar to that urged by Frank. It is rejected by Wasserstrom. The other procedure, which he regards as preferable, is a "two-level procedure of justification." "That procedure has as its rules of decision the rule which prescribes that a decision is justifiable if and only if it is deducible from the legal rule whose introduction and employment can be shown to be more desirable than any other possible rule." This procedure is "two-level" because it prescribes that two conditions must be met before the decision is reached. They are: (1) that "before any particular decision is deemed to have been truly justified, it must be shown to be formally deducible from some legal rule"; (2) that "before any particular decision is deemed to have been truly justified, the rule upon which its justification depends must be shown to be itself desirable, and its introduction into the legal system itself defensible." *Ibid.*, pp. 138, 172, 173. Wasserstrom's two-level procedure is close to that advocated by Llewellyn.

which each advocated differ, however, and must be analyzed separately.

The essence of Frank's position is the proposal that
judicial opinions become psychological reports of *how* the
decision was in fact reached. The need for such reports
stems from the fact that "the ultimately important influences in the decisions of any judge are the most obscure,
and are the least easily discoverable—by anyone but the
judge himself." His decisions "are tied up with intimate
experiences which no biographer, however sedulous, is
likely to ferret out, and the emotional significance of
which no one but the judge, or a psychologist in the closest
contact with him, could comprehend." Two means are
available to report this psychological knowledge. One is
"to get from our judges . . . detailed autobiographies con-
taining the sort of material that is recounted in the auto-
biographical novel." The other is the development of
"opinions annotated, by the judge who writes them, with
elaborate explorations of the background factors in his
personal experience which swayed him in reaching his
conclusions." In this way the "language of artificial,
rule-worded, published opinions" will be replaced by that
which reports "fully the true bases of decisions." The end
result will be an increase in predictability.[44]

Unlike Frank, Llewellyn felt that "the opinion has no
function of *describing* the process of deciding." Nevertheless, he believed that it could become a more accurate
predictive tool. The differences between the Grand and
Formal styles indicate how. Under the latter judges
"*sought* to write . . . as if wisdom (in contrast to logic)
were hardly a decent attribute of a responsible appellate
court."

[44] Frank, *Law and the Modern Mind,* pp. 123, 124, 159–160;
Frank, "Are Judges Human?" *U. Pa. L. Rev.,* LXXX (1931), 267.

Opinions run in deductive form with an air or expression of single-line inevitability. "Principle" is a generalization producing order which can and should be used to prune away those "anomalous" cases or rules which do not fit, such cases or rules having no function except, in places where the supposed "principle" does not work well, to accomplish sense—but sense is no official concern of a formal-style court.

The great defect of such opinions is the unnecessary unpredictability which is created. For example, by 1885 the Formal Style had driven *"conscious* creation all but underground." The result was that inevitable change and growth were viewed as "things to be ignored in opinions." "The effects not only on reckonability but on 'the law' during the early decades of the twentieth century, were devastating." [45]

The Formal Style has such destructive effects on reckonability primarily because it encourages the use of "illegitimate precedent techniques." They include the tendencies for opinions to ignore a relevant case; to distort the facts of prior cases "so as to make it falsely appear that the case in hand falls under a rule which in fact it does not fit, or especially that it falls outside of a rule which would lead in the instant case to a conclusion the court cannot stomach"; to interpret "the case in point beyond all recognition, so as to slip its force"; and to cite "a few alleged authorities which have little or nothing to do with the proposition for which they are cited." [46] The use of such procedures is an obstacle to prediction because it does not disclose either "the *reasons* not only for pruning a shoot, but for leaving it," or the "explicit principles of pruning, if there are any," or "the reasons for using one of the

[45] Llewellyn, *The Common Law Tradition,* pp. 131, 5–6, 38, 40.
[46] *Ibid.,* pp. 133–134.

legitimate techniques with any precedent or line of precedents rather than some other of the equally legitimate techniques." In essence, the illegitimate precedent techniques do not disclose the rationale for the particular choice made. Thus, where

> all you have is precedents, or rules phrasing decision, with the reasons obscure, then one lawyer can build a letter-perfect case on the language, or some language, announced in the process of actual decision; the opposing lawyer can show the language to be distinguishable stuff, and can bring other language. If lawyers are good, two technically letter-perfect cases are the rule, on just the Rules as They Stand. This is not certainty, *for lawyers.* . . . If the opinion does not tell the judge's successors and us *why* the technically solid argument of the loser had no business to be listened to, then uncertainty remains, *for lawyers,* as to whether this new precedent will be followed (or which part of it will be followed . . .) , or extended, or turned, and if turned, then turned in which direction; or distinguished down, and if distinguished, *how* and how far it will be distinguished.[47]

Under the Grand Style, however, these kinds of distinctions are drawn in the opinion. Thus lawyers are in a much better position to predict what the court is likely to do in the future. For this reason, the "Grand Style is [and was] the best device ever invented by man for drying up that free-flowing spring of uncertainty, conflict between the seeming commands of the authorities and the felt demands of justice." [48] Moreover, Llewellyn felt that in recent years the renaissance of the Grand Style had empirically verified this view. In 1942 he argued that its appearance in the last twenty-five years has meant that

---

[47] Llewellyn, *Jurisprudence,* pp. 125–126, 124.
[48] Llewellyn, *The Common Law Tradition,* pp. 37–38.

"modern appellate judicial decision is already the more predictable, for anyone who has eyes to see." Still further, in 1959 he contended that "the open and conscious quest for the reasonable rule *for the type-situation* . . . characterizes the work of the American State Supreme Court today." Based on samplings into the opinions of the Supreme Courts of New York, Massachusetts, North Carolina, Pennsylvania, Washington, and nine other Western, Southern, and Middle-Western states, he concluded that "the march toward recapture of the Grand Style is unmistakable, strong, steady, and increasing." Thus, he felt, a study of "current practices of distinguishing shows that purely technical distinguishing is today almost as extinct as the dear dodo. Today a distinction without a reason expressly given is rare; and almost always the reason given goes to reason of fact, which is reason of life, as seen by the court." Finally, Llewellyn claimed that

when I speak of overt resort to and discussion of sense as an opinion-daily phenomenon of current judging among American Supreme Courts, I do *not* mean merely such discussion in regard to the *application* of the rule. Neither do I mean such discussion merely in regard to a *choice* between two so-called competing rules or principles. I refer to open, reasoned, extension, restriction or reshaping of the relevant rules . . . done in terms of the sense and reason of some significantly seen *type* of life *situation.*[49]

Evaluation of Realist Norms for Opinions

The norms for opinions explained in the foregoing pages have elicited little systematic evaluation.[50] In part

[49] Llewellyn, *Jurisprudence,* pp. 310, 218, 219, 225–226, 219–220.
[50] A major exception to this generalization is Lon L. Fuller, "American Legal Realism," *U. Pa. L. Rev.,* LXXXII (1934), 429.

this is because the methods were advocated by a relatively small number of realists. Most of them were concerned with other problems. In part the failure of the proposals to be examined in any detail has resulted from the false assumption that none of the realists was interested in normative problems. Even so, it is easy to visualize the kinds of criticisms which could be advanced.

Two objections to Frank's reforms are apparent. In the first place, his proposals do not seem feasible. Judges are not psychoanalysts. They are not likely to become skilled enough in psychoanalytical techniques to be able to explain fully the "real" reasons for their decisions. Indeed, Frank himself once admitted as much. In an early article he confessed that "whether opinions can ever be so written [as valid psychological reports] it is hard to say: the writer is skeptical as to that possibility."[51] His skepticism seems warranted. In the second place, Frank's reforms may not be desirable. The judicial opinion has many functions.[52] Two seem to be of particular importance. The first is to justify the specific decision reached. The second is to for-

---

Fuller has been very critical of some doctrines of the legal realists. He was most sympathetic, however, to their reforms for opinions. "The intellectual torture which our courts inflict on legal doctrine will be obviated, when we have brought ourselves to the point where we are willing to accept as sufficient justification for a decision the 'non-technical' considerations which really motivated it. . . . This millennium . . . will bring not only a humanitarian reform in our treatment of legal doctrine, but also, I feel sure, greater certainty in the prediction of judicial action." In short, "Out of this evaluation would come greater certainty and greater justice for litigants." *Ibid.*, 435, 437.

[51] Frank, "Are Judges Human?" *U. Pa. L. Rev.*, LXXX (1931), 267.

[52] For an excellent analysis of the functions of judicial opinions, see Robert Leflar, "Some Observations Concerning Judicial Opinions," *Colum. L. Rev.*, LXI (1961), 810.

mulate a rule of law prescribing the legal classification of the type of factual situation involved in the instant case. Neither of these functions will be facilitated by the kind of voyages in psychoanalysis which Frank urged.

The case is different where as Llewellyn's reforms are concerned. He did not claim that the function of the judicial opinion is to describe the psychological process by means of which the decision is reached. His proposals are thus not open to the same kind of objections which can be advanced against Frank's. They are feasible. Also, they are not inconsistent with the basic functions of judicial opinions. Two questions can be asked, however, about the changes which Llewellyn recommended. One is whether their adoption will facilitate prediction *as much as* he claimed. The other is whether it is desirable for judges to be *as candid as* he suggested.

The first question stems from the fact that Llewellyn's estimate of the predictability which results from use of the Grand Style is not above question. To be sure, the conclusions of such an indefatigable investigator of the cases cannot be ignored. The fact that Llewellyn's samples are random also lends authority to his hypothesis. Still, he is somewhat imprecise about when the revival of the Grand Style began, how wide its renaissance has been, and the evidence which indicates how greatly predictability has been increased. The consequence is that more studies by experts in particular areas of law are required before the degree of validity of his account can be reliably determined. For example, Llewellyn may have tended to overgeneralize somewhat about the renaissance of the Grand Style. Thus, a knowledgeable lawyer has written me that "the restoration has occurred primarily in certain fields, constitutional law, labor law, for instance." He has gone on to say that "if you drove your weary way through the opinions of the New York Court of Appeals on contract cases, or almost any court on cases involving the parole evidence rule, you would find that the formal style flourishes like ragweed." He has also contended that the use of the Grand Style depends upon such nonuniversal factors as the remoteness of rules from reality, the knowledge of the court about the facts of the case, and the legal fluidity of the situation involved. The institutional traditions of the court and the intellectual abilities of the judges are also factors to be considered.[53]

Nonetheless, the *assumption* that decisions which are justified by Llewellyn's methods will probably be *more* predictable seems to me to be justified. Surely, such decisions will be more foreseeable than those reached through exploitation of the full freedom which the interpretation of prior rules affords, but justified by the Formal Style. Moreover, decisions reached and justified by the Grand Style have one other advantage. They will be at least as predictable as decisions reached by judges who felt that they had no alternative, but who logically had a choice for which a premise could have been found in the antecedent rules. The reason for that is the fact that lawyers cannot be certain of the policy reasons for such decisions. The judges may actually have felt that they had no alternative; but they also may merely have been reluctant to confess the pragmatic reason for their decision.

This last problem can never, of course, be completely eliminated. No one can ever be absolutely certain why a judge reached a particular decision. Human motives are too elusive. Nonetheless, opinions in which considerations

---

[53] Letters from Professor Ian R. Macneil of the Cornell Law School to the author, Aug. 19, 1964, and Sept. 29, 1964.

of policy are freely discussed will probably make future decisions *more* predictable. The reason is that opinions of this type are more likely to reveal why one among a number of possible decisions was reached. As such, they will provide more reliable clues to the future course of judicial behavior than would otherwise be available.

The other question arises from the possibility that judicial self-restraint in the *articulation* of the policy reasons for decisions may sometimes be desirable. It might be necessary, for example, to preserve traditional myths on which the power and prestige of courts allegedly depend. Too much overt discussion of policy considerations in opinions could make all too apparent the role of the "human equation" in the judicial process. Such is the argument of Martin Shapiro and Paul Mishkin.[54] It is an argument which is not beyond criticism and which has evoked a spirited reaction.[55] A less controversial and per-

[54] See Martin Shapiro, *Law and Politics in the Supreme Court: New Approaches to Political Jurisprudence* (New York: Free Press of Glencoe, 1964), pp. 24–32, and Paul Mishkin, "The High Court, the Great Writ, and the Due Process of Time and Law," *Harv. L. Rev.*, LXXIX (1965), 62–70. Shapiro and Mishkin do not agree on how "mythical" the myth is. Mishkin's point of view is very similar to that of Pound and Cardozo, while Shapiro's is virtually identical with that of the legal realists. Mishkin, pp. 60, 63; Shapiro, pp. 27–28, 31; and Shapiro, "Stability and Change in Judicial Decision-Making: Incrementalism or Stare Decisis?" *Law in Transition Quarterly*, II (1965), 134. The two men do agree, however, that the failure of judges to enunciate the policy reasons for their decisions is justifiable.

[55] See Arthur S. Miller, "Some Pervasive Myths about the United States Supreme Court," *St. Louis U. L. J.*, X (1965), 153; and Jack Ladinsky and Allan Silver, "Popular Democracy and Judicial Independence: Electorate and Elite Reactions to two Wisconsin Supreme Court Elections," *Wis. L. Rev.* (1967), 128.

haps more persuasive justification for some restraint has come from Robert Leflar. The essence of his view is that candor is an important, but not an absolute, value.

Candor is a virtue, in judicial opinions as elsewhere, and we need much more of it. But to "tell all," with complete and unmitigated candor, is not always a virtue in judicial opinions or elsewhere. Restraint may be a virtue too, for reasons sometimes of decency and sometimes of wise planning. The problem of when to be candid, when silent, and how candid to be, is one that antedates the invention of pen and ink.[56]

This problem is probably also one to which Llewellyn, in his largely justified revolt against the Formal Style, directed too little attention.

Criticisms of the Realists' Methods for Reaching Decisions

The method by means of which the realists felt decisions ought to be reached can be, and has been, subject to numerous criticisms. If the evaluation of rule-skepticism advanced in Chapter II is correct, then the most obvious of these objections is based on an erroneous premise. The pragmatic method urged by the realists cannot be criticized on the ground that the judge has no choice but to reach one decision. In most cases which are doubtful enough to be contested, litigated, and appealed, courts must choose between conflicting decisions. Grounds for each can usually be found among established rules. Their application to a specific set of facts does not unequivocally indicate which decision ought to be reached. Nonetheless, criticisms can be advanced which are not premised upon a

[56] Leflar, *op. cit.*, p. 819.

denial of this fact. Two of these objections are of particular importance. One is that the failure to recognize the wide range of choice usually available to courts is not necessarily undesirable. The other is that the realist method is incomplete. It fails to indicate how the fairness, justice, or wisdom of results can be measured. These two criticisms are of special significance because neither is inconsistent with the genuine insights of rule-skepticism. They conflict only with the normative inferences which the realists drew from it.

The first criticism is an excellent illustration of this point. Its advocates do not deny that judges are usually faced with competing decisions, each of which can be reconciled with established rules. Their argument is, rather, that the failure to recognize this range of choice can be desirable. Indeed, no less a realist than Llewellyn once advanced precisely this claim. In a celebrated passage in *The Bramble Bush* he implicitly attacked the notion that judges should consciously and universally search for what they regard as the wise, just, or fair decision. He began by admitting that it is the "job" of the judge "to decide which ladder [of doctrine] leads to the *just* conclusion, or to the *wise* conclusion—when he sees two clear possibilities. He does that job, and in the main he does it well." Yet, he went on to add that frequently the judge does not perceive the range of competing decisions which can be reconciled with the established rules. More important, Llewellyn insisted that this lack of vision is socially desirable. "Again we see wisdom made institutional, caught up and crystallized into a working system: by way of logic the weak judge is penned within the walls his predecessors built; by way of logic the strong judge can scale those walls when in his judgment that is needed.

And either phase, and both, promote the common weal." [57]

This argument assumes, of course, that legal myths can have socially desirable consequences. As such, it conflicts with the general position of Llewellyn and the other legal realists. It is very similar, though, to a point of view which Thurman Arnold elaborated upon again and again. Unlike most of the advocates of realistic jurisprudence, he denied that a frank awareness of the facts of legal life is necessarily good. In part his argument is that myths have value as means to preserve the power and prestige of courts. In part his contention is that they function as a useful restraint upon the exercise of judicial power.

For Arnold, "the great paradox of government consists in the fact that institutions lose vitality without ideals, in spite of the fact that all ideals may be made to look absurd by unemotional and practical statements." Man is an emotional creature with a strong wish to believe that what ought to be exists. He "can never escape from his moral self, and a cynical position brings the futility of disillusionment. Man is under the constant necessity of putting on ceremonial robes and watching himself go by. All the wealth of Midas will not make man happy if he cannot strut." Institutions without ideals cannot satisfy this "moral self." They are inherently unstable. It is for this reason that ideals, no matter how unrealizable or inconsistent with the facts, perform a vital function. "The student of government needs to understand that while the presence of the ideal element in law is a confusing factor, its omission leads to a spiritually unstable institution, backed by the harsh exercise of power, lacking that perma-

[57] Llewellyn, *The Bramble Bush: On Our Law and Its Study* (New York: Oceana, 1960), pp. 73, 74.

nence and strength which comes from unquestioning public acceptance." This is why, for example, "it does not matter to the security of the institution that the ideals are not 'true.' It is only important that they fit into the vague emotional notions of that part of the public whose acceptance is vital to the power of the institution, and without which it falls." [58]

What now needs to be emphasized is that these kinds of considerations led Arnold to criticize his fellow realists *even in the heyday of the movement.* Thus in his first book he argued that "the charge . . . so often made by realists, that law is inconsistent with its own notions is not an indictment but a commendation. The law fulfills its functions best when it represents the maximum of competing symbols." He elaborated more fully on this theme in a passage which merits quotation in its entirety.

It is child's play for the realist to show that law is not what it pretends to be and that its theories are sonorous, rather than sound; that its definitions run in circles; that applied by skillful attorneys in the forum of the courts it can only be an argumentative technique; that it constantly seeks escape from reality through alternate reliance on ceremony and verbal confusion. *Yet the legal realist falls into grave error when he believes this to be a defect in the law.* From any objective point of view the escape of the law from reality constitutes not its weakness but its greatest strength. Legal institutions must constantly reconcile ideological conflicts, just as individuals reconcile them by shoving inconsistencies back into a sort of institutional subconscious mind. If judicial institutions become too "sincere,"

[58] Arnold, "Law Enforcement—An Attempt at Social Dissection," *Yale L. J.,* XLII (1932), 12, 23; Arnold, *The Symbols of Government* (New York: Harcourt, Brace, 1962), pp. 125, 71.

too self-analytical, they suffer the fate of ineffectiveness which is the lot of all self-analytical people. They lose themselves in words, and fail in action.[59]

In light of this analysis, the criticisms which Arnold advanced against the realists in his celebrated memorial article on Jerome Frank are not surprising. He was warm in his praise of Frank as a person, an attorney, a judge, and a scholar. Nonetheless, he was critical of the appeal for avowed pragmatism as a norm for decisions. Such a view is "so utterly materialistic that it will not serve as a permanent basis on which to rest the authority of courts." Frank did not

give adequate consideration to the importance of authoritarian law based on human reasoning and respected with mystical faith. . . . This ideal is the cement which holds a free society together. The ideal of a judiciary which discovers its principles through the enlightened application of established precedents dramatizes that most important conception that there is a rule of law above men.

Indeed, in light of this Arnold went on to attack indirectly the patron saint of legal realism, Mr. Justice Holmes. "Law must be a 'brooding omnipresence in the sky.' This is an ideal which can never be attained, but if men do not strive for it the law loses its moral force." [60] The ideal may be an illusion; but "to dispel it would cause men to lose themselves in an even greater illusion, the illusion that personal power can be benevolently exercised." For this

[59] Arnold, *The Symbols of Government*, pp. 248–249, 44 (italics mine).

[60] Arnold, "Judge Jerome Frank," *U. Chi. L. Rev.*, XXIV (1957), 634.

reason, Arnold concluded that "realistic jurisprudence is a good medicine for a sick and troubled society. The America of the early 1930's was such a society. But realism, despite its liberating virtues, is not a sustaining force for a stable civilization." [61]

The Insufficiency of the Realist Method

The other major criticism is that the realist method for reaching decisions is insufficient, because it does not indicate *how* the fairness, justice, or wisdom of results are to be measured. According to Edward McWhinney, for example,

the American Legal Realists offered only a theory of the judicial process and had no firm set of values or objectively-verifiable criteria for the solution of concrete case problems once the fallacies of the orthodox theory of the judicial process had been exposed and the opportunities for creative, law-making choice on the part of the judicial decision-maker demonstrated. . . . Their primary function as a group, as they saw it, was to inculcate skepticism in the mind of judge, lawyer, teacher, and student. . . . What that solution [of cases] might be . . . did not matter as long as the decision-maker was fully aware of the . . . factors operating on his choice and did not conceal them in his opinion.[62]

To those who take this point of view, it is obvious that "there are objectively better or worse solutions of legal

[61] Arnold, "Professor Hart's Theology," *Harv. L. Rev.,* LXXIII (1960), 1311; Arnold, "Judge Jerome Frank," p. 634. For a view similar to Arnold's, see Cooperider, "The Rule of Law and the Judicial Process," *Mich. L. Rev.,* LIX (1961), 501.

[62] "Judge Jerome Frank and Legal Realism: An Appraisal," *N. Y. L. F.,* III (1957), 120. For a similar view, see Edgar Bodenheimer, *Jurisprudence: The Method and Philosophy of Law* (Cambridge: Harvard University Press, 1962), p. 127.

problems; that . . . valuation makes sense, that there is truth in the realm of ethics and law." [63]

The criticism that the realists paid insufficient attention to the problem of values is of particular importance for two reasons. In the first place, it reflects a point of view which has been widely shared in the postwar period. In the second place, it has been advanced even by those lawyers who are in other respects very sympathetic to the legal realists. Eugene V. Rostow, ex-Dean of the Yale Law School, is a case in point. His perceptive article on "Realistic Jurisprudence," which was first published in 1961, is illustrative. According to Rostow, "one of the most significant criticisms of the realist movement [is that] . . . the realists denied the problem of judging the goodness or badness of law, beyond the single issue of the correspondence between the law in the books and the law in action." Rostow has correctly indicated that "there is a paradox in this charge . . . for the legal realists were among our most devoted and effective reformers, both of law and of society." Nevertheless, he has pointed out that

during the past twenty years or so, the stress in the American literature about law has been on this part of the equation—the quest for standards and values in the process of guiding the evolution of "the law that is" into the law we think it ought to become. The formulation and acceptance of ends, these writers know, helps to fix the line of growth of the law. . . . Their work has helped to correct and offset the relative neglect of the problem of values which characterized the more positivistic outlook of the earlier legal realists.[64]

[63] Jerome Hall, *Studies in Jurisprudence and Criminal Theory* (New York: Oceana, 1958), p. 140.

[64] Eugene V. Rostow, *The Sovereign Prerogative: The Supreme Court and the Quest for Law* (New Haven: Yale University Press, 1962), pp. 18, 20–21.

It would be mistaken, of course, to explain this quest for standards and values simply as a reaction to legal realism. A variety of factors have been at work. Also, "it is impossible to state exactly when the new, current movement in American jurisprudence began." [65] At the same time, the existence of a greater conscious concern by American jurists with problems of value is indisputable.[66] Moreover, it is impossible to deny the impact of the impression that the realists were not sufficiently concerned with values in the emergence of the new movement.

Evaluation of the First Criticism

The argument for the desirability of the failure of judges to recognize the range of choice involved in most cases is not easy to evaluate. A really systematic appraisal is, indeed, beyond the scope of this book. The issues which arise are too numerous and complex. Nevertheless, identification and tentative evaluation of at least the major issues is desirable. Otherwise a reasoned judgment about the utility of the method urged by the realists is not possible. Three of the issues seem to be of special significance: (1) Is the traditional ideal, defined as the norm that decisions should be reached by the mechanical application of established rules to the facts, an effective means to induce uniformity and insure predictability? (2) To the extent that this ideal is effective, is it desirable? (3) Regardless of its prior effectiveness or desirability, is the old ideal still a credible norm for decisions?

Resolution of the first issue is, unfortunately, far from easy. The major reason for this is that it is difficult to know *why* decisions are uniform, to the extent that they

[65] Hall, *Studies in Jurisprudence,* p. 138.
[66] See *ibid.,* pp. 136–142.

are. As a result, the precise impact of belief in and use of the traditional ideal is hard to determine. The rule-skepticism of the realists, it was pointed out earlier, has correctly identified the wide range of competing premises which are *logically* available to courts in cases doubtful enough to be litigated, contested, and appealed. What is true *logically,* however, is not necessarily true *psychologically.* Judges may not always have been aware of the existence of competing decisions, each of which can be reconciled with established rules. Indeed, recognition of this possibility is the *raison d'être* of the realists' plea for greater judicial self-consciousness. Such a plea assumes, in other words, that the traditional method may have been too effective.

The problem stems from the difficulty of knowing *how* effective it has been *as a means to reach specific decisions.* In all probability, however, the old method is not nearly as effective as has been traditionally assumed. It seems unlikely that in cases doubtful enough to be litigated, contested, and appealed most judges have been too stupid to have perceived the range of choice open to them. It also seems improbable that they have failed to search consciously for what they felt to be the pragmatically best decision. Yet their behavior has still been uniform enough to make meaningful prediction possible. The inference to be drawn is that this uniformity is due to the impact of extralegal values rather than established rules. Such is, at least, the justified implication of rule-skepticism as defended in this study.

Determination of the extent to which the impact of the traditional ideal, where it has been effective, is desirable is also most difficult. Still, a strong case can be made for the proposition that the effect has not been wholly, or perhaps even primarily, beneficial. As Julius Stone has pointed out,

> Judicial unawareness of the leeways within the system of precedent, imports also inadvertence to the "judicial duty of choice." It has led to unjust or socially inapt decisions, made often with a reluctant sense of inevitability. . . . Too often still . . . at any rate on the appellate level, the sense of compulsion springs from caution, or from a baseless belief in the rigidity of precedent law.[67]

To be sure, unjust or socially inapt decisions have not only sprung from a "baseless belief in the rigidity of precedent law." Self-conscious awareness of the leeways within the system of precedent can be an instrument for justice; but it can also function as a tool of injustice. Judges who are fully aware of the range of decisions open to them can reach, as they have reached, unjust decisions. Nonetheless, awareness of the leeways probably does more good than harm. In the first place, it increases the likelihood that decisions are effective means to achieve desired values. It makes more rational, in other words, the process by which decisions are reached. In the second place, such awareness makes less likely the possibility that judges will feel compelled by established rules to reach what they regard as unjust decisions. It thus reduces the probability of at least one cause of judicial injustice.

To this extent Frank was justified to criticize the view stated by Llewellyn in *The Bramble Bush.* In a celebrated review of this work, Frank contended that Llewellyn has given a "too emphatically favorable appraisal of the social benefits of the old ways." For

[67] Stone, *Legal System,* p. 292.

the ignorant, unskillful judge . . . frequently blunders unwittingly out of the clutches of the bothersome precedent. . . . The skillful judge may be weak in courage or common sense. . . . The strong judge who is not skillful (or the skillful strong judge when too fatigued to use his strength and skill) may let himself be dragooned by a precedent into injustice. . . . The strong and/or skillful judge is not necessarily the scrupulous, conscientious, socially minded judge. . . . The dishonest judge . . . can easily cover up his conduct by . . . a skillful opinion . . . written for him.[68]

It would be fatuous to assume that all of these possibilities will be eliminated by greater judicial awareness of the leeways within the system of precedent. It is not fatuous to contend that the likelihood of some of them will be reduced.

The third question, like the preceding two, does not admit of a simple answer. On the one hand, the traditional ideal for decisions obviously retains some credibility. Otherwise informed scholars could not maintain with any plausibility that its public disavowal by judges would do more harm than good. On the other hand, the traditional ideal does not induce the kind or degree of credibility which prevents frequent change. Nor does it bar a significant degree of candor in the judicial avowal of change. To be sure, the precise extent to which such candor characterizes judicial opinions is difficult to determine. Still, a number of studies indicate that it is increasing. The research of Llewellyn on the revival of the Grand Style is one example. The work of Robert Keeton in torts is another. According to him,

[68] Frank, Review of *The Bramble Bush,* by Karl N. Llewellyn, *Yale L. J.,* XL (1931), 1125, 1123.

the most striking impression that results from the weekly outpouring of tort opinions handed down by appellate courts across the nation during the last few years is one of candid, openly acknowledged change.[69]

The real issue is, thus, *how* credible the traditional ideal is. Unfortunately, the issue is probably irresolvable at the present time. The required knowledge of the attitudes of bench, bar, and public is simply not available.[70] To admit that the old ideal is still to some degree credible is, however, one thing; to contend that it is desirable is another. The implication of the foregoing discussion is that the realist method is preferable. Search for the wise or just decision will not make judicial behavior more unpredictable and unjust. Such a method probably is, after all, that which most judges have used most of the time. Moreover, conscious awareness of how open the way

[69] Keeton, "Judicial Law Reform—A Perspective on the Performance of Appellate Courts," *Texas L. Rev.*, XLIV (1966), 1254. Also, see Keeton, "Creative Continuity in the Law of Torts," *Harv. L. Rev.*, LXXV (1962), 463.

[70] One of the few available empirical studies indicates, however, that the older ideal is not as credible to the public at large as has often been assumed. According to Ladinsky and Silver, "We found few evidences . . . of a prevalence of judicial mystery or majesty in Wisconsin. The 'ideological insulation' of the judiciary manifested in the general electorate does not appear to reflect the sophisticated rhetoric of legal and political analysis. Public acquiescence to judicial actions in the realm of policy-making hardly seems to be a function of the 'priestly' image promulgated by Lerner or Frank; neither is it a function of the 'Blackstonian' image proclaimed by Mishkin and Arnold. In the face of widespread disagreement with the substance of recent judicial innovations in public policy areas, public support seems more a matter of acquiescence or ignorance rather than positive endorsement, of respect for the judiciary as one kind of government official rather than as a distinctive office embodying unique functions and status." Ladinsky and Silver, "Popular Democracy," *Wis. L. Rev.* (1967), 167–168.

is for the search may reduce judicial injustice. At the least it will make the process by which decisions are reached more rational.

To argue that the realist method is preferable to the traditional method is not to maintain, however, a number of other things. In the first place, it is not to suggest that "fireside equities" ought always to prevail. They can be given, as Llewellyn's criticisms of Frank's position indicate, too high a value. In the second place, to defend the realists' method is not to contend that judges ought to ignore precedents or other types of established rules. Careful examination of their implications for the instant case is, indeed, highly desirable. Such a procedure indicates to the judge how other judges or government officials have resolved somewhat similar disputes; it shows the consequences of adopting one rule rather than another as the major premise for the decision; and it can act as a restraint on the completely unprecedented decision or rule. What such a procedure should not do, however, is to conceal from the judge the "fundamental truth" that "rules are not to control but to guide decision." [71]

Evaluation of the Second Criticism

The essence of the other basic criticism is that the realists failed to develop a set of values or criteria in terms of which concrete decisions ought to be reached. Is this charge true? If it is true, what explains this failure? Is the failure a ground for criticism? Each of these questions must be answered if the legacy of legal realism for our generation is to be fully grasped.

The most valid answer to the first question has been indicated at the outset of this chapter. The advocates of

[71] Llewellyn, *The Common Law Tradition*, p. 179.

"realistic jurisprudence" were not indifferent to normative problems. The kind of interest which the vast majority of them manifested is, however, instrumental in nature. Its focus is the methods by means of which decisions should be reached or justified. With the notable exception of Felix Cohen, the legal realists did not in their published writings give much space to systematic prescription of the values which specific decisions should reflect.

No simple explanation of this fact can be advanced. A number of different factors played a role. One is the not infrequent commitment of the exponents of "realism" to the ideal of a value-free science of law. A second is moral subjectivism. The view that no "firm set of values" or "objectively verifiable criteria" can be found is not uncommon among the realists. Typical of this strand of thought is the claim that the ultimates of traditional jurisprudence are but "phantoms drifting upon the stream of day dreams." [72] Men convinced of this are not likely to regard the quest for standards or values as of much significance. A third factor is skepticism about the utility of all general principles, legal or moral, as means to prescribe specific decisions in concrete cases. In 1905 Holmes wrote that "general propositions do not determine concrete cases." [73] His reference is to general propositions of law. What is true of these propositions may also be true of other normative utterances. Such is the view of Holmes, and to a degree of the realists. A fourth factor is the impact of pragmatism. Throughout this study its effect on the realist movement has been emphasized. One of the

[72] Underhill Moore, "Rational Basis of Legal Institutions," *Colum. L. Rev.*, XXIII (1923), 612.

[73] *Lochner* v. *New York,* 198 U.S. 76 (1905).

most important signs of this influence is a reluctance to specify the criteria by means of which the *value* of results or outcomes can be measured.

A final and paradoxical factor is the very interest of the legal realists in the reform of law. This interest induced a reluctance to formulate normative theory of the substantive type for two reasons. One is the general temper of the American reform movement in the 1920's and 1930's. In the period between the two great wars it took on a new form. Instead of relying on absolutes and moral appeals, reformers became tough-minded, relativistic, and experimental. The seeds of this outlook had been planted, of course, before 1920. After all, it is the essence of what Morton White has suggestively labeled the "revolt against formalism." [74] This revolt had been undermining the moralism of the traditional reform mentality long before 1920. But it was not until the interwar period that this hardboiled outlook became the dominant mood of practical reformers. As Richard Hofstadter has pointed out, then there was a relative reversal of the ideological roles of conservatives and reformers. Classically,

it has been the strength of conservatives that their appeal to institutional continuities, hard facts, and the limits of possibility is better founded; while it has usually been the strength of reformers that they arouse moral sentiments, denounce injustices, and rally the indignation of the community against intolerable abuses. Such had been the alignment of arguments during the Progressive era. During the New Deal, however, it was the reformers whose appeal to the urgent practical realities was most impressive. . . . It was the conservatives, on the

[74] See Morton White, *Social Thought in America: The Revolt Against Formalism* (Boston: Beacon Press, 1957).

other hand, who represented the greater moral indignation and rallied behind themselves the inspirational literature of American life.[75]

The other reason is the particular nature of the traditional jurisprudence against which the realists were in revolt. More specifically, it is the reluctance to avow the role of policy considerations in the process by which decisions are reached and justified. This attitude is not unknown even today; but it was much more common in the 1920's and 1930's. Because it was, the legal realists no doubt felt it more imperative to dissolve the iron chain of dogma which imprisoned traditional jurisprudence than to prescribe new norms for decisions. Only after it had been demonstrated that "the field of free play for Ought in appellate courts is vastly wider than traditional Ought-bound thinking ever had made clear," could "ought" questions become truly meaningful. Until that had been demonstrated, the main job of reformers was to show that the application of traditional legal norms to the facts cannot determine judicial decisions in most cases. Only then could courts be urged to seek consciously "for the wise decision," "for the fair or wise outcome." [76] Only then, too, could the prescription of norms of fairness or wisdom become a major job for jurists. Otherwise, it could be dismissed as irrelevant. The judicial function, it could be argued, is simply to deduce decisions by the application of established legal rules to the facts.

Is the absence of normative theory of the substantive type from the realist movement a ground for criticism? The answer to this question is not as simple as the critics

[75] Richard Hofstadter, *The Age of Reform: From Bryan to F. D. R.* (New York: Knopf, 1956), p. 315.

[76] Llewellyn, *Jurisprudence,* pp. 70, 72.

of the realists have assumed. Legal philosophers have for centuries tried to formulate "a firm set of values or objectively verifiable criteria for the solution of concrete cases." Values or criteria which all right-minded men can accept have yet to emerge. It is not likely that they will emerge. A normative jurisprudence which assumes that such values and criteria can emerge is doomed to failure. The realists were right to be distrustful of the relevance of vague absolutes to concrete cases. Their suspicion of "broad ultimates" is not without reason. Few rules or decisions relevant to and desirable for a specific society at a particular time can be "*dictated* by the philosopher's Natural Law." "A jurist's or lawyer's Natural Law will in a diversified world fail of its very function if its content be sought in formulations so broad as to apply to too many legal times, systems, and societies at once." [77]

Nonetheless, the emergence of a normative jurisprudence in the postwar era is a response to a genuine need. Some kind of guidance for judges is needed, if the range of choice which confronts them is as wide as the realists claimed. It is obviously not enough to inform the judge to search for the decision which has the wise, just, or fair outcome. Criteria are needed in terms of which his quest for such decisions can be guided and evaluated. Systematic analysis of such criteria is surely as important as development of means for the prediction of decisions. No unconditional answer can ever be given to the question of what kinds of decisions judges ought to reach. But to avoid conditional answers in terms of stated criteria is to ignore the most important of all questions: how men ought to live. Judges have values and they will use these values to reach and to justify their decisions. Their critics have

[77] *Ibid.*, pp. 112, 114.

values and they will use their values to criticize or to approve judicial decisions. To assert that nothing can be gained from systematic, conscious analysis of these values amounts to a kind of irresponsibility. The responsibility to make value-judgments cannot be avoided; it can only be concealed. To this extent, the failure of the realists to concern themselves with normative theory of the substantive type is a ground for criticism.

Contribution of the Realists

The normative theories of the legal realists, it has been argued, constitute one of their most important contributions to American jurisprudence. The methods which they proposed for reaching and justifying decisions are not, to be sure, beyond criticism. The issues which these methods raise are complex. All right-minded men will probably not solve them in the same way. Problems still remain to be resolved. Nonetheless, the instrumental norms urged by the realists constitute a notable achievement.

One reason for this has been spelled out by Felix Cohen. In 1935 he wrote that "it is the great disservice of the classical conception of law that it hides from judicial eyes the ethical character of every judicial question, and thus serves to perpetuate class prejudices and uncritical moral assumptions which could not survive the sunlight of free ethical controversy." He went on to point out that "it is perhaps the chief service of the functional approach that in cleansing legal rules, concepts, and institutions of the compulsive flavors of legal logic or metaphysics, room is made for conscious ethical criticism of law." Once it is realized that decisions "are not products of logical parthenogenesis born of pre-existing legal principles . . . then we are ready for the serious business of appraising law and legal institutions in terms of some standard of human values." [78] If the analysis advanced in the foregoing pages is correct, then the door which was opened for "conscious ethical criticism of law" was insufficiently explored by the legal realists. Nonetheless, it is no mean achievement to have opened the door. Judicial decisions are still discussed and evaluated, for example, in terms which cannot be reconciled with the insights of the legal realists. The search for "neutral principles" of constitutional adjudication is an illustration. The critical reaction to this kind of quest indicates the extent of the impact of the realists. Yet, the existence of the quest indicates that their analysis of the limitations of established rules has yet to be fully digested. In 1933 Cohen wrote:

The question before the judge is: "Granted that there are differences between the cited precedent and the case at bar, and assuming that the decision in the earlier case was a desirable one, is it desirable to attach legal weight to any of the factual differences between the instant case and the earlier case?" Obviously this is an ethical question. Should a rich woman accused of larceny receive the same treatment as a poor woman? Should a rich man who has accidentally injured another come under the same obligations as a poor man? Should a group of persons, *e.g.* an unincorporated labor union, be privileged to make all statements that an individual may lawfully make? Neither the ringing hexameters of *Barbara Celarent* nor the logic machine of Jevons nor the true-false patterns of Wittgenstein will produce answers to these questions.[79]

[78] *The Legal Conscience: The Selected Papers of Felix S. Cohen,* ed. Lucy Kramer Cohen (New Haven: Yale University Press, 1960), pp. 67, 74–75, 75.

[79] Cohen, *Ethical Systems and Legal Ideals,* p. 37.

Only one blind to current controversies could argue that this is even now universally recognized to be the nature of the question which confronts judges.

The other major contribution of the normative theories of the realists is to have helped pave the way for a more flexible legal system. It would be absurd to contend that the more liberal attitude of many current American judges is due only to the realist movement. Legal theory cannot be assigned such an impressive role. But it would be a mistake to suggest that the theories of the realists played no role. Both as teachers and as writers they had an impact. As Grant Gilmore has pointed out, the realists "created a professional climate of opinion which immensely facilitated the making of necessary adjustments within the traditional framework of our law. They did much to make of law a more useful and flexible instrument for the resolution of social conflicts." A similar theme was advanced by the late Hessel Yntema, who asserted that "the significant achievement of American legal realism has been to imprint in legal thinking the concept of relativity in the adaptation of positive law to social change." [80]

A movement to which both of these kinds of contributions can be ascribed merits a high standing in the annals of American jurisprudence. It is also a movement the significance of which is not limited to factual insights into the nature of the judicial process, or proposals for the scientific study of law.

[80] Grant Gilmore, "Legal Realism: Its Cause and Cure," *Yale L. J.,* LXX (1961), 1048; Hessel Yntema, "American Legal Realism in Retrospect," *Vand. L. Rev.,* XIV (1960), 329.

VI

Legal Realism in Perspective

No universally accepted criteria exist for the determination of the significance of intellectual movements. At least four standards are, however, rather widely accepted. The importance of a movement is frequently measured by the intrinsic validity, utility, impact, and originality of its ideas. To be sure, these yardsticks are not easy to apply. Right-minded and informed men cannot be expected always to reach the same conclusions. This possibility imparts a tenative and relative character to attempts to appraise the significance of any movement, including that examined in this study. Nonetheless, tentative and relative evaluations are preferable to none. Also, the improbability of universal agreement in the selection or application of criteria does not preclude the possibility of some consensus.

Significance of the Realist Movement

One conclusion to be drawn from this book is that, as judged by the standards of intrinsic validity and utility, the theories propounded by the legal realists are significant. The advocates of "realistic jurisprudence" demonstrated the limitations of established rules as means to determine decisions in most cases doubtful enough to be litigated, contested, and appealed; they opened juristic eyes to the often unpredictable and subjective character of the process by means of which the facts of a case are determined; they suggested fruitful means to make decisions more predictable; and they proposed valuable methods for reaching and justifying decisions. To be sure, these ideas in some instances raise issues as important as those which are resolved. Then, too, they often need to be qualified. The theories of the realists are neither as universally true nor as useful as was sometimes suggested. Indeed, they may not be as true and as useful as has been suggested in this book. Nonetheless, even a less sympathetic student of the legal realists than the author of this study would probably agree that their theories contain important insights and valuable proposals.[1] Moreover, the relevance of some of these insights transcends the judicial process of the modern nation-state: it extends, in addition, to decision-making in all human organizations.

[1] Robert E. Keeton is a good case in point. He has criticized the "current state of low esteem for doctrine" which he regards as "a heritage from the heyday of Realism." Still, he has pointed out that "from today's vantage point, it seems indisputable that there were ample grounds for dissatisfaction with the prevailing accommodation of creativity and continuity to which Realism was a reaction. Doctrine was commonly treated as an authoritative and closed system of concepts whose reasons for being were almost immune from re-examination, and whose particular applications were precedent almost beyond a power of retraction. That accommodation gave overwhelming emphasis to continuity, little range for judicial creativity, and less range still for candor about the creativity that occurred. In challenging that state of affairs, the Realist movement performed a service." "Creative Continuity in the Law of Torts," *Harv. L. Rev.,* LXXV (1962), 469.

Very few ideas are ever completely original. It has not been contended here that the thought of the legal realists merits this classification. The impact upon their movement of the climate of opinion in the 1920's and the 1930's has been stressed. Also, some of the keenest insights and most useful proposals of the legal realists can be traced back to Mr. Justice Holmes. Nevertheless, the sparkle of originality is not absent from their literature. The views of the realists had antecedents; but the systematization, application, and justification of these ideas are often relatively original.

The impact of the realist movement is difficult to measure with precision. The kinds of biographical, historical, and institutional studies which are required are simply not yet available. Nonetheless, enough material exists to suggest that realism has had significant effects. Jerome Hall has pointed out that "most legal scholars in the United States, from the late twenties on, have been realists in important respects; and the polemics of the thirties should not obscure that fact." [2] The ideas of the realists which have probably had the greatest impact are their insistence on the limitation of established rules as means to determine specific decisions; their plea for the need to consider "extralegal" factors in the prediction of decisions; and their pragmatic approach to the evaluation of legal rules and judicial decisions. Also, it is apparent that the realists provided a stimulus to the utilization of scientific methods in legal education and the study of law. At the same time, it is necessary to point out that what may be true of most legal scholars is not true of all lawyers. The "victory" of the realists has been partial rather than complete.

[2] *Studies in Jurisprudence and Criminal Theory* (New York: Oceana, 1958), pp. 136–137.

The Decline of Realism

The inevitable question to be asked in this connection is why a movement of such clear significance is no longer the dynamic force which it once was. Unfortunately, the question is far easier to raise than to answer. A number of different factors have probably contributed, in greater or lesser degree, to the decline of realism as a movement. One of the most important is the death of its major figures, such as Herman Oliphant, Underhill Moore, Walter Wheeler Cook, Felix Cohen, Karl Llewellyn, and Jerome Frank. Another factor is the change in the climate of opinion in the last twenty-five years. Edwin W. Patterson has written that realism "was a true child of the period . . . between the World Wars, when skepticism of tradition, reverence for science and faith in man's ability to make his world better by inquiry and effort were articles of the American academic creed." [3] These articles of faith no longer have *as* vital an appeal as they once did. A third factor is the transformation which occurred in the American legal system since the 1920's and 1930's. Realism was clearly a response, in part, to the problems created by a case-law system which often lagged dangerously behind the times. Few would deny that in the last thirty years this system has become much more responsive to the needs of a society characterized by very rapid socioeconomic change. The understandable result is that a movement such as realism, in which the plea for responsiveness plays such a cardinal role, no longer seems quite as relevant.

Probably the most important factor is, however, the failure of the realists to take the steps implied by some of

[3] *Jurisprudence: Men and Ideas of the Law* (Brooklyn: Foundation Press, 1953), p. 556.

their most brilliant insights. Their ideas are not only negative. Moreover, they have a value and relevance not limited to any particular period of history. Nonetheless, these ideas have implications which were not systematically investigated. The most convincing evidence of this fact is the emergence in the postwar period of judicial behavioralism, policy science,[4] and a normative jurisprudence. Each of these movements is focusing upon problems which are genuine only if some of the central ideas of the legal realists are accepted. The mere existence of such movements indicates, however, that the implications of these ideas were not adequately investigated by the exponents of "realism."

Conclusion

Every movement has its limitations, and the limitations of legal realism should not obscure its significance. The distinctive doctrines of its advocates not only have had an important impact, but possess a high degree of validity,

---

[4] The most outstanding advocate of an outright policy-oriented approach to the study of law is, of course, Myres S. McDougal. See Harold D. Lasswell and Myres S. McDougal, "Legal Education and Public Policy: Professional Training in the Public Interest," *Yale L. J.*, LII (1943), 203; McDougal, "Law as a Process of Decision: A Policy-Oriented Approach to Legal Study," *Natural Law Forum*, I (1956), 53; McDougal, "The Law School of the Future: From Legal Realism to Policy Science in the World Community," *Yale L. J.*, LVI (1947), 1345. According to McDougal, "It is . . . the opportunity, and the obligation, of . . . law . . . schools, to emerge from the destructive phase of legal scholarship—indispensable though the destruction was—and to center its energies upon conscious efforts to create the institutions, doctrines, and practices of the future. . . . The time has come for legal realism to yield predominant emphasis to policy science. . . . It is time for corrosive analysis and inspired destruction to be supplemented by purposeful, unremitting efforts to apply the best existing scientific knowledge to solving the policy problems of all our communities." *Ibid.*, p. 1349.

utility, and originality. Moreover, these doctrines were developed in articles and books marked by an unusual zest and vigor. The realists may at times be wrong, yet they are seldom dull. They were men who not only had important things to say, but who also articulated their thought in lively, lucid, and at times brilliant language. A movement of which all of this can be said merits both admiration and further study.

Index

INDEX